To arthur nash

best wishes

Gordon arti

LAW, LIBERTY AND CHURCH

Law, Liberty and Church examines the presuppositions that underlie authority in the five largest Churches in England – the Church of England, the Roman Catholic Church, the Methodist Church, the United Reformed Church and the Baptist Union. Examining what has influenced their development, and how the patterns of authority that exist today have evolved, Gordon Arthur explores the contributions of Scripture, Roman Legal Theory, and Greek Philosophy.

This book shows how the influence of Roman legal theory has caused inflexibility, and at times authoritarianism in the Roman Catholic Church; it explores how the influence of reason and moderation has led the Church of England to focus on inclusiveness, often at the cost of clarity; it expounds the attempts of the Free Churches to establish liberty of conscience, leading them at times to a more democratic and individualistic approach. Finally Arthur offers an alternative view of authority, and sets out some of the challenges this view presents to the Churches.

ASHGATE NEW CRITICAL THINKING IN RELIGION, THEOLOGY AND BIBLICAL STUDIES

The *Ashgate New Critical Thinking in Religion, Theology and Biblical Studies* series brings high quality research monograph publishing back into focus for authors, international libraries, and student, academic and research readers. Headed by an international editorial advisory board of acclaimed scholars spanning the breadth of religious studies, theology and biblical studies, this open-ended monograph series presents cutting-edge research from both established and new authors in the field. With specialist focus yet clear contextual presentation of contemporary research, books in the series take research into important new directions and open the field to new critical debate within the discipline, in areas of related study, and in key areas for contemporary society.

Law, Liberty and Church

Authority and Justice in the Major Churches in England

GORDON ARTHUR

ASHGATE

Published by
Ashgate Publishing Limited
Gower House
Croft Road
Aldershot
Hampshire GU11 3HR
England

Ashgate Publishing Company
Suite 420
101 Cherry Street
Burlington, VT 05401-4405
USA

Ashgate website: http://www.ashgate.com

British Library Cataloguing in Publication Data
Arthur, Gordon, 1963-
  Law, liberty and church : authority and justice in the major churches in England.—(Ashgate new critical thinking in religion, theology and biblical studies)
  1.Authority—Religious aspects—Christianity 2.Justice,
  Administration of (Canon law) 3.England—Religion
  I.Title
  262.8'0942

Library of Congress Cataloging-in-Publication Data
Arthur, Gordon, 1963-
  Law, liberty, and church : authority and justice in the major churches in England / Gordon Arthur.
    p. cm.—(Ashgate new critical thinking in religion, theology, and biblical studies)
  Includes bibliographical references and index.
  ISBN 0-7546-5437-0 (hardback : alk. paper)
  1.Church—Authority. 2. Authority—Religious aspects—Christianity. 3. Christianity and justice—England. 4. England—Church history. I. Title. II. Series.

  BT88.A48 2006
  262.8—dc22
                                                              2005034562
ISBN-10: 0-7546-5437-0
ISBN-13: 978-0-7546-5437-7

Printed and bound in Great Britain by MPG Books Ltd, Bodmin, Cornwall.

Contents

List of Tables

Preface

This is a study of authority in the Church, of how it operates, and of some of its foundations. It takes in subjects such as legal theory, history and Canon Law in addition to theology. While this is written as a scholarly work, I have not assumed familiarity with these subjects, and I have tried to write in a way that is accessible to non-specialists. We shall encounter several works not written in English. While I have, where possible, quoted the original texts, I have included a translation of any text I have quoted in Latin or Greek. I have, however, replaced ſ and ∫ where they occur in the original texts with the modern *s*, and expanded all contractions of *n* or *m* represented by a line above the preceding vowel (for example, I have replaced *frō* with *from*).

There are, of course, several people I wish to thank, and without whom this project would not have been completed. Firstly, I should like to express my gratitude to Drs. Brian Horne, Steve Holmes and Murray Rae, and the late Professor Colin Gunton, who have supervised this project and given me much encouragement along the way. I must also thank the many other members of King's College, London, both staff and students, who have given me advice, and made helpful comments on and criticism of my work. Any errors that remain, however, are my responsibility alone.

I am grateful to Mrs. Sheila Hingley, Librarian at Canterbury Cathedral, and to Mrs. Judy Powles, Librarian of Spurgeon's College, for allowing me to use their respective libraries, and for guiding me to the (often obscure) information for which I was looking. I am also grateful to my father David for bailing me out financially on more than one occasion, and to the King's College, London, Theological Trust for its generous financial support towards the end of this project. Finally, I would like to thank Mrs. Tricia Hart for proof reading the text.

Soli Gloria Deo.

Gordon Arthur

List of Abbreviations

ASB: The Alternative Service Book, 1980.
BCP: The Book of Common Prayer.
CIC: Friedberg and Richteri: Corpus Iuris Canonici.
CPD: The Constitutional Practice and Discipline of the Methodist Church.
ECAS: The English Church Attendance Survey, 1998.
NIV: The New International Version of the Bible.
NRSV: The New Revised Standard Version of the Bible.
REB: The Revised English Bible.
SCG: St. Thomas Aquinas: Summa Contra Gentiles.
SGM: The Synodical Government Measure, 1969.
SO: Standing Order.
ST: St. Thomas Aquinas: Summa Theologica.

Introduction

Authority in the Church has long been an important and divisive issue. How the Church should regulate the conduct of its members and make decisions has been debated for centuries, and the debate has been particularly vigorous since the Reformation. In this study, I propose to examine authority by studying some of the assumptions that underlie its exercise. I take it as an axiom that the mission of the Church is to point people towards God, and to proclaim the truth of the Gospel. In doing so, it attempts to maintain the faithful in the truth, and enable and encourage them to live just and righteous lives in the sight of God. The structures of the Church must themselves reflect God's justice and righteousness if they are to do this effectively. The next two chapters will explain the differences between authority and power, and examine the current doctrines of authority of the major Churches in England, to put what follows into its proper theological context.

The Episcopal Churches in the West have traditionally worked out their authority structures through Canon Law. We shall examine their concepts of canonical jurisprudence, and compare them with theories of justice and patterns of authority from the Old and New Testaments, Greek Philosophy, Roman Law, Germanic Law and English Law. I shall not attempt a detailed historical study here; rather I shall select key points on the journey and attempt to trace the developing patterns of authority through them. The non-Episcopal Churches have generally rejected Canon Law. We shall explore the reasons for this, and see what structures they have put in its place. We shall examine whether they perform the same function as Canon Law, and if so, in what ways they operate.

Before embarking on this study, however, I must explain why I have chosen to examine the Roman Catholic Church, the Church of England, the Methodist Church of Great Britain, the United Reformed Church and the Baptist Union of Great Britain as the five major Churches in England. My criteria for these selections are as follows:

1. The Churches must be Trinitarian.
2. They must form a contiguous group, and have weekly attendances exceeding 100,000.
3. Each major ecclesial structure (Episcopal, Presbyterian, and Congregational) must be represented.
4. No more than one Church of each denominational group should be included.

The first criterion excludes Jehovah's Witnesses, Mormons and Scientologists, all of which have more members than the URC, the smallest Church we consider.[1] The second criterion is not so straightforward, since different Churches calculate their size in different ways. The Roman Catholic Church uses Mass attendances, the Church of England uses Parish Electoral Rolls,[2] and the other Churches have lists of members. It is therefore difficult to compare like for like when using the statistics produced by the individual Churches.

I have therefore based my selections on the 1998 English Church Attendance Survey (Brierley, 2000, hereafter ECAS), which recorded actual worship attendances in September 1998. For comparison, I will also list the membership statistics for late 1998 produced by the individual Churches. According to the *UK Christian Handbook: Religious Trends* (Brierley, 1999), the membership figures for some major Churches in 1998 are given in Table 1.1.

Table 1.1: British Membership Figures For Some Major Churches

Church	Membership
Church of England	1,345,000
Roman Catholic Church in England	1,021,900
Methodist Church (GB figures)	353,332
Orthodox Churches (UK figures)	202,236
Baptist Union of Great Britain (GB figures)	144,000
United Reformed Church (GB figures)	93,665

The Methodist, Baptist and United Reformed Churches also publish detailed statistics from local Churches, together with local, regional and national totals for each year. An English membership figure for 1998 can be obtained for each Church from these figures. These figures are listed in Table 1.2:

---

1   Brierley (1999), p. 10.2.

2   The Electoral Roll of a Parish Church is the list of members of and regular worshippers at the Church. It is not the same as a secular Electoral Roll.

Table 1.2: English Membership Figures For These Churches

Church	Membership
Church of England	1,345,000
Roman Catholic Church	1,021,900
Methodist Church	336,274[3]
Orthodox Churches (UK figures)	202,236
Baptist Union of Great Britain	128,441[4]
United Reformed Church	88,710[5]

The equivalent figures from ECAS are given in Table 1.3.

Table 1.3: English Church Attendance Survey Figures For These Churches

Church	Attendance
Roman Catholic Church	1,230,100
Church of England	980,600
Methodist Church	379,700[6]
Baptist Union of Great Britain	232,200
United Reformed Church	121,700
Orthodox Churches	25,200

It is clear from this that the quoted membership numbers for the Orthodox Churches greatly exceed their actual attendance, so under criterion two, I have not included them in this study. I have similarly excluded Pentecostal Churches, since ECAS reports that the largest Pentecostal group, the Assemblies of God, has 59,900 worshippers,[7] significantly less than the threshold in criterion two. This group of Churches satisfies my third criterion, in that the Roman Catholic Church and the Church of England are Episcopal, the Baptist Union is Congregational, and the URC is largely Presbyterian in structure.[8] Chapters 8 and 9 of *Religious Trends*, and chapter 2 of *The Tide is Running Out* (Brierley, 2000), confirm that the Methodist

---

3   Methodist Conference (1999a), p. 67.

4   Baptist Union (1999), p.173.

5   United Reformed Church (1999a), p. 23.

6   Brierley (2000), p. 37. This figure includes other Methodists, but Brierley states (p. 38) that over 98 per cent of these are members of the Methodist Church of Great Britain.

7   Ibid., p. 42.

8   The URC's structure is a hybrid of the Presbyterian and Congregational models. I shall argue later that the Presbyterian model is dominant.

Church, the Baptist Union and the URC are by far the largest Churches of their type in England, thus satisfying my fourth criterion. These, then, are the reasons for my selection of these five Churches.

It is my thesis that the doctrines of authority adopted by the Churches we consider fall short of the New Testament doctrine of authority. I shall place particular emphasis on the juridical side of authority in this study. The Churches have developed a wide variety of structures, based on a number of influences, of which Scripture is a major source, but by no means the only one. The Roman Catholic Church has been influenced substantially by Roman legal theory, and has adopted a monarchical structure based on the Roman Empire, with a legal system developed from Roman Law. This has led to a certain inflexibility, and has at times led to authoritarianism. The Church of England, influenced by English Civil Law, has concentrated on reason and moderation, leading to a sometimes indistinct structure that seeks to keep Evangelicals, Catholics and Liberals living together in relative harmony.

The Free Churches have adopted structures that could be seen as more democratic, in an attempt to enable everyone to be as free from authoritarian control as possible. This has at times led them into individualism. There is, however, little sign of democracy either in the New Testament, or in civil government at the time the Free Churches began, so I shall argue that there is suggestive, if not conclusive evidence that this is due in part to Aristotle, and I shall further argue that the alleged Roman Catholic dependence on Aristotle, particularly in the writing of St. Thomas Aquinas, is exaggerated. We begin our study by examining authority in the New Testament, and by setting out where the Churches stand on authority now.

Chapter 1

Authority in the New Testament

Introduction

At the outset of this enquiry, it will help to set out the distinction between authority and power. Dictionaries are not always helpful in this context: The *Collins English Dictionary* includes in its definitions of power: 'control or dominion or a position of dominion, or authority'. Its definition of authority begins: 'the power or right to control, judge or prohibit the actions of others'.[1] This illustrates the connection between power and authority well, but does nothing to clarify the distinction. Paul M. Harrison (1959) defines power as 'the ability to carry out one's will despite the inertia or resistance of others; it is the ability to influence or control the actions of others even though there is no institutional sanction for this control'.[2] Authority, by contrast, is 'formalized or institutionally recognized power'.[3] T.A. Lacey (1928) argues that authority is personal and moral, not official and legal, while power is the reverse.[4] Authority, then, is power combined with authorisation: those with authority have the right to exercise power, and are accountable to those who authorise them to act.

Richard T. de George (1985) explores the nature and limits of authority. He distinguishes between several types of executive and non-executive authority. My main concern in this study is with executive authority. While it is clear that Church leaders often have great moral authority, and other authors I cite later will refer to some types of non-executive authority, such as epistemic, competence or exemplary authority[5] (Church leaders often have such authority as a result of their personality or training), my main concern here is with the way the Churches make decisions and exercise discipline. Legitimate executive authority in the Church is, in my view,

---

1 Butterfield (2003), pp. 109 and 1275.

2 Harrison (1959), pp. 60–61. Harrison takes this (secular) definition from Weber (1947), p. 152.

3 Ibid., p. 61. Richard de George (1985, pp. 14–21) and Gerard Mannion (in Hoose, 2002, pp. 19–36), distinguish between *de facto* and *de jure* authority. Their *de facto* authority corresponds to power in this study, while their *de jure* authority corresponds to what I describe as authority.

4 Lacey (1928), pp. 1–3. Lacey also thinks that both power and authority were given to the apostles, who had legislative, disciplinary and administrative functions (pp. 43–50). The great Councils, however, had only moral authority (p. 23). We shall examine this issue further in chapter 5.

5 See de George (1985), pp. 26–61.

operative authority, and it is generally performatory, rather than imperative. While in some situations it may be necessary for the Church to issue directives and those who do so may carry imperative authority, they cannot legitimately use coercion to implement these directives.

The nature of authority in the Church is central to how the Church understands herself. Most branches of the Church believe they take their concept of authority largely from Scripture. They believe that all authority comes ultimately from God, the creator, redeemer and sustainer of the Universe. Christ, as founder, has authority over the Church, but He passed on some of that authority to the disciples during His earthly ministry. He gave them authority to bind and loose sins (both on earth and in heaven), and He told them that they would sit on thrones in His Kingdom, judging the Twelve Tribes of Israel. The Church claims that she is the inheritor of this authority. Some Churches believe that the apostles handed down this authority to their successors and they to theirs: that the Apostolic Succession is at the root of Ecclesiastical Authority. Others, which do not recognise this version of the Apostolic Succession, believe their authority comes directly from Scripture. We shall explore these views in more detail later, but first we must set out what the New Testament has to say on the subject. Since the focus of this study is authority in the Church, I shall limit the discussion to places where the New Testament talks of the exercise of power and authority by humans within the Christian community. I shall omit passages that instruct Christians to obey secular rulers or talk of powers in the heavenly realms. While there are a number of terms used to denote authority in the New Testament, the most important of these for our purposes are *dunamis* and *exousia*, which can refer to both human and spiritual powers. We shall examine how the New Testament writers use these words. While recognising that both have a much wider range of meanings, we shall concentrate on their application to the organisation of the Church.

Authority and Power

The primary meaning of *dunamis* is the ability or capacity to do something. It signifies power and competence.[6] In the New Testament, the focus of this power is Jesus, who bears the power of God through the Holy Spirit.[7] Luke in particular sees the Messiah in terms of His prophetic power, rather than as the traditional Kingly Messiah of the Old Testament. He therefore emphasises that God's essence is power, and so endowment with power is linked with the gift of the Holy Spirit. Jesus is able to exercise that power, thereby revealing His *exousia*. Luke also follows the general Synoptic usage, which sees the miracles as acts of power, through which God's dominion invades the world through the person of Jesus Christ. John's Gospel, while in accord with this, places more emphasis on the uniqueness of Christ and also emphasises that the power expressed in the Christ-event is the active power of God, initiating the new aeon and supporting Christ in His whole existence. This power is

---

6   See Kittel (1964b), pp. 284–317.
7   Luke 4:14.

particularly demonstrated in His death, resurrection and exaltation. It will be fully demonstrated at His return.

The apostles, who were given power and authority (*dunamin kai exousian*) and sent out to preach the Gospel and to heal the sick,[8] stood in the place of Jesus and continued His work. This power was the power of Christ, which He possessed during His earthly ministry, and as such, it was the power of God. Jesus expressly promised this power to the disciples through the presence of the Holy Spirit.[9] The purpose of this power is to develop and build up the community, in which those in bondage to sin and guilt can be released, and faith can be nurtured. As Christ is present in these communities,[10] they also share in His power, which protects and preserves the community, while transforming and strengthening it, bringing about a lasting and indissoluble relationship with Christ. This relationship in turn feeds into the conduct of the community, which develops a new way of life, that of Christian love. This power can also express itself through the gifts of the Spirit, including miraculous works and healing.[11]

Exousia, by contrast, denotes the ability to perform an action to the extent that there are no hindrances in the way, as distinct from *dunamis*, which as we have seen denotes intrinsic ability. It also indicates authorisation given by a higher power, but this authority may be illusory unless the agent so authorised or the authorising power has the intrinsic ability (*dunamis*) to enforce any such actions. It is therefore often impossible to separate *exousia* from *dunamis* entirely. The latter sense of *exousia*, as authorisation, either by God or by human authorities, predominates in the New Testament. It is also used in the plural to describe authorities such as the Sanhedrin and officials of the Roman government.

Specifically, in the New Testament, it represents the power that decides, and that is active within a legally ordered context. It can also denote the freedom given to the community. Taking these in turn, *exousia* signifies first the absolute possibility of action that belongs to God alone, and of which He is the source. This *exousia* is demonstrated supremely in the Creation, which bears witness both to the existence and the *exousia* of the Creator. Secondly, the *exousia* and power of God are demonstrated within the sphere of nature, which is seen as an ordered totality. However, authority of this sort is not limited to God. Revelation speaks of angels and scorpions having authority, and Acts talks of Satan having authority.[12] Creaturely authority, however, is limited.

Jesus as God has unrestricted, divinely given power and authority to act. He freely chooses to exercise this authority in accordance with the will of the Father. This authority is universal, but it applies particularly to humanity. Jesus chose to exercise

---

8   Luke 9:1–2.

9   Luke 24:48–49.

10 Matthew 18:20.

11 See Luke 24:48–49 and 1 Corinthians 12:4–11.

12 Acts 26:18 and Revelation 6:8, 9:3, 9:10, 9:19, 14:18, 16:9 and 18:1. Revelation 9 implies that the scorpions receive their power and authority to hurt others from God.

this authority through a life of service, and by laying down His life for humanity. This was a free choice, and He claimed authority from the Father to receive His life back again in the Resurrection.[13] Thus, *exousia* does not just designate authority, it also carries the connotation of freedom, that the Son has authority to act on behalf of the Father and is free to choose how He exercises that authority.[14] In the Great Commission, Jesus claims full authority in heaven and on earth, indicating His exaltation as Christ and Lord.[15]

As man, Jesus expressed His authority by forgiving sins, expelling demons and healing the sick, activities for which both *exousia* and *dunamis* were necessary. His teaching also carried *exousia*, in the sense that it was prophetic, which distinguished it sharply from the teaching of the scribes,[16] who shared the common view at the time that there were no longer any prophets, and therefore saw their own teaching as exposition not prophecy. This prophetic preaching claimed divine authority, to which Jesus' signs and miracles bore witness. It therefore presupposed a divine commission, and the power and authority that go with it, to preach that the Kingdom of Heaven is near. There is therefore an intimate link between the bearer of divine authority, the power of healing and forgiveness, and the presence of the Kingdom of God. When applied to the Church, the essential feature of authority is that the Church owes its existence and nature to Christ, Who enables the faithful to enter the Kingdom and to act on His behalf. This authority cannot be used in an arbitrary manner: it must be used responsibly, in accordance with His will. In particular, *exousia* refers to the freedom the community of the faithful receives to live under grace, and not according to the Law. While all things are permitted to believers, not all things are beneficial,[17] and Paul urged the Corinthian Christians not to allow their liberty (*exousia*) to become a stumbling block for the weak,[18] or to develop into authoritarianism. This liberty is not freedom to do as one likes: it is freedom from sin to serve and glorify God.

With this in mind, we first consider the passages in the New Testament that speak directly of the exercise of human authority within the Christian community and in the Kingdom, of which the Church can be seen as the herald. All but one of these passages are from the Gospels, because in general, the epistles, particularly those written before the Gospels, tend to be less specific about what authority in the Church entails. Paul, for example, urges leaders to lead diligently and to act as servants of Christ and stewards of God's mysteries, and urges the people to respect their leaders,[19] but does not develop the theme further. Hebrews exhorts the faithful to respect and obey their leaders, but offers no guidance on how they should lead.[20]

---

13 See John 10:18 and 17:2.
14 Compare Bauer (1979), pp. 277–9.
15 Matthew 28:18.
16 Matthew 7:29, Mark 1:22.
17 1 Corinthians 6:12.
18 1 Corinthians 8:9.
19 Romans 12:4, 1 Corinthians 4:1 and 1 Thessalonians 5:11.
20 Hebrews 13:7 and 17.

The writer to Timothy commends good leaders as worthy of a double stipend, and offers advice about how to deal with a number of specific pastoral situations, but beyond urging gentleness, does not appear to offer a theory of authority.[21] We must therefore concentrate on the Gospel accounts, which offer more detailed principles for Church government, and which the Churches acknowledge as the foundations for their theologies of authority.

The New Testament

Matthew 16:17–19

Davies and Allison (1991) believe that, while the surrounding material comes from Q, these three verses come from M as a unit.[22] They acknowledge that this could lead to the conclusion that Matthew has the original text here, and that Mark has edited his version of Peter's confession of Christ.[23] They oppose this idea, however, since the evidence from the rest of the Gospel suggests that Matthew is dependent on Mark. They see the recording of the establishment of the new community acknowledging Jesus' true identity as the essential point of the text, which they also see as deeply rooted in the Messianic teaching of the Old Testament.[24] In summary, they argue, Matthew records the realisation of the promises made to David in this passage.

They point to a parallel between verse 18 of this passage, in which the founding of the Church is associated with Peter, and Genesis 17, in which the founding of Israel is associated with Abraham. In both cases, the name of the person involved (Abraham = 'father of multitudes' and Peter = 'rock on which the Church is built') symbolises the key function each is to perform. This view is buttressed, they tell us, by Isaiah 51:1–2 in which the Israelites were invited to consider the rock from which they were hewn, and to consider Abraham and Sarah who gave them birth. This may have been the basis for John the Baptist's warning that God could raise up children for Abraham from the stones by the River Jordan.[25] They argue that this passage shows the realisation of the Baptist's prediction, as God founded his new people on Peter, not Abraham.[26] If this interpretation is correct, it naturally follows that the rock

---

21　1 Timothy 5:1–2 and 17.

22　Davies and Allison (1991), pp. 602–43. By contrast, Luz (2001, pp. 355–60) sees this passage as a redaction of several separate sources by Matthew.

23　Mark 8:27–30.

24　Particularly in 2 Samuel 7:4–16 and 1 Chronicles 17:3–15, in which Nathan prophecies that one of David's descendants will rule over Israel as king, will be God's son, will build the temple, and will rule forever. This oracle was understood to refer both to Solomon and to the eschatological king.

25　Matthew 3:9.

26　Compare Kittel and Friedrich (1968), pp. 98–9 and 105–8. Luz (2001, pp. 362–3) rejects both this interpretation, and the tradition that Peter was the foundation stone of the Church, parallel to the foundation stone in the Holy of Holies on which the temple was built.

is Peter himself, and not his confession of faith or Jesus, as various commentators have suggested across the years.[27] Luz (2001) adds that the New Testament idea of the Church as a building is parallel to the Old Testament language of the house of Israel. In both cases, the image of a building symbolises the faith community and indicates that its foundations are solid.[28]

The main objection to this position is that one might have expected the word play in Greek to revolve around *Petros* (masculine) – *petrō* (masculine), rather than *Petros* (masculine) – *petra* (feminine). The masculine *petrō*, however, refers to a small stone, while the feminine *petra* refers to a large rock. It is likely that both are translations of *Kefa* [Cephas]. We should also note that the word *ekklēsia*, which is translated 'church', indicates the whole congregation of God here, rather than a local Church.

Turning to the keys, Davies and Allison argue that the keys signify the power to bind and loose sins, by which, following Rabbinic tradition, they understand to declare what is permitted and what is forbidden.[29] While in this passage Peter alone is being addressed, we shall see shortly, when we discuss Matthew 18, that this power was not given to Peter alone. The authority given in this passage, however, is implicitly wider than the authority given in chapter 18. It seems that Peter has, in effect, been appointed chief rabbi of the new community and given authority to teach the whole community. Davies and Allison see a parallel with Matthew 23:13, in which Jesus accuses the scribes and Pharisees of shutting the doors of heaven by teaching false doctrine. They also note that in Matthew 28:18–20 the apostles are commanded to make disciples of all nations and teach them to observe Jesus' commands.

There may also be an allusion to Isaiah 22:20–22, in which Isaiah tells Shebna, the comptroller of the king's household, that the Lord has decided to replace him with Eliakim, and 'I shall place the key of David's palace on his shoulder; what he opens none will shut, and what he shuts, none will open'. While this may appear to support the view that the keys were intended to admit or exclude people from heaven, Davies and Allison argue that Matthew has reinterpreted this passage in 16:19 to harmonise the illustration of the keys with its use in Jesus' debate with the Pharisees in 23:13. All this supports the view that preaching and teaching were the primary functions of the apostles. Similarly, Luz understands binding and loosing as interpreting the law, in such a way that people are enabled to enter heaven. He is unwilling, however, to exclude the possibility that this passage refers either to Church discipline, or to forgiveness of sins.

If it is fair to read binding and loosing as primarily a teaching function, then, it seems to follow that Peter is neither just a representative disciple, as many Protestants have claimed, nor is he necessarily the first holder of an office that many others would

---

27 For an extensive examination of this point, see Webster (1999).

28 Luz (2001), pp. 362–70.

29 Compare von Campenhausen (1997), pp. 126–7.

subsequently hold, as Roman Catholic tradition has maintained.[30] Instead, Davies and Allison claim, he has a unique rôle in salvation history, in that his faith was the means by which God brought a new people into being. Luz adds that while there is no evidence that Matthew knew of a Petrine office, he did envisage that Peter's ministry would continue through the ongoing missionary activity of the Church.

Matthew 18:15–20

Davies and Allison attribute verses 15–17 to Q[Mt]. They attribute verses 19–20 to M, and they treat verse 18 as a reworded version of 16:19. They see this passage as a disciplinary procedure to deal with serious and intentional, but not public, sins.[31] In Luke 17:3, Jesus simply tells the disciples to rebuke those who sin against them, and if they repent, to forgive them. Matthew goes into more detail. First, if one Christian sins against another, the innocent party should try to persuade the offender of his sin by demonstrating his guilt. If the offender heeds his brother (clearly the result hoped for), he is restored to fellowship. If not, the second stage is another conversation, this time with witnesses who can confirm the offence. If this fails, the local Church (*ekklēsia*) is charged to support the disciple in his final attempt at reconciliation, and only then is the offender expelled.

Davies and Allison interpret binding and loosing here in the same sense they do in Matthew 16:17–19, but they note that in this passage it is more restricted. While in 16:17–19 Peter was given authority to bind and loose the whole Christian community by issuing authoritative rulings on what is or is not permitted, in this passage Jesus is talking to the Twelve. The local Churches are also given authority here to judge the behaviour of individual Christians, although Davies and Allison do not think this applies to the earlier rebukes. In both passages the decisions have the authority of heaven. The power of the local Church, however, depends on the spiritual harmony (*sumphōneō*) of its members, a harmony that must include the practice of forgiveness.[32] Luz, by contrast, argues that declaring what is permitted and what is forgiven does not fit in this context, and that binding and loosing here, where expulsion from the community is envisaged, must mean retaining or forgiving sins. He points out that throughout the history of the Church, this passage has been interpreted as a model for discipline by both Catholics and Protestants, and emphasises that such action involves the whole Church, and not just its office-bearers. He also emphasises the need for the whole process to be rooted in prayer, in which the Church remains dependent on God and seeks His will.

Davies and Allison also note that verse 20 has been subjected to opposite interpretations by different sections of the Church: if Christ is present when two

---

30 If the parallel with Abraham holds, we might note that there is no record of anyone in Israel claiming to be the successor of Abraham in the way the popes have claimed to be successors of Peter.

31 Davies and Allison (1991), pp. 781–91.

32 Ibid., pp. 787–8.

or three are gathered, one might ask how much more is He present in a council of bishops (Roman Catholic), but then again, if two or three gathered together is enough to ensure Christ's presence, one might also ask what need there is for an institution (Free Churches). Davies and Allison see no grounds for dogmatism in favour of either approach in this passage. Finally, they point out that reproving fellow Christians is a delicate business that needs to be undertaken in a spirit of love and humility. Matthew places this passage after a discourse about humility and not offending others, and follows it with another about reconciliation and forgiveness. They see this as proof of Matthew's deep pastoral concern.

Matthew 19:27–29

Davies and Allison (1997) assign verse 28 of this passage (along with its parallel Luke 22:28–30, which we shall consider shortly) to Q, and see it as drawing on the illustration in Daniel 7:9, in which there seems to be one throne set up in heaven for the Ancient of Days, and another for the Son of Man. By extension, then, the Twelve will sit on thrones alongside Christ. Davies and Allison hold that *krinontes*, has the same range of meaning as the Old Testament *shafat*, which has the double sense of 'to rule' and 'to judge'. They therefore understand it as government, not judgement or condemnation, and see it as a process extending over a long time. Thus, the Twelve enter into God's Kingly power, and become rulers alongside Him in the age to come.[33]

Luke 22:24–32

C.F. Evans (1990) comments that Luke at this point is following Mark closely, except that he has unaccountably omitted Mark 10:35–45, which we will discuss shortly, even though there is similarity in thought and language between the two passages. In Evans' opinion, the differences are such that it is more likely that Luke has reproduced an independent tradition, using some of the same wording, rather than transferring the passage from Mark in a revised form suitable to Jesus' parting address to the Twelve. He argues that while the point of the equivalent passage in Mark is that those who are supposed to rule over the Gentiles actually act as tyrants, and their great men have dominion over them, but that must not be the case among the apostles, Luke's point is that in the Gentile world it is kings who rule their subjects, and those in authority are hailed as benefactors, but among the apostles the greatest should behave as if he were the youngest or newest in the group (*neōteros*), and the leader as the one of lowest rank, the servant of all (*ōs ho diakonōn*). Thus, while an apostle may be a benefactor to others, this is not a consequence of his position, in

---

33 Davies and Allison (1997), pp. 53–63. They add that Matthew does not seem particularly interested in the details of future cosmological states. For an alternative view see Luz (2001), pp. 516–8.

which he is expected to serve others.[34] Elsewhere in the New Testament, it is clear that the *neōteroi* were at the beck and call of others, and they may have performed the lowlier tasks.[35]

Joseph A. Fitzmyer (1985), also sees this passage as a Lucan composition, combining elements of Q and L. Addressing a dispute between the disciples, he tells us, Jesus begins with an appeal to normal pagan experience: the kings of the pagans lord it over them (*kurieuousin*), and the important make their power felt. They allow themselves to be called benefactors, a title often given in the Hellenistic world to gods, princes and Caesars. The apostles, however, must not behave in this way, but those who wish to be great must minister to others, must act as though they were of least significance. Fitzmyer emphasises that this injunction is not egalitarian: it does not eliminate distinction or rank in the Church. Rather, it insists that greatness must serve lowliness, in an inversion of the secular order.[36]

While Evans acknowledges Luke's debt to Daniel 7:9, he sees its influence on Luke as less apocalyptic than on Matthew. The apostles, who have remained faithful all along, will share in the divine kingdom, in which they will sit on thrones. They, representing the true Israel, a new eschatological Twelve Tribes, will share in the judging (*krinontes*) of the empirical Israel. Evans acknowledges the possibility that 'judging' may imply 'rule', and sees this possibility as parallel to the promise of Revelation 3:21.[37] Fitzmyer agrees that the apostles will be given thrones because of their perseverance, but translates *basileian* as 'kingship' rather than 'kingdom'. Thus, he thinks, Luke is emphasising that the apostles will share in Christ's regal glory, rather than that they will sit in judgement over Israel. He agrees that this passage refers to Daniel 7:9, believes that Q is Luke's source for the reference to sitting on thrones, and agrees that this judgement should be taken in the Old Testament sense of ruling.

Of the final section of this passage, Evans comments that Peter's leadership of the apostles is nowhere stated in Luke's Gospel, but here it is simply assumed. Satan has demanded to test all the apostles, yet Jesus prays particularly for Peter, that when he has repented of his explicit denial of Christ, he may strengthen his brothers (*stērison tous adelphous sou*) who have only implicitly denied Him by running away. The language used here is used elsewhere in the New Testament to express various kinds of confirmation or establishment in Christian faith and practice.[38] In this context, Evans adds, the word 'brethren' is used in a restricted sense, and applies only to the apostles. Fitzmyer adds that while Peter's commission to strengthen his

---

34 C.F. Evans (1990), pp. 795–7.

35 1 Timothy 5:1–2, 11 and 14, Titus 2:6, and particularly 1 Peter 5:5–7 and Acts 5:6.

36 Fitzmyer (1985), pp. 1412–26.

37 C.F. Evans (1990), pp. 798–803. This probably indicates that Evans does not think Q is Luke's source here, although he does not explicitly say so.

38 Romans 1:11 and 16:25, 1 Thessalonians 3:2 and 13, 2 Thessalonians 2:17, James 5:8, 1 Peter 5:10, 2 Peter 1:12 and Revelation 3:2.

brothers applies in the first case to the apostles, it also foreshadows his missionary role in the Church.

Matthew 18:1–5

Davies and Allison (1991) and Luz (2001) are agreed that this passage is based on Mark 9:33–37, and they agree that verses 3–4 were inserted by Matthew. The key verse in this passage is verse 4.[39] Both agree that it is based on Matthew 23:12, which Davies and Allison (1997) attribute to Q.[40] Luz points out that children (*paidioi*) were often seen as incomplete human beings who needed training, were incapable of judgement, and had only slightly higher status than slaves.[41] It indicates that greatness and exaltation in the Kingdom is the result of both humility and the renunciation of status on earth.

Mark 10:35–45 and Matthew 20:20–28

The Greek text of these two passages is virtually identical, and the four commentators I shall cite are all agreed that these two texts are linked, so we will discuss them as a pair rather than individually. None thinks that Q is the source of these accounts, and all agree that Mark's text is earlier, so we will consider it first. Craig A. Evans (2001) argues for the unity of the whole passage in Mark, as an embarrassing episode that would not have been preserved but for Jesus' teaching in response to it.[42] C.S. Mann (1986) argues that it is composed of two separate accounts, with Jesus' response being attached by the community to the story of James and John because the subject matter matches.[43] They are agreed that the reference to sitting on thrones in Jesus' coming glory refers back to Jesus' earlier statement that the apostles would sit on thrones judging the Twelve Tribes of Israel, which we have just discussed.[44] Jesus then reminded the disciples of the realities of leadership at the time: rule often became tyranny and the great used their power for their own advantage, exercising total control over their subjects (*katexousiadzousin*). In other words, greatness in the secular world was exercised through coercive power. He emphatically rejected this as a leadership style among His followers.[45] Those who wish to be great must serve others, and anyone who wishes to be first must be the slave of all. The syntax of this couplet indicates a Semitic parallelism, in which the second half explains and clarifies the first. It is therefore unnecessary to press the difference in meaning

---

39 Davies and Allison (1991), pp. 752–9, Luz (2001), pp. 425–6.
40 Davies and Allison (1997), pp. 264–6 and 279–80.
41 Luz (2001), pp. 427–8. Compare Galatians 4:1–2.
42 Evans (2001), p. 114.
43 Mann (1986), p. 411.
44 Matthew 19:28 and Luke 22:28–30.
45 Paul also refused to follow this secular model of leadership. See 2 Corinthians 1:24.

between *diakonos* [servant] and *doulos* [slave] as the sense is clearly intended to be the same. Instead, Jesus offered his own lifestyle as a model for leadership.

Turning to Matthew's account, Davies and Allison point out that Matthew's language to describe the conduct of rulers is stronger than Luke's (both Matthew and Mark use *katakurieuousin* instead of the weaker *kurieuousin*), and that the first–century Mediterranean reader would inevitably assume the rulers in question were the Romans, whose example was not to be followed. Instead, those who lead in the kingdom must act as though they had no rights of their own, and existed solely for others, following the example of Christ, Who is the outstanding model of the first becoming last.[46] Luz adds that to debate whether Jesus is contrasting authority in the Church (*exousia*) with secular authority in general or with tyranny in particular is to miss the point. In his judgement, the issue for Jesus is that there should not be any 'being great' or 'being first' in the Church at all. Luz expresses his concerns that this passage has almost never been understood as a basis for Church organisation, being seen instead as a standard for individual behaviour. He questions whether there should be any distinction between priests/pastors and the laity, or indeed any structure at all. He acknowledges that in an institutionalised Church some form of authority is inevitable, but argues that all denominations must take seriously the need to develop constitutions based on service.[47] It will become clear later that while I do not wish to go quite this far, I have a great deal of sympathy with Luz's position.

John 20:21–23

George R. Beasley-Murray (1987) comments that one cannot deal with this passage without recalling its parallel in Matthew 16:19. He accepts that most commentators interpret binding and loosing in Matthew's version as forbidding or allowing certain actions, but adds that the idea of binding and loosing as judgement, specifically declaring those brought before them guilty or innocent, and therefore forgiven or unforgiven, is gaining ground. This interpretation is in harmony with John's version of this saying, in which it is clear that forgiveness is the issue. There is no indication, however, whether this power was exercised by leaders or by the whole congregation in John's Churches.[48]

J.H. Bernard (1928) believes that Jesus' words throughout this passage refer primarily to the Twelve. He believes that the second sentence reproduces the words of the final prayer at the Last Supper,[49] and they also point forward to the parting commission in the last sentence.[50] This sending of the Twelve had similarities with the sending of Jesus by the Father. Christ had told the Twelve at the beginning of the Farewell Discourses that anyone who received those He sent received Him, and that

---

46 Davies and Allison (1997), pp. 83–101.
47 Luz (2001), pp. 544–7.
48 Beasley–Murray (1987), pp. 383–4.
49 John 17:18.
50 John 20:23.

those who received Him received the Father.[51] Bernard argues that in John's Gospel this kind of language is addressed only to the apostles, and not to the wider group of disciples.[52]

Jesus then breathed on the Twelve and gave them the Holy Spirit, with authority to bind and loose sins. While He gave the Spirit to the whole Church, Bernard argues, He gave it particularly to the apostles. Only those who could discern whether repentance was genuine or not could pronounce sinners forgiven or unforgiven, and this gift of discernment was given particularly to the apostles.[53] Thus, the commission to bind or loose sins also applied to the apostles alone, and not to the Church as a whole. Bernard sees the reference to binding and loosing as an echo of Matthew 16:19 and 18:18, which we have already discussed. John's Gospel has nothing to say about passing on this authority to others. There is no doubt, however, that the apostles interpreted this passage as justification for handing on this authority nevertheless, and that early bishops saw themselves as successors to the apostles.

C.K. Barrett (1960) also emphasises the parallels between the Father sending Jesus and Jesus sending out the apostles, arguing that provided the Church is obedient to Jesus, the apostolic mission of the Church confronts the world with both a human institution, and with Jesus the Son of God. He also believes that the thought behind binding and loosing is the same as that behind Matthew 16:19 and 18:18, which he takes to mean declaring sinners forgiven or unforgiven.[54]

John 21:15–17

Beasley-Murray comments that this passage deals with the one issue in the entire Gospel where members of different confessional groups not only divide, but find difficulty in even understanding the answers of the others. He finds no difficulty in associating shepherding with ruling, but is surprised that so few associate 'shepherd' with 'bishop', which was understood in a similar way in the New Testament Church. He therefore finds a parallel with 1 Peter 5:1–5, which we shall discuss shortly, and concludes that the key to feeding the sheep is acting as their pastor. He does not, however, find authority for any universal ministry in this text.[55]

Bernard comments that in this passage, Jesus changes Peter's ministry from one of simply catching men to one in which he also guides and guards them in their new spiritual environment. The image of Peter's ministry changes from fisherman to shepherd, in which he must follow the example of Jesus, the Good Shepherd.[56] He sees as an anachronism the interpretation that identifies the lambs with the faithful

---

51 John 13:20.

52 Bernard (1928), pp. 674–81. He cites Justin, Origen and Cyprian as early supporters of this position.

53 Compare Acts 5:1–11 and 8:14–24, but see also 1 Corinthians 12:10: this gift was not given to the apostles alone.

54 Barrett (1960), pp. 473–5.

55 Beasley-Murray (1987), pp. 404–9.

56 John 10:11–16.

laity and the sheep with other pastors, but accepts that the third of these commissions to Peter entrusts the whole flock to his care.[57] Barrett accepts that this passage is a prediction of what Peter would become in the Church, namely the great pastor who would die a martyr's death, but he says nothing about the Petrine primacy as such.[58]

1 Peter 5:1–5

This passage appears to link the thought of our other passages on authoritarian uses of power with that of those that talk of shepherding. It is therefore particularly significant for our attempt to understand the relationship between these two elements of authority in New Testament thought. John H. Elliott (2000) comments that this letter addresses a situation in which the early structures of the Church were still evolving. Thus, he thinks, at this stage there was no formal idea of office and no fixed structure of ministry. Instead, the model of the community as household predominates here, with the elders of the community playing the rôle of the household managers.[59]

In both Israel and the Hellenistic world, elders served as community functionaries. In Israel, they served as village, city or community leaders in addition to their duties in the synagogue and, for some, the Sanhedrin. In the Greco-Roman world generally, elders were not office-holders; rather they were heads of household, and other senior people of honour and significance. Their authority was informal, representative and collective.[60] Elliott thinks the term elder was gradually widened to include those senior in the faith, thereby including all who could have any form of oversight over the congregation. He therefore sees no need to affirm that elders held any form of office in the Churches addressed by this letter, in contrast to the Pauline Churches in which elders were appointed.

In this passage, elders are instructed to shepherd the flock of God. Elsewhere in the Bible this metaphor entails leading, guiding, gathering, feeding and defending a flock, either literally or figuratively.[61] In a secondary sense, it can also mean ruling,[62] although in the Old Testament it is only used of the Messianic king, never the ruling king.[63] While the prophets often denounced human rulers as unfaithful shepherds leading the people astray, God also promised to 'send shepherds after my own heart',[64] or one shepherd over all the people, namely the Messiah, who was to reassemble Israel. In the New Testament, congregational leaders are referred

---

57 Bernard (1928), pp. 705–7.

58 Barrett (1960), pp. 485–6.

59 Elliott (2000), pp. 810–41. Compare 1 Timothy 3:4–6 and Achtemeier (1996), pp. 320–34.

60 For a fuller discussion of this point, see Campbell (1995), particularly pp. 7–18.

61 Literally: Luke 17:7; figuratively: Ezekiel 34:10, John 21:15–17, Acts 20:28 and Revelation 7:17.

62 2 Samuel 7:7, Isaiah 44:28 and 63:11, Ezekiel 34 and Matthew 2:6.

63 Kittel and Friedrich (1968), pp. 487–8.

64 Jeremiah 3:15.

to as shepherds only in Ephesians 4:11.[65] Paul J. Achtemeier (1996) believes this command is derived from John 21:16, with Peter understood as mediator of this tradition.[66] He points out that Paul gives a similar charge to the elders at Ephesus in Acts 20:28–30, when he tells them to keep guard over the flock entrusted to them by the Holy Spirit, guarding them against attacks from outside and divisions from within caused by distortions of the truth.

Elders are charged to look after (*poimanate*) the flock of God. Elliott explains that the Greek word used for flock in verses two and three (*poimnion*, also used in Luke 23:12 and Acts 20:28–9 but nowhere else in the New Testament) is a diminutive, meaning little flock, and referring to the believing community. The qualification 'of God' indicates that the flock is not theirs, but God's, and that they are therefore under-shepherds of the chief shepherd, Jesus. This oversight, Elliott tells us, encompasses instruction in the faith, moral guidance, and protection of the flock, organisational leadership and management of the community's resources.[67] They must exercise this leadership according to three principles.

Firstly, elders must lead willingly, not under compulsion. This may indicate that one became an elder by designation or election, and that some became elders somewhat reluctantly, whether out of modesty or because of the burdens of leadership (such as the cost of acts of benevolence, or the likelihood of being singled out for special abuse in times of persecution). The author, however, suggests that responsibility should be taken on willingly, in accordance with what God wants.

Secondly, it is to be done not for shameful gain, but out of devotion. The contrast here is between calculation of personal gain and spontaneous eagerness to serve. Christian leaders generally received payment for their work, whether in the form of meals and shelter, clothes or other material honour, and they also had some responsibility for community funds and property. The temptations to take advantage of such a position for personal financial gain would have been ever present. Instead, elders were to be motivated by a desire to give, not an itch to get.

Thirdly, elders were not to lord it over (*katakurieuontes*) their charges (*tōn klērōn*), but to serve them by setting an example (*tupoi ginomenoi*). Notice here that the author has adopted the strong language of Matthew's and Mark's Gospels to describe domineering. Paul would not even use the weaker language of Luke to describe his position in Corinth.[68] Elliot tells us these similarities cannot be traced to textual dependence, and must therefore represent an early tradition on ministry. The use of this tradition here, he thinks, shows that there was already a tendency to associate issues of leadership, ministry and shepherding with Peter. Instead, the elders are to lead by example, offering a moral role model after the pattern of Jesus, and living a lifestyle for others to follow. This may indicate that they are, in part,

---

65 *Poimenas*, usually translated pastors. Compare Kittel and Friedrich (1968), pp. 497–8.

66 Achtemeier (1996), pp. 325–6.

67 Compare 1 Timothy 3:1–7 and 5:17–19, and Titus 1:5–11.

68 2 Corinthians 1:24.

continuing Christ's ministry, and perhaps that they will have to give an account of their stewardship of the flock to Him in due course. Their charges, and also the flock, are probably those over whom the elders have authority, rather than minor clergy assigned rôles by the elder or bishop.

Finally, the younger men (*neōteroi*) are charged to submit (*hupotagēte*) to the older (*presbuterois*). This may indicate that the whole of the congregation should submit to the elders, or that those new in the faith should submit to those mature in the faith. In either event, those young in years or in the faith are urged to submit to their more experienced brethren. This submission is not blind obedience, but finding one's proper place within the Church. The fact that this is not elaborated indicates that there is less emphasis in the author's mind on subordination as such than the fact that even though leaders must not be overbearing, the congregation may not on that account ignore what they say. Humility is urged on all, not just the leaders. Despite the need for authority within the Christian community, arrogance is excluded, as everyone is urged to give place to fellow Christians.

Conclusion

It is clear that there is a core consensus behind these passages, despite their differing origins and emphases, and we can draw from them several points of agreement concerning Church government. The first thing to say is that there is no place for authoritarian government in the Church. Relationships in the Church must be founded on humility, not self–assertiveness. As we have seen, Matthew and Mark emphasise that secular leaders are tyrants, exercising coercive power, while Luke emphasises that kings rule the nations and are seen as benefactors. In all three descriptions, the ruler considers his own interests first. By contrast, the Evangelists emphasise that authority in the Church must reverse this order, with those in positions of leadership placing the interests of others before their own. Leaders must follow Christ's example of sacrificial love for those in their care.

Secondly, there seems to be a consensus among the commentators we have discussed that binding and loosing involves at least forgiving and retaining sins. This is most clearly apparent in John 20, but it is also likely to be true of Matthew 18 and possibly 16:17–19 as well. It is, however, difficult to believe that where there is a clear Rabbinic precedent, as there is in the case of binding and loosing as declaring particular activities permitted or forgiven, Matthew did not have this at least in the back of his mind when he was writing his Gospel. It seems that the tide of scholarship is flowing in the direction of the Johannine understanding even when Matthew is discussed, but I am nevertheless persuaded that binding and loosing in these passages involves both declaring sinners forgiven or unforgiven and declaring activities permitted or forbidden, thereby combining the functions of teaching and discipline. Thus, it would seem that today's leaders of the Church also have responsibility both for moral teaching and for exercising discipline.

There also seems to be wide agreement that the power of binding and loosing was given not just to Peter, but to the Twelve, and that the Twelve were charged to exercise their power through the local Church, which in turn was charged to promote reconciliation between those offended and their offenders. There are, however, some differences between the two situations. Peter seems to have been given power to bind and loose the whole Church, which would support the view that binding and loosing in Matthew 16 refers to teaching rather than discipline, while the others are seemingly given authority to bind and loose only within their own communities, which would imply a stronger emphasis on discipline than teaching in Matthew 18, as is clearly the case in John 20. We might reasonably conclude from this that both the local Church and the universal Church have authority, but that there needs to be a balance between the local and the universal Church when authority is exercised.[69] It seems that the references to the disciples sitting on thrones judging the Twelve Tribes of Israel are largely eschatological, and that they do not make a significant contribution to our understanding of how the Churches should conduct themselves now.

Finally, we consider Peter. It seems that Peter's position was different from that of the other apostles. He seems to have been given the keys in a wider sense than the others, and Jesus may also have indicated that Peter was to be the foundation of the Church; that his faith was to be the means by which God brought a new people into being, possibly in the same way He brought Israel into being through the faith of Abraham. It is evident that Peter held a special position in the Twelve, and it is widely accepted that he was seen as their leader. He also played an important part in the missionary work of the Primitive Church. However, there is no indication in the New Testament that Peter's position was seen as an office. Nor is there any indication that he could, or in fact did, pass his position on to anyone else. Certainly, others continued his ministry, and many saw themselves as his successors, but it seems probable that they had no more authority than the successors of the other apostles. There is no evidence in the New Testament that either Jesus or Peter foresaw or intended the subsequent development of the Petrine Office. It seems instead that Peter's role in salvation history was unique and unrepeatable.

Having established this, then, we are in a position to examine the claims to authority of the major Churches. The Churches use the passages we have discussed to support their claims to moral and spiritual jurisdiction. If Christ in any sense gave the Church authority to bind and loose in either of the ways I have detailed above, she is entitled to judge what is sinful and what is not, and to prescribe the appropriate penalties. The way each Church does this, however, will be affected by how she understands justice, and its aims and presuppositions. Such ideas, not surprisingly, vary. Roman, English, Greek and Hebrew jurisprudence are all different. The application of authority will also vary according to the degree of individualism, centralisation and corporateness in the concept of judgement in each Church.

---

69 For a similar view, see Hill (1988), chapter 2. Hill also argues that authority is seen only in terms of service, and that it is shared by all the members of the Primitive Church.

Chapter 2

Authority in the Major English Churches

Introduction

With this Biblical picture in mind, then, we turn to authority in the Church. As we have seen, the Bible repudiates the authoritarian and coercive models of authority used by secular rulers, and we should therefore expect authority in the Church to operate in a noticeably different way from this. We should expect leaders in the Church to exercise mainly moral, rather than legal or judicial authority. They should exhort those they lead to do what is right, maintain them in the truth and direct them towards God.[1] We should also expect to find structures of authority in each Church that assist leaders to perform this function.

The Roman Catholic Church

The Second Vatican Council has defined the Roman Catholic view of authority.[2] Most of the relevant material is in *Lumen Gentium*, the dogmatic constitution on the Church, but we will also need to consider *Dignitatis Humanae*, the decree on religious freedom. The only post-Conciliar official document on authority issued to date, *The Theological and Juridical Nature of Episcopal Conferences* (John Paul II, 1998b)[3] provides a pastoral application of the principles of the Second Vatican Council to particular episcopal conferences, but does not affect our argument here. While the Council provides the theoretical framework, the practical application is to be found in the *Code of Canon Law* (Canon Law Society, 1997), which sets out to embody and apply the theology of Vatican II to the practical governance of the Church. We shall examine the extent to which the practice fits the theory in detail in chapter 5. In this chapter, we shall simply produce a summary of the Code to illustrate the way it implements the principles of the Council.

---

1   Maintaining the faithful in the truth, particularly in times of controversy, may require the exercise of legal or judicial authority as well as moral authority. See McKenzie (1966), pp. 3–18.

2   Tanner (1990), pp. 820–1135.

3   This document states that while bishops may make declarations in their own dioceses, unanimity is required for conferences to make declarations in the name of the conference. It also seeks to regulate the statutes of episcopal conferences and ensure they are consistent with Canon Law.

Vatican II

Christ, the Council Fathers tell us, set up His Holy Church as a visible structure, a community of faith, hope and love through which He pours out grace and truth on everyone. This society is equipped with a hierarchical structure, and it is not separate from the mystical body of Christ. Rather, the two form one complex reality comprising a human and a divine element.[4] This dual analogy of the Church reflects the dual nature of Christ. In Him, the assumed human nature serves the divine Word as a living instrument of salvation inseparably joined with him. Similarly, the social structure of the church serves the Spirit of Christ who vivifies the church towards the growth of the body. This Church, which Christ entrusted to Peter to feed, and to the apostles to govern and spread, subsists (*subsistit*) in the Roman Catholic Church, governed by Peter's successor and the bishops in communion with him. Its boundaries, however, are not coterminous with the Roman communion.

Christ governs the Church, through the pope and the bishops, by the bonds of profession of faith, the sacraments, ecclesiastical government and communion. He established His Church as one flock under one shepherd. He sent the apostles, just as He had been sent, and willed that their successors, namely the bishops, should be shepherds in his church right to the end of the world. The popes, as successors of Peter, govern the whole Church with an infallible magisterium, as a permanent and visible foundation for unity of faith and communion. Those in the hierarchy, however, serve their brothers and sisters, and co-operate with them in the pursuit of salvation. The pope and the bishops constitute an apostolic college, similar to the original college of Apostles. The ancient practice of maintaining communion among the bishops, and particularly with the bishop of Rome, in unity, charity and peace reveals the collegial character of this body. It is revealed when the bishops gather in councils, particularly Ecumenical Councils, to discuss important matters and resolve them by consensus after listening carefully to all involved, and when they gather to consecrate a new bishop.[5] Bishops have proper, ordinary and immediate authority in virtue of their consecration: they are not vicars of the pope, although they cannot exercise this authority until he appoints them to their dioceses, and he can limit their authority for the good of the Church or the faithful.

Bishops delegate some of their authority to other clergy, appointing them as coadjutor or auxiliary bishops, giving them pastoral offices within the diocese, or appointing them as parish priests. All bishops, in virtue of their consecration, are members of the episcopal college, and are entitled to attend Ecumenical Councils.

---

4   Ibid., p. *854. This is a modified restatement Pius XII's encyclical *Mystici Corporis* (1943, p. 12), which teaches that the one, holy, catholic, apostolic Roman Church is the true Church and is the same as the mystical body of Christ. Pius repeated this in his later encyclical *Humani Generis* (1950, p. 10).

5   Ibid, p. *866. This view may be unjustifiably idealistic: there is substantial evidence that some early Councils were anything but peaceful and charitable, that agreement was far from unanimous, and that their success in suppressing the heresies they condemned was limited.

Nevertheless, the episcopal college only has authority when united with the pope, who, by virtue of his office, has full, supreme and universal power over the church, a power he is always able to exercise freely. This power extends to the college of bishops, in which the apostolic college continues to exist, provided it remains united to the pope and acts with his consent. It is exercised most fully in an Ecumenical Council, which must be called by the pope, who alone can confirm its decrees.

Lay people do not, in general, share in this authority. They can, however, and sometimes should, advise the priests on matters within their competence or expertise concerning the good of the Church. They should do so through the proper channels with courage, prudence and respect for the truth. They should accept the decisions made by their pastors, who should willingly make use of the prudent counsel of the laity, and allow them the freedom and space to act in the service of the Church.[6] Nevertheless, people acknowledge God's law through their consciences, through which they are directly accountable to God, and which they are bound to follow. Thus, no one should be forced to act against their conscience or prevented from acting according to it.[7] The Council fathers restate the doctrine of Vatican I that popes can make infallible pronouncements. The First Vatican Council placed strict limitations on the use of infallibility: the pope had to speak in his official capacity as shepherd and teacher of all Christians, and his definition could only cover maters of faith and morals.[8] Vatican II restated, clarified and extended these limits, concluding that the pope, acting as supreme shepherd and teacher of the faithful, proclaims in a definitive act a doctrine on faith or morals:

> For then the Roman pontiff is not delivering a judgment as a private person, but as the supreme teacher of the universal church, in whom the church's own charism of infallibility individually exists, [when] he expounds or defends a doctrine of the catholic faith.[9]

The bishops can also participate in making infallible statements with the pope, when they agree among themselves and with him on matters of faith or morals and pronounce their judgement as definitive. Such judgements have the same status as divine revelation. The people of God also share in the prophetic rôle of Christ, through the anointing of the Holy Spirit. Consequently, the whole body of Christ cannot err in matters of faith. When all, from the bishops to the last of the faithful laity, agree on such matters, they cannot be mistaken.[10] Before making *ex cathedra* pronouncements, the pope and the bishops must work sedulously through the appropriate means duly

---

6 Ibid., p. *879. Todd (1962, p. 222) suggests that petrified convention is an obstacle to fuller lay participation. McKenzie (1966, pp. 117–22) argues that over–management by the clergy can leave the laity with no room to act.

7 *Dignitatis Humanae*. Ibid., p. *1003.

8 *Pastor Aeternus*. Ibid., p. *816.

9 *Lumen Gentium*. Ibid., p. *869–70.

10 Ibid., p. *858. The Council assumes that such agreement is inspired by the Holy Spirit and guided by the magisterium. While Christians outside the Roman communion often have difficulty with Roman views of infallibility, the weaker view that the whole

to investigate this revelation and give it suitable expression. Once the bishops make such definitions, however, all Christians are bound to treat them as revealed truth. The aim of these provisions, which are a corrective to Vatican I, is to ensure that infallible pronouncements are only made after universal agreement is reached. In effect, if the Church makes an infallible statement, it believes it is acting through the Holy Spirit, and putting its seal on what the faithful already believe.

The Code of Canon Law

We will examine the current Code of Canon Law in more detail in Chapter 5. At this stage, we need only summarise how it implements the principles of Vatican II. The Code states that the pope has supreme, full, immediate and universal ordinary power, which he can always freely exercise, in the Church. Bishops, cardinals and others, aided by the Roman Curia, assist the pope in the performance of his office. The Synod of Bishops falls directly under the authority of the pope. Metropolitans and bishops have immediate, proper and ordinary authority within their jurisdictions, but they can only exercise this authority in hierarchical communion with the pope and the other members of the College of Bishops.

The College of Bishops delegate some of this authority, within each parish, to parish priests. The bishop is the sole legislator at the Diocesan Synod, and only he can publish its decrees, or appoint vicars general or episcopal vicars to assist him in his diocese. The moderator of the diocesan curia, the financial administrator, the pastoral council, and parish priest can only act under his authority. Lay people do not share in ecclesiastical power or authority,[11] which in catholic ecclesiology comes with ordination, but those with suitable character or knowledge can discharge certain ecclesiastical functions, or act as expert advisors to the councils in the Church. Different provisions apply to members of Religious communities, but they are also under authority, whether they are answerable to their Diocesan Bishop, or directly under the authority of the pope.

When it comes to the purpose of authority, the Apostolic Constitution *Sacrae Disciplina Leges*, promulgating the 1983 Code of Canon Law, tells us that 'the Catholic Church has been wont to revise and renew the laws of its sacred discipline so that ... these laws may be truly in accord with the salvific mission entrusted to the Church'.[12] It goes on to explain that the Code 'looks towards the achievement of order in the ecclesial society, such that while attributing a primacy to love, grace and the charisms, it facilitates at the same time an orderly development in the life both of the ecclesial society and of the individual persons who belong to it'.[13] This is a clear

---

Church cannot err commands much wider assent. Compare Moltmann and Küng (1981), p. 56.

    11 Norman Doe (1996, p. 57) comments that 'Lay members of the faithful may co-operate in the exercise of this power, but they do not possess it'.

    12 Canon Law Society (1997), p. xi.

    13 Ibid., p. xiv.

statement that a concern for pastoral need underlies the Code, and that its structures are intended to achieve growth in the Christian life.

This view of authority, then, is top-down. Power and authority flow down from Christ, through the pope, who is supreme pastor and legislator of the Church, and the bishops, to the lower clergy. Lay people do not carry institutional authority, but may have moral authority to advise as a consequence of their expertise or lifestyle. The clergy, however, while they may have a moral duty to listen to such advice, have no such duty to accept it. While the view of the pope as chief shepherd to the faithful, continuing Peter's ministry as chief rabbi to the faithful, sits well with the Biblical picture of Church leadership, the hierarchical and official structure is more problematic. We have seen that the New Testament offers no clear evidence that Jesus intended the Church to be hierarchical, or indeed that he intended it to have any institutionalised form of Church government. It is particularly difficult to reconcile a highly developed hierarchical structure with Biblical passages that emphasise that those leading the Church should not only not seek any personal position, but by contrast they should act as though they were the newest and youngest of Christians.[14] We have also seen that while Peter's ministry had to be continued by his successors, as the apostolic ministry generally needed to be continued by the successors of all the apostles, there is no clear evidence of a Petrine office as such to be handed on.[15]

Accountability presents a further problem. Upward accountability is clearly present, with clergy responsible to their bishops, who are in turn responsible to the pope, who appears only to be responsible to God. Lay people are not directly accountable to the hierarchy, so long as they follow the teaching of the Church. However, there does not seem to be any accountability downward. As we have seen, Matthew 18:15–20 indicates that the whole Church has a share in the discipline of offenders, which carries with it a share of authority, and the popes have for centuries described themselves as servants (literally, slaves) of the servants (slaves) of God. It would seem, therefore, that the hierarchy should also be accountable in some degree to the laity. There is currently no evidence that this accountability exists.

It is true, however, that the structures that the Roman Catholic Church has developed into its current hierarchy came into being quite early, probably in the second century. We shall explore how this came about, and what influences were most prominent, in Chapter 5. It seems, then, that the hierarchy of the Roman Catholic Church is insufficiently accountable, and that the Church at times overemphasises the institutional side of its life.

The Church of England

The Church of England has not issued a definitive statement on authority. Instead, it works with a dispersed model of authority, drawn from several sources. Its position is set out in the preface to the Declaration of Assent required of all clergy:

---

14 Matthew 20:20–28, Mark 10:35–45 and Luke 22:24–32.
15 Above, chapter 2.

The Church of England ... professes the faith uniquely revealed in the Holy Scriptures and set forth in the catholic creeds ... it has borne witness to Christian truth in its historical formularies, the Thirty-nine Articles of Religion, *The Book of Common Prayer* and the Ordering of Bishops, Priests and Deacons.[16]

The rule of thumb is that Scripture is the supreme authority, but it is mediated by tradition and reason. This line is taken up by the Doctrine Commission (1981):

The Church of England does not indulge in ringing, authoritative, doctrinal formulations. There are plenty of people within it, in official positions or otherwise, who do make formulations, and sometimes in more than ringing tones. But none of them is entitled to speak with final authority.[17]

It was the view of the 1948 Lambeth Conference that this dispersed model of authority with many interacting elements offered mutual support, mutual checking and mutual redressing of errors or exaggerations to the many-sided fullness of the authority committed by Christ to the Church. The conference recognised in this multiplicity of sources through which authority could be mediated 'God's loving provision against the temptations to tyranny and the dangers of unchecked power'.[18] Taking these sources in order, we have already examined what the Bible has to say about authority in Chapter 2. Further, the Apostles', Niceno-Constantinopolitan and Athanasian Creeds deal principally with the Trinitarian nature of God, and say nothing directly about the authority of the Church. The characteristic view of the Church of England on this matter, then, is set out in the Thirty-nine Articles, the Book of Common Prayer (BCP) and the Ordering of Bishops, Priests and Deacons.

It seems to follow from this that the Church of England grounds its doctrine of authority in both its liturgy and its theology. While the BCP contains a great deal of doctrinal material, it contains little evidence of an explicitly English Anglican view of Church authority. Thus, we will need to examine the Thirty-nine Articles and the Ordinal.[19]

The Thirty-nine Articles

Seven articles are relevant here. The first three of these articles deal specifically with the authority of Scripture. Article VI states that the Scriptures contain everything necessary for salvation, and that no one should be required to believe anything neither

---

16 Canon C15. Church of England (2005), p. 99. Emphasis original.

17 Doctrine Commission (1981), p. 231.

18 Anglican Communion (1948), p. 85.

19 Canons A4 and A5 take the BCP Ordinal as doctrinally standard, although it is rarely if ever used. The ASB Ordinal, which is used, is much more specific about authority. The preface to the ASB (p. 10) acknowledges that the BCP remains a doctrinal standard, but states that nothing in the ASB erodes the historical foundations of the faith. In the light of this, it seems reasonable to regard the ASB as an authoritative interpretation of the BCP, and I shall therefore refer to both Ordinals.

contained nor implied in them as an article of faith or necessary for salvation. Article VIII states that the Nicene, Athanasian and Apostles' Creeds ought thoroughly to be believed, since they can be proved by most certain warrants of holy scripture. Article XVII states that we must receive God's promises as they are set out in the Bible, and that we must follow the will of God as set out for us in His Word.

The next two Articles we consider talk specifically of authority in the Church. Article XX, *Of the authority of the Church*, states that the Church may authorise rites or ceremonies, and has authority to resolve controversies of faith. It may not expound one part of Scripture so that it conflicts with another, however, nor may it decree or require others to believe anything not contained in or implied by Scripture. Article XXI states that General Councils are assemblies of fallible men, and that therefore they may err, and sometimes have erred, even in matters concerning God. Even if they claim that their pronouncements are necessary to salvation, their declarations have neither force nor authority unless they can be proved from Scripture. Article XXXIV discusses tradition. It does not require total uniformity of tradition and ceremony: such things have always varied from time to time and place to place. Each national or particular Church may establish, amend or discontinue ceremonies or rites set up by human authority. Such ceremonies must not be repugnant to the Word of God, and must be designed for general edification. The Church may also rebuke those who do not comply for undermining authority and wounding the consciences of the weak. Finally, Article XXXVII states that the sovereign's government extends to the ecclesiastical realm as well as the civil realm. This does not give the sovereign the power to preach or administer the sacraments as though he or she were a bishop or priest, rather it affirms what the Article takes to be a Biblical principle that the jurisdiction of a Godly monarch is not restricted to the state.

In these articles, then, the Church of England emphatically declares that the Bible is the supreme source of authority in the Church. It is very clear that nothing repugnant to Scripture is acceptable, and that nothing not stated in or implied by Scripture is or may be required. Within these constraints, the Church has authority to authorise her own liturgy, to require her priests to follow it, and to decide controversies concerning matters of faith. She also reserves the right to discipline those who do not follow the rules.

The Ordinal

The preface to the BCP Ordinal states that 'It is evident unto all men diligently reading holy Scripture and ancient Authors, that from the Apostles' time there have been these Orders of Ministers in Christ's Church; Bishops, Priests and Deacons'.[20] In its notes to the Ordinal, the ASB states that the Church of England maintains

---

20 BCP, p. 553. This, of course, is a defence based on tradition rather than Scripture. Cranmer's statement may have been defensible in 1550, when the Ordinal was written, and between 1552 and 1662 when it was inserted into the Prayer Books, but it is no longer tenable.

the threefold ministry of bishops, priests and deacons, each ordained by bishops according to authorised forms of service with prayer and the laying on of hands. Bishops are ordained by the archbishop of the appropriate province and two other bishops; priests and deacons by a single bishop.

The most important parts of the ordination service for our purposes are the declarations, the vows, and the charges at the giving of the Bible (or New Testament). In the BCP, the bishop-elect promises to instruct the people, teaching them the Scriptures and driving away false doctrine, to be faithful in ordaining, sending or laying hands on others, and to show himself gentle and merciful towards the poor and needy. The ASB expands on this, stating that the bishop is called to lead in serving and caring for his flock, and to work with them in the oversight of the Church.[21] He is a chief pastor, who shares with his fellow bishops responsibility to further the unity of the Church, uphold discipline, and guard her faith. He must baptise, confirm, and preside at the Eucharist. He must administer discipline mercifully. He must have a special care for the needy and the outcast, and he must declare the forgiveness of sins to those who turn to God. He must pray for, teach, and govern his flock, following the example of the Apostles, speaking in the name of God and interpreting the Gospel of Christ.

In the BCP Ordinal, the bishop-elect affirms his calling, and accepts that Scripture contains everything necessary for salvation. He agrees to be diligent in prayer, to live a Christian lifestyle, and to be a faithful witness to Christ. In the ASB Ordinal, he also declares his assent to Anglican doctrine, agrees to promote Christian unity, and agrees to accept the discipline of this Church and faithfully to exercise authority within it. In the BCP rite, after ordination, at the giving of the Bible, the new bishop is charged to reflect on the Scriptures, and to act as a shepherd towards the flock, not a wolf; to feed them, not devour them. He is charged to hold up the weak, heal the sick, bind up the broken, reclaim the outcasts and seek the lost, being merciful to all. The ASB charges him to 'Receive this Book; here are words of eternal life. Take them for your guide. Keep watch over the whole flock in which the Holy Spirit has appointed you shepherd. Encourage the faithful, restore the lost, build up the body of Christ; that when the Chief Shepherd shall appear, you may receive the unfading crown of glory'.[22]

In the BCP, the bishop exhorts the new priests to be messengers, sentinels and stewards of the Lord. They must teach and admonish their congregations, feed and provide for the Lord's family, seek out God's people among the lost and guide them to Christ. The ASB adds that priests are called to work with the bishop and other priests in serving and shepherding those to whom they are sent, to minister to the sick, prepare the dying for death, and join the faithful in common witness to the

---

21 This is, at least in principle, a collaborative model of Episcopacy. G.R. Evans (1990, p. 28) comments that this model presupposes that 'The bishop has no powers apart from the community within which he serves, and every member participates in its authoritative actions'.

22 ASB, pp. 394–5. Compare Acts 20:28–29 and 1 Peter 5:1–4.

world. They must proclaim the word of the Lord, baptise, and prepare the baptised for confirmation. They must preside at the Eucharist, lead the people in prayer and worship, pray for them and bless them in the name of the Lord. Before ordination, in both rites, candidates affirm their calling, and accept that the Scriptures contain everything necessary for salvation. They agree to be diligent in prayer, to live a Christian lifestyle, to promote Christian unity, and to be a faithful witness to Christ. Unlike bishops, however, they accept the discipline of the Church and agree to obey their Ordinary. In the ASB rite, they also make a formal declaration of assent to Anglican doctrine. After ordination, at the giving of the Bible, new priests are given authority to preach the Word and administer the Sacraments. In the ASB rite, the bishop invites the priest to 'Receive this Book, as a sign of the authority which God has given you this day to preach the gospel of Christ and to minister his Holy Sacraments'.[23]

The BCP declaration at the ordination of a deacon states that deacons are called to serve in the Church, assisting in leading worship, particularly at the Eucharist, reading Scripture, catechising the youth, preaching, if licensed by the bishop, and baptising when necessary. They should also assist the priest to care for the sick, poor and needy. The pre–ordination affirmation for deacons in the BCP is shorter than that for priests, but the wording of the sections common to both is the same. The ASB affirmation is identical to that for priests, except for the different job title. After ordination, at the giving of the New Testament, new deacons are invited in the ASB rite to 'Receive this Book, as a sign of the authority given you this day to speak God's word to his people. Build them up in his truth and serve then in his name'.[24]

There are some interesting differences here. The ASB takes up Paul's comment from Acts 20:28 that the Holy Spirit appoints bishops as shepherds over the flock, yet it states that the bishop is called to work with the people in the oversight of the Church. This suggests a shared ministry, in which the bishop has authority only within the community he leads, and by their consent. This may suggest that while the bishop is called and appointed by God, he cannot exercise his ministry except in collaboration with those he supervises and to whom he ministers. The Biblical testimony that priests/elders and deacons are also appointed by the Holy Spirit is indirect, however. There is no statement concerning presbyters or deacons parallel to Paul's statement about bishops. However, in the New Testament the laying on of hands, which always accompanied such appointments, is generally associated with the giving of the power of the Spirit.

The ASB states that priests receive authority to preach and administer the Sacraments from God. Yet, they cannot exercise their ministry without the authority of the bishop. Canon C8, *Of ministers exercising their ministry*, states that the bishop confers this authority on priests and deacons at their installation or licensing, not at

---

23 Ibid., p. 363. In the BCP rite (p. 582), the bishop invites the priest to 'take thou authority'.

24 ASB, p. 349. Again, in the BCP rite (p. 566), the bishop invites the deacon to 'take thou authority'.

their ordination.[25] Article XXVI states that ministers act in Christ's name and by His authority. While priests receive their authority from God, then, they act as vicars of the bishop, who can withdraw the authority to exercise a particular ministry for just cause. Deacons also receive authority to preach, but neither Ordinal states the source of their authority. The ordination services for priests and deacons require that the congregation be told that those whose duty it is to examine such things believe that the candidates are apt and meet (BCP), or duly called to serve God in this ministry (ASB), and asked to agree to the ordination of the candidates. It therefore appears that while priests and deacons receive their authority to exercise their ministry from the bishop, their authority comes ultimately from God,[26] and it is mediated through the Church.

This, then, is a mixed model of the Church. It has both top-down and bottom-up elements. It is top-down in that it is hierarchical. Bishops promise to obey archbishops, priests and deacons promise to obey bishops and other senior clergy. Clergy cannot be appointed without the consent of the bishop, who has a continuing responsibility to supervise them. Nevertheless, since the bishop shares oversight with the congregations over which he presides (in part through the work of churchwardens, who are the representatives of the bishop and the crown in the parish), there are also bottom-up elements in the English Anglican view of authority. The bishops, for example, cannot ordain clergy without the support of the people. At the presentation of candidates for the diaconate or priesthood, the BCP allows the congregation to object, and in the ASB rites for all three forms of ministry, the congregation is asked 'Is it your will that he/they be ordained?' If a substantive objection is made, or assent is not forthcoming, the service cannot proceed. As we have already noted, the bishop's authority depends to some extent on the consent of the local churches in his diocese. This mixed model is also reflected in the structure of General Synod. We shall discuss its workings more fully in Chapter 6.

Synod is made up of three houses: bishops, clergy and laity. Any Measure or Canon must be approved by all three houses and Parliament before receiving Royal Assent. Only the House of Bishops can propose Doctrinal Measures, and Synod can only give final approval to the House of Bishops' text: they cannot alter it. Parliament can also veto Measures, but it cannot alter them. Neither clergy nor laity on their own can impose their wishes on the Church.

I have been unable to find a clear statement on the purpose of authority by the Church of England, but we can derive an Anglican view from a number of sources. The ASB tell us that at the ordination of a bishop, the archbishop prays that the bishop–elect might receive humility, and use his authority to heal, not to hurt, and to build up, not to destroy. Similarly, priests are charged at their ordination to build

---

25 Church of England (2005), p. 89.

26 The report of the 1978 Lambeth Conference (Anglican Communion, 1978, p. 76), when discussing Episcopal authority and synodical government, states: 'All authority comes from God and that which is given to the Church involves all the people of God in responsibility and obedience'.

up the congregation in faith, and do all in their power to bring their congregations to loving obedience to Christ. The 1948 Lambeth Conference states that God, the ultimate authority, demands of all his creatures entire and unconditional obedience. The bishop is the mediator of this authority in the Church, and he seeks to lead his diocese to God, exercising his authority in humble submission, as one under authority himself.[27] The 1978 Lambeth Conference describes the Church as a place of healing and restoration, which helps to make people whole.[28] Finally, the Anglican Roman Catholic International Commission, in *The Gift of Authority III* (1999), states that 'authority enables the whole Church to embody the Gospel and become the missionary and prophetic servant of the Lord'.[29] None of these last three documents represents the official position of the Church of England, although English Anglican bishops were members of the committees that produced all the documents, but when these are combined with the quotations from the Ordinal, they do suggest that the Church is concerned that authority should be used to facilitate pastoral care and spiritual growth.

This complex approach to authority does, however, seem to lead on occasion to the Church avoiding issues rather than dealing with them. One obvious recent example of this is the failure to address the issue of women bishops when the Church of England decided to ordain women as priests in 1992. Since the Church does not accept the Roman position that bishops have the fullness of orders, while priests have only basic orders, it would seem to follow that anyone who can be a priest can, in principle, be a bishop. This principle, however, currently applies only to men. While one might argue that Roman Catholic structures and doctrine are often too rigid, the Anglican structure, with all its different sources of authority and its many checks and balances, can seem rather labyrinthine. It is not clear that the effects of this have been an unmixed blessing. A more serious problem is that this model of authority often makes it difficult to find out what the Church of England thinks, even on matters that are relatively uncontroversial.

On occasion, the Church of England has even produced statements that are deliberately ambiguous, with a view to preserving communion between Evangelicals and Anglo-Catholics. The BCP Communion service contains a classic example of this. On delivering the bread, the priest says: 'The Body of our Lord Jesus Christ which was given for thee, preserve thy body and soul unto everlasting life: Take and eat this in remembrance that Christ died for thee, and feed on him in thy heart with faith by thanksgiving'. The first half of this statement, prescribed by the 1549 Prayer Book, seems to presuppose the Real Presence, while the second, which replaced it in 1552, emphasises spiritual memorial (*anamnēsis*). Subsequent Prayer Books combined the two statements, presumably in an attempt to satisfy both those who affirm the Real Presence and those who deny it. The statement made by the priest while delivering the chalice has the same structure and history. Ambiguity of this

---

27 Anglican Communion (1948), p. 85.
28 Anglican Communion (1978), p. 57.
29 ARCIC (1999), p. 25.

sort can impede the Church's ability to exercise the teaching function of the keys. If the Church is not sure itself what is permitted and what is forbidden, it is in no position either to enlighten the faithful, or to exercise effective discipline. Despite this, the Church of England does seem to have achieved a workable balance between a top-down and a bottom-up model, but its structures sometimes appear to hinder, rather than to help clarity in its teaching. While the Anglican desire to be a broad Church has served it well over the centuries, and helped to preserve its unity, its comprehensiveness perhaps needs to be tempered by a clearer sense of purpose in its Church government.

The Methodist Church

It is not always easy to ascertain the doctrine of the Methodist Church. From their earliest days, Methodist societies have been voluntary associations, and their members have been defined by their mission to spread scriptural holiness, rather than by any particular doctrinal framework: Methodists were and are defined more by what they do than by what they believe. When the Oxford Institute on Methodist Theological Studies held a symposium on the doctrine of the Church in 1962, the first paper was entitled *Do Methodists Have a Doctrine of the Church?*[30] Its answer was yes and no: at first there was no need for one, and while Methodist ecclesiologies developed later, even in the 1960s there was no generally agreed ecclesiology. Despite this, the Methodist Church has laid down doctrinal standards for its members, and successive Conferences have made declarations to elucidate them. These standards are set out in the *Constitutional Practice and Discipline of the Methodist Church* (1988/2005, hereafter CPD), which explains that they 'are not intended to impose a system of formal or speculative theology ... but to set up standards of preaching and belief'.[31]

It states that the Methodist Church rejoices in the inheritance of the apostolic faith and loyally accepts the fundamental principles of the historic creeds and of the Protestant Reformation. It explains that Methodism has maintained the Evangelical faith, based upon the divine revelation recorded in Holy Scripture, from the beginning. The Methodist Church acknowledges this revelation as the supreme rule of faith and practice, and pledges itself to remain faithful to the doctrines contained in Wesley's Notes on the New Testament and the first four volumes of his sermons. Other doctrinal declarations come from the Methodist Conference, which is also the final authority within the Methodist Church on the interpretation of Methodist doctrine. We must therefore look first to John Wesley, and then to acts of Conference, for the Methodist view of authority.

---

30 Kirkpatrick (1964), chapter 1.
31 Deed of Union, section 2, clause 4. CPD p. 213.

John Wesley

Wesley did not preach directly on authority in any of the sermons that became doctrinally important. He did, however, refer to important passages on authority in several sermons, and in his *Notes on the New Testament*. Two of these are important for our purposes: Sermon 4, *Scriptural Christianity*, and Sermon 74, *Of the Church*. Wesley divided *Scriptural Christianity* into four sections. The first three sections set out his views of the beginning of Christianity, its early spread, and its covering the earth.[32] The fourth section, a 'plain practical application' which we shall now consider, caused a major row and cost Wesley his right to preach to the University of Oxford.

Its thrust was that Scriptural Christianity nowhere existed, and that Oxford was in urgent need of reform. It was widely seen as a censure of the whole university. Wesley asked rhetorically if the authorities were one of heart and soul, showing the Lord abroad in their hearts, whether they were filled with the Holy Spirit, and full of the words of God, expressing dignity and love in all their actions. He asked whether the fellows taught their charges to love God, and all humanity for His sake, and whether they did so with every talent and with all their strength. He asked whether ministers of the Gospel were always concerned to serve God, trusting that they were inwardly moved by the Holy Spirit to minister to others, exalting God and edifying His people; whether they lorded it over God's heritage, or were willing to act as the servant of all, forsaking all worldly cares and studies; whether they were willing to suffer affronts and rejoice in Christ's reproach, or whether they resented correction. He asked whether the students were humble, teachable and advisable, or stubborn, self-willed, heady and high-minded; whether they pursued their studies with diligence or wasting days in gaming. He ended with a prayer that God should reform them to their first love. It is not surprising that this caused offence – no one likes to hear that they are a habitual sinner – but it is difficult now to see why this sermon caused such a reaction. Wesley's only crime seems to have been that he held up the Gospel before the University, and showed it by how far it fell short.

Wesley briefly took up the theme of service in *Of the Church*, which concentrates more on who the Church is than on what it is. All Christians are called to walk in lowliness, having in us that mind which was also in Christ Jesus, endeavouring to walk in the bond of peace, and clothed with humility.[33] In his *Explanatory Notes Upon the New Testament* (1976) Wesley explains his views on authority more fully. He tells us that when Christ told the Twelve they would sit on thrones, judging the Twelve Tribes of Israel, he made no condition, yet clearly a condition was implied, since Judas did not gain his throne, but it was taken by another.[34] On the application of this authority, Wesley emphasises that the Twelve imagined that the leaders in the

---

32 Wesley (1984), pp. 174–80.
33 Wesley (1986), pp. 53–5.
34 Notes on Matthew 19:28. Wesley (1976), p. 95.

Kingdom of Heaven would act like secular rulers. Jesus was trying to correct this idea.[35]

The disciples were to be benefactors to humanity, not by governing, but by serving.[36] They should not act in a haughty or domineering manner in matters concerning personal conscience, but rather should be examples to the flock, remembering that they, like their charges, were part of the one flock under the chief shepherd.[37] When it comes to the power of the keys, Wesley believes that in Matthew 16:18–20, Peter's profession of faith is the rock on which the Church is built, and that the keys were given to the Twelve, and not to Peter alone. All the acts of discipline performed by the apostles, he tells us, were undoubtedly confirmed in heaven.[38] Commenting on Matthew 18:18, he tells us that binding on earth consists of excommunicating the offender, without civil penalty, and loosing consists of absolution.[39] Commenting on John 20:21–23, he suggests that the tenor of the Gospel indicates that the apostles were expected to forgive the sins of the penitent, and to retain those of the impenitent.

He realises that this poses a problem: those who repent are immediately forgiven by God, whether or not they receive sacerdotal absolution later. From this he concludes that the power of the keys implies the declaration of the Christian terms of pardon, and the exclusion and readmission of offenders from the fellowship. The important thing to notice for our purposes is that Wesley was keen to affirm that the purpose of ministry and authority is service, not rule. We must now consider what the Methodist Church has said itself about authority.

Declarations of Conference

Called to Love and Praise (Methodist Conference, 1999b) is the current Conference statement on the Church. It states that:

> First, for the Christian the supreme authority is Christ, and to him there are vital, dependent witnesses, of which Scripture is the most important. Second, an eschatological perspective is vital: in this life we travel by faith, and faith is not the same as certainty, or it would not be faith. On such a journey, absolute or infallible authorities are not immediately accessible. But, thirdly, our experience and discernment, nurtured, stimulated and corrected by the witness of Scripture and tradition help to confirm the truth that is in Christ. In such a way Christians may have 'sufficient authority', or light, by which to travel.[40]

Sufficient authority is a concept developed by Rupert Davies (1968) in response to F.D.E. Schleiermacher's challenge that the dogmas and doctrines that many consider

---

35 Notes on Matthew 20:25. Ibid., p. 98.
36 Notes on Luke 22:26. Ibid., p. 287. Wesley does not comment on Mark 10:42–44.
37 Notes on 1 Peter 5:3. Ibid., p. 886.
38 Ibid., pp. 81–2.
39 Ibid., p. 90.
40 Methodist Conference (1999b), p. 6.

the essence of religion are the result of religious experience, inner convictions, which carry no authority for others.[41] Since others have received different 'revelations', Davies asks on Schleiermacher's behalf, how can we know that ours are trustworthy? Is it not utter irreligion to believe what others tell us, or to believe what we find in sacred writing? This leads Schleiermacher to the conclusion that, while doctrine is valuable, it is also derivative, and that the only authority we can trust is that of inward feeling, which authority is unassailable.

However, Schleiermacher seems to neglect the possibility that experience can be given, and have a real basis in something external to the person, and he denies that what others tell us can be a source of authority in religion. This excludes both personal testimony and the written word as sources of authority. While it seems true that religion is incomplete if not experienced, we might note that courts of law are far less convinced that personal testimony, which is also often a report of experiences, is useless in criminal trials (even trials for capital offences). He also seems to presuppose that supporters of the Enlightenment oppose religion for purely rational reasons. It is far from clear that this is true.[42] Further, Methodist Minister Kenneth Wilson, points out that such isolation is hardly attractive, and that any confidence we might have in such an approach is swiftly undermined in the light of experience, since our convictions need to be tested, and this puts us back where we started.[43]

Similarly Schleiermacher's claim in his earlier work *The Christian Faith* (1928) that religion is essentially contemplative denies that religion has anything to do with action, and separates it from ideas and principles. By maintaining this dichotomy, he separates religion from all branches of knowledge, including theology. It is far from clear that this sharp distinction between religion and theology can be maintained, or that religious knowledge should be in a different category from any other knowledge, and this therefore seems a false dichotomy. Even if Schleiermacher is right that religious knowledge is in some way different from other knowledge, all forms of knowledge, from mathematics to the humanities, have to rely at some stage on unprovable assumptions, which seems to place them in the same predicament Schleiermacher attributes to religion: their foundations are uncertain.[44] Schleiermacher consistently argues that feeling is at the core of religion. In doing so, he seems to surrender too much to Enlightenment thinking by reducing religion to religious experience, a view of religion that has never been widely held, not to mention the fact that his view may appear entirely subjective, and therefore, to many, unreliable.

---

41 Davies (1968), pp. 48–56. Schleiermacher's comments are from p. 87 of *On Religion* (1958).

42 Schleiermacher (1958), pp. 31, 36 and 46.

43 Timms and Wilson (2000), p. 39.

44 Schleiermacher (1928), pp. 3–128.

To avoid the perceived problems raised by Schleiermacher, Davies proposes 'a measure of authority which is sufficient for the spiritual and intellectual needs of the Church and its members'[45] as follows:

> Granted that we cannot know the truth of the Christian Religion *for certain,* or the truth of any particular doctrine *for certain,* we can be enough convinced of their truth to live by them without awareness of any contradiction between them and the rest of what we believe to be true: and an 'authority' which can convince us in this way and to this extent is 'sufficient'.[46]

Davies denies that the Bible, the Church, the pope, the Creeds, the consensus of the Universal Church, reason or spiritual insight have sufficient authority. For him, the only such authority is Christ, to whom the others are or can be trustworthy witnesses. Together, however, provided they tell the same story, the witnesses can also acquire sufficient authority. This, then, is the concept of sufficient authority used by the Methodist Conference.

Section 2.3.14 of *Called to Love and Praise* states that 'Spiritual authority "resides in the Church as a whole, in so far as the Church is indwelt by the divine spirit" (Matthew 16.19; 18.18; John 20.22–3)'.[47] This is expressed within Methodism through an interdependent connexionalism, with each level having representative bodies governing it. This connexional form of government, it states, precludes both independency and autocracy as modes of Church government. Leadership in the New Testament Church was interdependent and collaborative. The structures of the Methodist Church give a special place in decision-making to the ministers, who have oversight, and encourage contributions from experts on particular subjects, but it is ultimately the whole people of God who make decisions through their representatives. Nevertheless, once Conference or another representative body has made a decision, no further local consent is required for its implementation.

Methodist structures illustrate the collaborative nature of ministry through the Circuit, in which a minister usually has responsibility for more than one Church, and in which the Superintendent can normally call on more than one minister and several lay preachers; and the District, which links local and national structures. Two other things which seem to follow from the Methodist understanding of ministry, but which the declaration does not spell out, are that while the minister's authority is conferred through the members of the Church, it comes from Christ, and that such authority belongs to the office of ministry, not the individual minister.[48]

This last point is made in the statement on authority agreed by Roman Catholics and Methodists in March 1978. Both parties agreed that institutions have officers who have authority by virtue of their official status. They agreed that such officers should also have personal authority as a result of prophetic insight or lives of obvious

---

45 Davies (1968), p. 212.
46 Ibid. Emphasis original.
47 Methodist Conference (1999b), p. 18.
48 Kirkpatrick (1964), pp. 133–4.

sanctity.[49] The major point of disagreement between the two communions concerns the extent of that authority, with Roman Catholics asserting papal infallibility, and Methodists claiming only sufficient authority, as we have seen.

Called to Love and Praise informs us that Methodist structures preclude autocracy. Other texts, however, cast doubt on this statement. Section 29 (b) of the Deed of Union states that the President of Conference may, if he or she thinks it 'necessary or expedient', remove, transfer or appoint any minister to or from any station 'in such manner as he or she thinks fit'.[50] Any such move has the effect of an act of Conference. Should anyone wish to protest at such action, it would seem that they have no opportunity, since SO 160 permits only the President to summon an extra meeting of Conference, and then only in a great emergency. The next chance to censure a President for using this power arbitrarily or maliciously, would seem to be at the next Conference, at which the President retires anyway. While in a crisis it might be necessary to remove an individual from a particular situation quickly, it is difficult to see why the normally extensive checks and balances that operate in the Methodist Church do not also apply here. In this situation, the President's powers could seem rather excessive.

In *Called to Love and Praise*, the Methodist Church states that it believes that the Church should be structured for mission, and able to respond pragmatically when new needs or opportunities arise.[51] This clearly reflects a concern for authority to be applied in a pastorally sensitive way. The Church also raises the question of how effectively its structures continue to fulfil this objective. Section 4.7.10 is devoted entirely to this question, raising three challenges: firstly, whether Methodist structures help members to grow in holiness, secondly, whether the Church is in danger of allowing its structures to become ponderous and inflexible, and thirdly, whether in replacing these structures there is a danger of concentrating on the pastoral needs of settled congregations and becoming inward-looking. It considers, however, that the Holy Spirit continues to lead the Church to adapt its structures to face new situations and challenges, and urges Methodists not to be too resolute in defending the traditional structures of the Methodist Church against such change.

This structure, again, is a mix of the top-down and bottom-up. As we have seen, the Methodist Church sees its polity as primarily bottom-up, with the national structures being made up of representatives from local Churches and regional bodies. These delegated assemblies in general, and Conference in particular, then act as executive bodies on behalf of the wider Church. Methodist doctrine is clear, as are the ways in which it is formulated and the structures by which authority operates.

A few issues arise from this discussion, however. Firstly, if the Church sees its polity as bottom–up, it could be questioned why the President of Conference has such extensive powers in emergencies without appropriate checks and balances on them. Even though the President of Conference has been given these powers by the wider

---

49 *Statement on Authority*, Roman Catholic/Methodist Committee (1981), p. 17.

50 CPD, p. 228.

51 Methodist Conference (1999b), pp. 50–53.

Church through the Conference, it seems that there is a failure of accountability here, since the use of these powers, even if unjustified, does not appear to be subject to review by anyone else.

Secondly, there is a need to guard against unrestrained democracy, which may lead to local Churches and their members doing what they want, rather than coming together in Jesus' name and seeking God's will in a spirit of harmony. In a structure where decisions are made by delegate voting, there is a constant need to emphasise the necessity to seek the Holy Spirit when making decisions, as the Church's documents clearly indicate.

Finally, the Methodist Church seems strangely lacking in confidence that a robust doctrine of authority can be devised, despite the clear Biblical teaching that Christians do have authority, and that this authority is recognised in heaven. While the Methodist Church has accommodated Schleiermacher's critique of authority to the extent of defining its theology to avoid the perceived problems Schleiermacher addresses, I have been unable to find any non–Methodist statement of authority in which Schleiermacher is even mentioned.

The United Reformed Church

The United Reformed Church (URC) is the result of the amalgamation of the Congregational Church of England and Wales, the Presbyterian Church of England, the Re-formed Association of Churches of Christ, and the Congregational Union of Scotland. While two-thirds of the Churches that formed the URC in 1972 were Congregational, and most of the others were Presbyterian, the URC included a small number of Churches that were formerly members of the Baptist Union of Great Britain. The Churches of Christ, which joined in 1981, also had Baptist roots, and therefore we might expect to find a hybrid structure in the URC, with Congregational and Presbyterian elements both visible in the polity.

The most important documents of the URC are to be found in *The Manual* (2000). The *Basis of Union* is the foundation document of the Church.[52] In section 12 of this document, the URC 'acknowledges the Word of God in the Old and New Testaments, discerned under the guidance of the Holy Spirit, as the supreme authority for the faith and conduct of all God's people'.[53] In section 18, the URC acknowledges its duty, under the authority of Scripture and in corporate responsibility to Jesus Christ, to be open to the leading of the Holy Spirit and, if necessary, to make new declarations of faith. It accepts the Apostles' and Nicene Creeds as witnesses to the catholic faith, and also recognises its own heritage of faith as 'stating the Gospel and seeking to make its implications clear'.[54] The URC, then, takes its stand on Scripture as the supreme authority in the Church, but acknowledges that its formative documents are also authoritative, in that they expound and apply the Gospel. The most influential of

---

52 United Reformed Church (2000), section A.
53 Ibid., p. A2.
54 Ibid., p. A5.

these documents are the *Westminster Confession* and the *Savoy Declaration*.[55] Two sections of the *Confession* are relevant: chapter 31, *Of Synods and Councils*, and *The Form of Presbyterial Church Government*. Section 3 of chapter 31 states that synods and councils of ministers may resolve controversies of the faith and make regulations for orderly worship and Church government. They may also exercise discipline in cases of maladministration. If their decisions are consonant with God's Word, they should be received with reverence and submission. However, synods are fallible, and therefore their declarations may not be made rules of faith and practice, but may assist in both.

This seems to be saying that if, and only if, the decrees of Councils agree with Scripture, they are to be received as an ordinance of God, carrying both the authority of Scripture and the authority of the Council, but caution is required lest the Church fall into error, because synods have sometimes reached the wrong decisions. Here we see the centrality of Scripture in the Presbyterian tradition. Notice, however, that provided synods stick to Scripture, they can overrule individuals' liberty of conscience, much stressed elsewhere in the *Confession*, for the good of the Church. *The Form of Presbyterial Church Government* explains that the offices in the Church are pastors, teachers, other church-governors [elders], and deacons. The pastor has a ruling power, which he shares with the elders. Deacons are commissioned to see to the needs of the poor. These offices are conferred by the Presbytery. Christ gave the apostles the keys of the Kingdom, and 'hath since continually furnished some in his Church with gifts of government, and with commission to execute the same, when called thereunto'.[56] Discipline has three stages: rebuke, exclusion from Communion, and expulsion.

The *Confession* finds Scriptural authority for Presbyteries and congregational assemblies, although these congregational assemblies consist only of elders – they do not include the whole congregation. It also finds authority for provincial and national synods. It concludes: 'It is lawful, and agreeable to the word of God, that there be a subordination of the congregational, classical [of the Presbytery], provincial, and national assemblies, for the government of the Church'.[57] This polity is mainly top-down. There is a hierarchical structure of councils, with national assemblies superior to local assemblies. Each person in a position of authority receives that authority directly from Christ, although ordination by the Presbytery is a prerequisite. The local Church has no voice in the process unless it chooses to oppose a candidate for ordination and shows due cause for doing so. Authority comes with the office of ministry; it is not personal. It comes from Christ through His calling, rather than from the Church through either the historic Episcopate or the Church Meeting.

---

55 Thompson (1990), pp. 10–117.

56 *Of Church–Government, and the several sorts of Assemblies for the same*. Ibid., p. 49. This places the power of the keys in the hands of the ministers, rather than in the hands of the laity.

57 *Of Synodical Assemblies*. Ibid., p. 53. No Scriptural citation is given for this section. The Section in square brackets is mine.

The *Savoy Declaration* has no equivalent to chapter 31 of the *Westminster Confession*,[58] and therefore our interest in it here is limited to *The Institution of Churches and the Order Appointed in them by Jesus Christ*. This states that all power in the Church ultimately derives from Christ, by the appointment of the Father. Each local Church has all the power it needs to maintain order and discipline as instituted by Christ. No body more extensive than the local Church has any authority, although synods may be called to give advice on matters of debate. No standing or permanent synods are required. The officers in the Church – pastors, teachers, elders and deacons – who exercise this authority, are elected by all and draw their authority from the local Church.[59] This, then, is a bottom-up view of authority. Authority is vested in the local Church, which elects officers to minister to it.

The URC, having inherited this dual heritage, has tried to combine the best of both systems. As we have seen, authority in the URC ultimately derives from Scripture, but in practice, its application rests with a number of different councils, within both the local and the wider Church. The URC understands itself primarily as a conciliar Church, and its structure reflects this. Section 10 of the *Basis of Union* describes how the URC applies this authority. It states that while the Church will uphold the rights of personal conviction, 'it shall be for the Church, in safeguarding the substance of the faith and maintaining the unity of the fellowship, to determine when these rights are asserted to the injury of its unity and peace'.[60] This is expanded in the *Structure of the United Reformed Church*, section B of *The Manual*. Section 1.(3) of the *Structure* reads as follows:

> The oversight of the United Reformed Church shall be the concern both of the local church and wider representative councils. The councils of the United Reformed Church shall be:
> a. the church meeting and elders' meeting of each local church;
> b. the council of each district to be known as a district council and of each area of ecumenical cooperation to be known as an area meeting;
> c. the synod of province or nation to be known as a provincial or national synod; and
> d. the General Assembly of the United Reformed Church.
> These four parts of the structure of the United Reformed Church shall have such consultative, legislative and executive functions as are hereinafter respectively assigned to each of them and each shall be recognised by members of the United Reformed Church as possessing such authority, under the Word of God and the promised guidance of the Holy Spirit, as shall enable it to exercise its functions and thereby to minister in that sphere of the life of the United Reformed Church with which it is concerned.[61]

---

58 I am indebted here to Bray (1994) for his comparison of the *Westminster Confession* and the *Savoy Declaration*.

59 Ibid., pp. 112–3. Here the keys are in the hands of the laity, although some of this authority is delegated to the minister.

60 United Reformed Church (2000), p. A2.

61 Ibid., pp. B1–B2. The *Structure* never explicitly identifies what it considers the Church's legislative functions, but it seems that these functions are restricted to General Assembly. We shall return to this issue in chapter 8, where we shall discuss it in more detail.

This is then spelt out in detail. The URC's structure contains both top-down and bottom-up elements. We shall concentrate on General Assembly and the local Church. Assembly embodies the unity of the URC, and acts as the central organ of its life and the final authority, under the Word of God and the promised guidance of the Holy Spirit, in all matters of doctrine and order and in all other concerns of its common life. This enables it to interpret all forms and expressions of the polity, practice and doctrinal formulations of the URC including the *Basis* and the *Structure* and to determine when rights of personal conviction are asserted to the injury of the unity and peace of the Church. It also makes decisions on reports and other recommendations, and regulates theological colleges. It may alter the *Basis*, the *Structure*, or its own Standing Orders, hear appeals, or make decisions affecting the whole of the URC.

In the local Church, the Church Meeting is the governing body. It is responsible for local mission, ecumenical relationships, calling a minister, accepting and transferring members, and receiving and authorising action on reports from other councils of the Church. It elects elders to ensure that the spiritual life of the Church and the fabric of the Church building are kept in good order, and to represent the local Church in the wider councils of the URC. Unlike the traditional Presbyterian arrangement, however, the elders are responsible to the Church Meeting, and cannot implement decisions without its consent. While at first sight this may seem similar to Methodist polity, with the URC's Church Meeting performing a similar rôle to the Methodist Church Council, there is an important difference. No decision made by any of the wider councils of the URC can be implemented without the consent of the Church Meeting of the relevant local Church. The fact that decisions are made by people who are ultimately delegates of their local Churches does not guarantee implementation, although an unreasonable refusal to implement such a decision would inevitably lead to a pastoral intervention.

The URC, in its *Basis of Union*, explains that its purpose is fourfold. First, it seeks to make its life a continual offering of itself and the world to God through Jesus Christ (the worshipping function). Second, it seeks to receive and express the life of the Holy Spirit in the local Church and the wider fellowship, and there to declare the reconciling and saving power of the Christ-event (the teaching function). Third, it seeks to live out the ministry of caring, forgiving and healing love of Jesus (the pastoral function). Fourth, it seeks to bear witness to Christ's rule over the nations in all the variety of their organised life (the prophetic function). This seems to be as close as the URC gets to spelling out what authority is intended to achieve.

It is difficult to see how the exercise of authority could come under what I have called the worshipping function, and authority in the sense we are considering it does not easily fit into what I have called the teaching or prophetic functions as the URC understands them.[62] Thus, the purpose of authority seems to be most fully

---

62 While authority might fit into the teaching function of (say) the Roman Catholic Church, the URC's understanding of teaching concentrates more on the inspiration of the Holy Spirit in preaching and in the interpretation of Scripture than on authoritative exegesis

contained in the third function: 'to live out, in joyful and sacrificial service to all in their various physical and spiritual needs, that ministry of caring, forgiving and healing love which Jesus Christ brought to all whom he met'.[63] If this is a fair reading, it would seem that the URC also shares the concern that authority should be used to promote spiritual growth.

We therefore see that the URC has, as expected, a hybrid polity. It is Presbyterian in that the wider councils of the Church can make decisions on behalf of local Churches, and in that each Church has a group of elders who share the leadership of the Church with the minister. It is Congregational in that the Church Meeting, rather than the elders, is the governing body of the local Church. While the elders can recommend action, and in practice such recommendations are usually followed, in the URC the Church Meeting has the right to overrule the elders whenever it sees fit.

The URC is still exploring the tensions between the Presbyterian and Congregational models of Church, and the problems arising from them. It seems committed to the mix of top-down and bottom-up structures in its decision-making, but it has not developed a way of dealing with the fact that its current structure allows the local Churches legitimate authority to ignore decisions of the wider Church. This undermines its claim that General Assembly is the final authority on doctrine, order and the common life of the Church. In this situation, there is clear downward accountability, in that the local Churches can easily hold any of the wider councils to account if they disagree with them, by simply ignoring their decisions. Upward accountability, however, is impaired by the fact that although the wider councils, and particularly General Assembly, have executive powers and authority, this authority is ineffective if a local Church chooses not to accept their decisions. This structure is clearly unbalanced, and it therefore seems that the URC has yet to integrate its top-down and bottom-up structures satisfactorily. It remains to be seen whether the URC will eventually give priority to the Congregational model, by restructuring the way its wider councils operate and retaining the effective veto of the Church Meeting, or to the Presbyterian model, by insisting that decisions of General Assembly are implemented, even where a local Church has doubts or reservations about those decisions.

The Baptist Union

If we faced difficulties in ascertaining Methodist doctrine, these problems are greatly magnified when it comes to Baptist doctrine. Baptist Churches have traditionally placed great stress on the freedom of individual conscience. This militates against the formation of a single Baptist doctrine on most issues. The Baptist Union does not often issue guidance to Churches. What guidance it does issue is purely advisory,

---

backed by tradition. What I have called the prophetic function applies mainly to those outside the Church.

63 Ibid., p. A2.

and the Churches need not accept it. The Baptist Union has, however, published documents about authority. B.R. White (1976) tells us that like all other Christians, Baptists believe that authority ultimately derives from God in Christ.[64] This authority is primarily transmitted, he argues, through Scripture, through the contemporary thinking of the Church, through individual Christians and, interestingly, through tradition. White points out that the New Testament is in itself a deposit of tradition. Paul, for example, was concerned to pass on the tradition of the Lord's Supper to the Christians at Corinth.[65] He insisted that they should hold on to the tradition he had taught them about Christ's death, burial, resurrection and the post-resurrection appearances. It is also clear that the Spirit has spoken to men like John Wyclif, Martin Luther and John Calvin: in fact, He has been continuously active through the centuries. If this is accepted, and if we accept that the Spirit manifests the truth of God, we seem committed to accept that tradition has some value.

While this is a long way from the Roman view of tradition, even the influential (Reformed) *Second Helvetic Confession* of 1566 accepted that the teaching of the Fathers and Councils should be accepted provided they agree with the Scriptures.[66] Authority, however, has to be applied in the local Church. Baptists have traditionally adopted a radically Protestant model of the Church, which, as we shall see in more detail in chapter 7, acknowledges only three stages in the use of authority: two rebukes and then exclusion. If early Baptists were chaste and honest, paid their taxes and worshipped regularly, it seems their Church required little else of them. Authority derives from the congregation, and it is expressed through elders (of whom the minister is one) and deacons. Early General Baptists also asserted that there could be an order of 'bishops or messengers' above these officers.[67]

Baptists have generally been egalitarian in principle, believing that the Holy Spirit may speak to the Church through any of its members, and therefore that everyone should have a chance to be heard when there are decisions to be made. In practice, however, the minister, elders and deacons are likely to have a greater voice than others in how the Church operates, both because of their personal characters and (in the case of the minister) because of his or her professional training. Both of these sources of authority, however, are subordinate to Scripture: if a minister, elder or deacon lives an unscriptural life or fails to preach the Gospel, the result will be a loss of authority. Within the wider Church, there are local and national associations. There were differences between early Baptists on the position of the associations: Calvinist Baptists argued that such councils had only advisory power, while General Baptists thought they had the right to 'hear and determine as also to excommunicate' when hearing disputes.[68] Baptists from both groups were agreed, in general, on the

---

64 White (1976), pp. 5–19.
65 1 Corinthians 11:23–25.
66 Cochrane (2003), pp. 226–7.
67 From articles 31 and 39 of *An Orthodox Creed, or a Protestant Confession of Faith* published in 1679. Lumpkin (1969), pp. 298–334.
68 From article 39 of the *Orthodox Creed*. Lumpkin (1969), p. 327.

need for associations: in this way, Baptists express their interdependence as well as their independence.

In the 1948 *Declaration on the Church*, the Baptist Union states that it believes that a local Church 'lacks one of the marks of a truly Christian community if it does not seek the fellowship of other Baptist churches, does not seek a true relationship with Christians and churches of other communions and is not conscious of its place in the one catholic Church'.[69] No association, however, can coerce a local Church, and no local Church can coerce another: they can offer advice, which the receiving Church is expected to consider seriously, but each Church makes its own decisions. The Baptist Union of Scotland (1985) distinguishes between authority and power: power is coercive, while authority invites voluntary acceptance of its guidance. If authority becomes authoritarian, it loses part of its prestige. Authority is therefore entirely consistent with freedom, which Baptists have always greatly prized. While the authority of the Church is vested in the members, the result is a theocracy, not a democracy: the members are there to discover God's will, not to do what they like.[70] This view of authority has long been established in national Baptist constitutions. This can be seen from *The Constitutions of the Baptist Union* (Sparkes, 1996). Resolution 10 of the 1813 Constitution of the General Union of Baptist ministers and Churches disclaims any authority over or supervision of local Churches. Section 1 of the 1835 Constitution, then of the Baptist Union of Great Britain and Ireland, recognises that each Church has, within itself, the power and authority to exercise discipline, rule and government, and do all other things necessary for its edification under Christ's law. The declaration of Principle in section 3 of the 1873 Constitution states that every separate Church has liberty to interpret and administer the laws of Christ.[71]

Section 3 subsection 1 of the 1904 Constitution states that the basis of the Union is 'That our Lord Jesus Christ is the sole and absolute authority in all matters pertaining to faith and practice, as revealed in the Holy Scriptures, and that each Church has liberty to interpret and administer His Laws'.[72] This is repeated word for word in the 1926 Constitution.[73] The current Constitution was adopted in 1991, this time by the Baptist Union of Great Britain. In this, the wording has again changed. It now reads:

> That our Lord and Saviour Jesus Christ, God manifest in the flesh, is the sole and absolute authority in all matters pertaining to faith and practice, as revealed in the Holy Scriptures, and that each Church has liberty, under the guidance of the Holy Spirit, to interpret and administer His Laws'.[74]

---

69 Hayden (1980), p. 8.
70 Baptist Union of Scotland (1985), pp. 5 and 14–15.
71 Sparkes (1996), pp. 8–14.
72 Ibid., p. 23.
73 Ibid., p. 32.
74 Ibid., p. 51.

Thus, we can see a development of the self-understanding Baptist Union. In 1813, it seems, the Union was defined as much by what it was not as by what it was. Now the Union understands its basis through positive theological statements. It is interesting to note that while the nineteenth-century constitutions emphasised the liberty of the local Church and its independence from outside oversight, the twentieth-century constitutions, while restating that liberty, have shifted their focus away from the local Church and placed more emphasis on Jesus Christ as revealed in Scripture. They have also become increasingly nuanced. This may suggest an increasing confidence in associations among Baptists, who were at first extremely suspicious of them. It may be that the Baptist Union, having overcome early concerns about its intentions, has, during the twentieth century, gained the confidence to give positive advice, agreed by delegates of its member Churches, about issues central to the faith.

Paul Harrison (1959) examines the relationship between the local Church and the association.[75] He points out that since authority resides in the local Church, and the local Churches do not, in general, delegate their authority to associations, the officers of such associations have no authority to act on behalf of the Churches. They are, nevertheless, appointed to particular committees, and expected to work for the Church, and they are influential as a result of their position, so it seems that they have power without authority. If they are to do their appointed jobs, he argues, they must act illegitimately, since Baptist theology does not allow them the authority they need to operate.[76] Furthermore, under the Baptist Union constitution, the officers control the Assembly agenda, which gives them a disproportionately large say in policy decisions, because the Assembly is likely to be so large and unwieldy that making informed decisions becomes extremely difficult.[77]

The Faith and Unity Executive Committee and Doctrine and Worship Committee of the Baptist Union set out to explain the relationship between the local Church and the wider Church in terms of covenant communities (Fiddes, 1994). They argue that while Baptists have no difficulty in seeing the local congregation and the fellowship of all believers as Church, Baptists should also affirm the ecclesial nature of assemblies of Churches, with covenant responsibility to make decisions and prophetic criticisms, to sponsor mission and to exercise oversight (*episkope*), albeit in a different way. Marks of this covenanting would include a means of including local Churches in appointing representatives to these assemblies, in recognising and

---

75 Harrison's study is based on the American Baptist Convention in the 1950s, but many of his comments have wider relevance. We shall concentrate on their application to British Baptist Churches.

76 Harrison (1959), pp. 60–62.

77 With 1,813 English Churches in the Baptist Union in 1998 (Baptist Union, 1999, p. 173), each of which is entitled to send its minister and at least one other delegate, in addition to the officers of the Union and other delegates (Sparkes, 1996, p. 52), the theoretical size of the Assembly would be around 4,000.

appointing oversight, and a commitment to give weight and trust to the decisions of the larger bodies.[78]

They argue that the wider structures reflect the aim and nature of the Church Meeting, although the Assembly and the Council are two different expressions of the covenant relationship, and neither can simply be equated with the Baptist Union. They argue that the declaration of principle is the written form of this covenant, that the Council and Assembly are related in 'a balance of mutual trust',[79] which can only be won, not imposed. This requirement for trust prevents the Council from imposing its own agenda on the Assembly. The decisions of Assembly cannot be imposed on local Churches, but must be tried and accepted at the local level. Similarly, they urge local Churches not to ignore decisions of Assembly lightly, since they believe that local Churches express covenantal unity, and that each Church needs fellowship with others in order to discover the purpose of Christ.

Baptists recognise disciplinary authority only in its most limited sense, taking the form of two rebukes for sin, followed by expulsion if necessary, should the sinner prove impenitent. Since to attempt to drive sinners away from salvation would be contrary to the Gospel, the only possible intention of this form of authority can be to shock offenders into repentance, and thence to restore their broken relationships with God and with their fellow Christians. Thus, in the Baptist Churches, the use of authority is also intended to heal consciences and to reclaim the lost. For them, the local Church contains all the elements required to be a Church – it is not dependent on wider oversight – and the local Churches are united in that all are responding to the same Gospel. While the Baptist Union sees association as an essential element of being Baptist, local Churches are free to leave one association and join another if they have doctrinal disagreements with the association they leave.[80] However, as we have seen, the Bible seems to indicate that there are both local and universal components of authority. It might therefore be questioned whether the Baptist view that the local Church contains all the essential elements of the Church (a view also shared by Congregationalists) can be sustained. While Baptists do recognise a duty to associate, and therefore to have wider Church structures, they deny such structures any share in authority. It is not clear to what extent Baptist Churches can model their structures on the New Testament, in which the fellowship of believers is seen as an organic whole, while at the same time maintaining such a loose fellowship amongst themselves.

Conclusion

This, then is where the Churches stand on authority now. As we have seen, each denomination expresses authority in its structures in a different way, and each

78 Fiddes (1994), pp. 10–14. The text refers to *episkope* on several occasions.

79 Ibid., pp. 15–22.

80 For example, a Church might leave the Baptist Union and join the Federation of Independent Evangelical Churches.

structure has its own weaknesses. We must go on to examine how this diversity of views came about, and what factors influenced its development. This examination will take in legal and political theory, as well as theological developments, and will examine the roots from which each Church sprang. Having done so, we will then be in a position to analyse the effect these developments have had on the Churches' views of authority.

Chapter 3

Justice in the Bible, Roman Law and Greek Philosophy

Introduction

We have seen in the last chapter that the Churches we are examining have interpreted the Biblical texts on authority in several different ways. I believe that these differences are caused, at least in part, by differences in the understanding of the related concepts of judgement and justice. If the Churches disagree on the nature of justice, they will also disagree on its application. I take it as an axiom for this chapter that any system of justice must be largely coherent, and dedicated to achieving a particular end. It must have clear objectives and it must be set up specifically to achieve them.

Justice in the Church

If the Church is to use her authority to forgive, or not to forgive, sins in a manner true to its Biblical origins, it is essential that her ideas about what justice is, including its aims and underlying assumptions, are Biblically based. If the Church has drawn on ideas that run counter to the New Testament, her view of authority is likely to be a syncretism of Biblical and secular viewpoints, possibly leading to mistaken or inappropriate ideas of authority. My task in this chapter is to examine ideas of justice in early Hebrew, Roman and Greek thought. While the early Roman writers clearly show the signs of an authoritarian approach, the Greeks show little sign of individualism. Instead, in Aristotle, they show the dawning of libertarianism, which I believe is one source of democratic ideas of Church government. In Greek thought, life is often seen as the unfolding of tragic fate. Aristotle seems to be the major exception to this. I shall argue that Radical Protestants introduced individualism into the Church, under the influence of both the political circumstances of the day and their interpretation of the theology of Zwingli. We shall trace the progress of democratic and individualistic ideas through the Reformation to the Independent Churches in chapters 6 and 7. This will take in political and historical developments in addition to theological issues.

This chapter sets out some early views of justice. I shall examine judicial systems in four different contexts: Roman Law, Greek ethical philosophy, the Torah, and the New Testament. I shall concentrate more on the early forms of Roman Civil Law, since these reveal the differences from Biblical principles more sharply than the later forms, which have greatly softened. I shall then canvas the views of three early philosophers, and I shall seek to extract principles of justice from this study. I will then use them in subsequent chapters to evaluate later ideas of justice and authority.

What is Justice?

The Old Testament

In the King James Version of the Old Testament, the words 'justice', 'righteousness' and 'equity' frequently appear together. Justice and righteousness appear in the same verse 37 times, justice and equity six times, righteousness and equity four times, and all three words appear together three times. There is clearly a link between these words. We are therefore dealing with a cluster of related ideas, including acting ethically, right conduct and character, impartiality, vindication of the innocent, due process, uprightness, evenness and truth. In almost every case, the words translated justice or righteousness are derived from *tsaddiq*, *tsedaqah* and *tsedeq*. Similarly, the words for equity are almost always *meshar*, *mishor*, *yosher* and *yasher*. We must now explore what these words mean in their Old Testament context.

Botterweck, Ringgren and Fabry (2003), explain that there are two main schools of thought about the root *tsedeq*. One view sees righteousness and justice in a legal sense, as concurrence with a standard or norm, emphasising God's justice. The other views them as synonymous with deliverance and salvation, describing it as a relationship with God, rather than success or failure in meeting a judicial standard or norm.[1] They add that the latter view has traditionally been the more widely held, and that most scholars have seen righteousness as a primarily relational term, involving a real relationship between two entities. As a consequence of this relationship, the just or righteous person is the one who acts rightly, who takes refuge in God's righteousness and for whom God intervenes. Righteousness is a gift, leading to salvation. It produces a capacity to do good, leading to well-being for oneself and others.

Moving from the general to the specific, they state that in its verb form, *tsedeq* means 'be just/righteous' or 'emerge as just/righteous', often in a dispute against another person, but never before God. This can include both victory and exoneration in legal disputes. In its masculine substantive form, *tsedeq* refers to the ordered, divine principle of justice and righteousness, and can sometimes evoke the idea of active intervention, in the sense of deliverance or vindication. It also emphasises the righteousness of God's order. One can strive for *tsedeq*, through claiming what is rightfully due, a principle which, as we shall see later, is fundamental to many ideas of justice. In its feminine substantive form, *tsedaqah*, it goes further and attributes righteousness to humans, both in corporate form as the people of God,[2] and

---

1   Botterweck, Ringgren and Fabry (2003), pp. 243–56.
2   Deuteronomy 6:25 and 24:13.

to individuals like Abraham and Phinehas.[3] *Tsedaqah* can refer both to divine and human action. From God, it is positive, salvific activity. In humans, it is the exercise of human righteousness arising from God's activity. In some passages, it can mean 'legitimate claim'.[4] While *tsedeq* and *tsedaqah* are often interchangeable, they are not exact synonyms. *Tsedeq* emphasises correctness and order, while *tsedaqah* emphasises function and activity.

Botterweck and Ringgren (1990), explain that the root *yasher* refers literally to a physical quality, usually referring to something straight, as opposed to crooked, right, as opposed to wrong, or level, as opposed to undulating.[5] It is more commonly used figuratively, and this use can be described in two ways: 'straight' and 'level'. The dominant ethical sense of *yasher* denotes right, honest and upright conduct that does not stray out of bounds into the crooked ways of the dishonest. It can also indicate that things are progressing smoothly, in the sense that there are no problems or obstacles to an undertaking, for example, that God is making rough places into level ground. As we shall see later, a level playing field and equality of opportunity are essential components of many ideas of equity. Thus the concepts of justice and equity in the Old Testament are rooted in Jewish ideas about the nature of God, and offer objective standards against which human actions can be judged.

Rabbi K. Kahana Kagan (1955) explores how these concepts have been used in wider Jewish thought. He sets out two political theories of government: law imposed from above (top-down), and social contract (bottom-up), and argues that the latter is characteristic of Hebrew thought. This theory, of which Rousseau's *Social Contract* (1968) is the most famous, but not the only example, holds that the people agree to obey a ruler, who in turn agrees to provide order. Kagan finds the roots of social contract theory in the Biblical concept of covenant.[6] In Kagan's view, the Hebrew concept of the social contract is associated with the high ideas of freedom, righteousness and equality. Absolutism and coercion do not appear in Jewish Law. It is based on the covenant of Sinai and the consent of the community. Even the king was not a lawgiver – he was subject to the law and could be held to account just like everyone else. Prophets often denounced kings who misbehaved to their face: Samuel protested against Saul, Nathan against David, Elijah against Ahab, Elisha against Jehoram, and Jeremiah against Zedekiah. The principle of equality before the law is an essential element – Jewish social life and laws did not depend on the concept of status. So is the principle of freedom. The covenant was established when the Israelite people accepted it.

---

3   Genesis 15:6 and Psalm 106:30–31.

4   For example, Genesis 30:33, 2 Samuel 19:28, Nehemiah 2:20, Isaiah 5:23 and Amos 5:7.

5   Botterweck and Ringgren (1990), pp. 465–9.

6   Kagan (1955), p. 94, citing Borgeaud (1894), p. 78. Chilton and Neusner (1995, p. 23) state that only the Scriptural law codes governed all Jews everywhere, and that different groups interpreted these codes differently. It would therefore be misleading to speak of 'Jewish Law' as a uniform system. They also argue (p. 31) that in Jewish thought, Scripture is a source of facts, which must be selected and applied to any given situation.

Kagan finds other related concepts of justice in the Talmud – furthering human happiness and the alleviation of human suffering, the improvement of human moral and ethical standards, the consent of the governed and individual freedom. The overarching principle for him, however, is the notion of equality and ethics in their widest application.[7] We seem to have a mix of the top-down and bottom-up approaches here. To explore how this might work out in practice, I propose to examine the idea of Jubilee. The laws of Jubilee are set out in Leviticus 25 and 27, and restated in Isaiah 61. I shall concentrate on Leviticus 25:15–16 and 39–41. The writer explains that the price paid for a field must take account of the years until the Jubilee, because its owner is selling a series of crops, not the field.[8] He also tells us that if one Jew sold himself to another Jew, due to poverty, he must be treated as a hired man rather than a slave.[9] It was not the person or property that was sold, but his/her/its use. Different rules applied for Gentiles, who could be treated as property and enslaved forever, and for houses inside walled cities, which could only be redeemed for a year after their sale. The general principle, however, is clear: everything returned to its original owner, and everyone was set free, every second or third generation. Note that when a bound labourer was released the whole family went free. This is quite different from the normal rules of slavery, under which an individual might be set free or buy freedom for him/herself, while their owner kept their spouse and any children. The aim of these provisions seems to be to ensure that no one gets too rich at the expense of those less wealthy, and that no one stays too poor for too long. In short, it seems to aim for a level playing field – providing people with equal opportunities is its goal.

Dale Patrick (1985) offers an alternative view of the Old Testament concept of justice.[10] He believes that the Israelite system of justice began with unwritten law, and that the modern Judaistic concept of law began to develop only when the law was written down around the time of Jeremiah. His starting point is Deuteronomy 16:20. Patrick argues that the Judges were charged to acquit the innocent and condemn the guilty.[11] They were to set things right, restoring the community to health by recognising the righteous party and penalising the offender in proportion to his offence. The Book of the Covenant[12] has several prohibitions directed both to judges and to witnesses, such as 'You shall not spread a false report ... You shall not follow a majority in wrongdoing ... You shall not pervert the justice due to your poor in their lawsuits ... You shall take no bribe'.[13] There is, however, no command to consult lawbooks or to apply the letter of the law, which would suggest that the

---

7   Ibid., pp. 131–3. Compare Leviticus 24:22.
8   Leviticus 25:15–16.
9   Leviticus 25:39–41. Compare Exodus 21:2.
10 Patrick (1985), chapter 7.
11 Compare Deuteronomy 25:1–4.
12 Exodus 20:23–23:19.
13 Exodus 23:1a, 2a, 6a and 8a.

failure to do so was not seen as a threat to justice. Instead, everyone is warned not to obstruct justice.

This codified the practice Moses adopted on Jethro's advice when he was overloaded with cases – Moses chose trustworthy and unbribeable men to help him share the load. In later Biblical passages there is evidence that principled reason, not a system of laws, leads to justice. Abraham saw that the destruction of Sodom would be a travesty of justice if even ten righteous men were killed.[14] The daughters of Zelophehad appealed successfully to Moses against the transfer of their father's estate to his brothers,[15] setting a precedent based on intrinsic justice rather than accepted convention. Most striking, however, is the episode in which Joab, through the offices of a wise woman from Tekoa, induced David to pardon Absalom for murder – a pardon contrary to every law and principle of scripture.[16]

On this evidence, Patrick believes that 'the law which the judicial system enforced was an unwritten law woven into the fabric of society and discovered in the course of judicial deliberation'.[17] He argues that the texts do not attempt to give a comprehensive set of rules. They come across as sermons, exhorting the faithful to right conduct. He regards most of Deuteronomy's provisions on slaves as utopian, since had they been adopted, he thinks, slavery as an institution would quickly have been abolished. Idealistic provisions such as these and the year of Jubilee, he believes, would have found no place in the Book of the Covenant or the Holiness Code[18] if either had been intended as practical lawbooks. Patrick dates the change from unwritten to written law to the reign of Josiah, and the rediscovery of the Book of the Law.[19] He finds no attempt to cite lawbooks in Amos, Hosea, Isaiah or Micah (their definitions of God's law are often fairly general), but they begin to appear in Jeremiah (who is much more specific).[20] This change began the process that led to the identification of the written law with the Divine Law, and eventually to the canonisation of the Torah.

Hans Boecker (1980) points out that we should expect to find development in the Old Testament concept of justice, since it evolved over a period of around 2,000 years.[21] Israelite law began as family and tribal law: in ancient times, the father had unlimited authority over his family and his property. He alone had the power to settle disputes and dispense punishments. It will become clear when we examine early Roman Law that this is not an exclusively Israelite idea. In Israel, however, the idea did not last long. Some of the father's authority was ceded to the elders of the city or tribe. They heard disputes, usually at the city gates, and could invite any citizen (but not women, children or resident aliens) to join them in hearing and deciding the

---

14 Genesis 18:23–33.
15 Numbers 27:1–11.
16 2 Samuel 14:1–24.
17 Patrick (1985), p. 198.
18 Leviticus 17–26.
19 2 Kings 22.
20 For example, 7:6, 7:9 and 17:19–27 (these are Patrick's examples).
21 Boecker (1980), p. 28.

case. Their aim was to settle disputes so that prosperous coexistence was possible – to effect reconciliation. They intervened as little and as infrequently as possible. They did not have an abstract idea of justice like the Romans or Greeks. Even the famous 'life for life, eye for eye, tooth for tooth, hand for hand, foot for foot, burn for burn, wound for wound, stripe for stripe'[22] seems to be intended to limit retaliation. It aims to maintain a proper balance, rather than allowing blood feuds to spiral and escalate as they often did in other cultures.[23] We can see, then, from all our sources, that equity is deeply entrenched in Jewish Law. This is not true of many other systems of jurisprudence. In both Roman and Greek thought, the concept of equity was developed to counter the social consequences of a strict adherence to the law. Jewish Law is monistic – justice and equity are two sides of the same coin, the others dualistic – justice and equity are separate, and have to be held in tension.

The New Testament

When it came to expressing the idea of *tsedeq* in Greek, the writers of the New Testament, following the practice of the translators of the Septuagint, most often adopted the terms *dikaios*, *dikaiosunē* and their cognates. Of these, *dikaiosunē* is the more important for our purposes. This translation is not without problems, however, since *dikaiosunē* was widely understood in Greek thought either as one of the cardinal virtues, or as a legal term, not as a relationship between God and humanity.[24] While it does occasionally refer in the New Testament to God's just judgement and rule, it most often refers to the right conduct of humans that follows the will of God and is pleasing to Him. As Walter Bauer (1979) puts it, *dikaiosunē* is 'uprightness, justice as a characteristic of a judge … in a moral and religious sense: uprightness, righteousness, the characteristic required of men by God'.[25] Once again, the fact that the basic relationship with God is always in view distinguishes this use of *dikaiosunē* from the secular Greek usage, and links it firmly with the Old Testament usage. The main difference is that in the New Testament, and particularly in the writings of Paul, *dikaiosunē*, rightness before God, is a gift of grace, and the result of Christ's action on the cross, not the consequence of observing the Law. It therefore follows that in New Testament theology, one can be righteous before God, but only through the action of Christ, and never in one's own right.

However, *dikaiosunē* is not the only term for justice in the New Testament. *Krisis* [the act of judgement] and *krima* [the judicial verdict] are also translated 'justice', but they correspond too closely with judgement and condemnation to be appropriate to this enquiry. These terms deal largely with what is wrong, while our main interest

---

22 Exodus 21:23b–25.

23 In practice, however, the Rabbis rejected the idea that physical injury should be inflicted and substituted the payment of compensation. See Cohen (1995), p. 327.

24 Kittel (1964), pp. 192–205. Compare Botterweck, Ringgren and Fabry (2003), pp. 262–3.

25 Bauer (1979), p. 196.

is in what is right. As we have seen in connection with *tsedeq*, however, these ideas cannot be entirely divorced from the concept of justice in either the Old or New Testaments. Jesus clearly supported the ideas of justice in the Covenant. In Matthew's Gospel we hear Christ saying, 'Do not suppose that I have come to abolish the law and the prophets; I did not come to abolish but to complete. Truly I tell you: so long as heaven and earth endure, not a letter, not a dot, will disappear from the law until all that must happen has happened'.[26] The New Testament differs from the Old about how justice should be administered: in the Old, everyone should be treated equally and fairly. In the New, liberality and generosity is the ideal.[27]

In the Sermon on the Mount, Jesus also extended the scope of the Ten Commandments – anger may incur the same penalty as murder,[28] and lustful thoughts are equivalent to adultery,[29] for example. Bauer (1979) indicates that the anger in question (*orgidzomenos*) is premeditated anger, indignation, or wrath, nursed by the inveterate to keep it warm. Contempt for others, in the form of personal insults, is just as bad – it can leave one liable to Gehenna. Similarly, the word for lust (*epithumēsai*) implies premeditation, forbidden activity, longing for the thing desired – looking at a woman with the intention of having improper thoughts about her, coveting her. We are not only prohibited from harming our neighbour, but also prohibited from wishing harm upon him/her. We must forgive our neighbour's sins, not three times, as the rabbis recommended,[30] or even seven times, but 'seventy times seven'[31] – there should be no limit to our forgiveness, just as there is no limit to God's forgiveness. In its juridical context, then, *dikaiosunē* encompasses the Old Testament understanding of *tsedaqah*, but goes beyond it, requiring generosity of spirit towards others, not just giving them their due.

Patrick sees this change in emphasis as a reaction to the identification of Divine Law with the written codes of the Torah. Both Christ, in the Sermon on the Mount, and Paul, in Galatians and Romans, acknowledge the existence of Divine Law and shape their thinking accordingly. Yet both are very critical of the first–century interpretation of the law – Christ of its legalism, and Paul of its purpose.[32] Both arrive at much the same position: the law cannot save, but God freely offers salvation through Christ. Paul, in particular, rejects the idea that Christians are bound to observe Old Testament law, but he also states in Romans 7:7–12 that the law is holy, just and good. Paul might seem to be contradicting himself, but Douglas Moo (1996) believes that Paul is arguing that while sin has taken full advantage of the opportunity to deceive Israel into thinking it could attain life through the law, the law itself cannot be charged with anything wrong.[33] James Dunn (1988) explains

---

26 Matthew 5:17–18.
27 See, for example, Matthew 5:38–42.
28 Matthew 5:21–23.
29 Matthew 5:27–28.
30 Davies and Allison (1991), p. 793.
31 Matthew 18:21–22.
32 Patrick (1985), pp. 205–6.
33 Moo (1996), pp. 431–41.

that Paul seems to be saying that the law is holy, just and good in such strong terms that it seems he thinks it deserves approbation from everyone, not just from Jews.[34] It does not seem that Paul is being inconsistent here. He seems to be saying that while the law cannot bring salvation – only faith in Jesus can do so – and no one should be bound to observe it, the law is of great benefit to both Jews and Gentiles.

The extra element of justice in the New Testament, then, is generosity. One should observe the spirit of the law and do so generously, rather than rigidly sticking to the letter. This concept of justice, with which we shall compare Roman and Greek ideas, is distributive in emphasis, not retributive. It seeks to provide everyone with equal opportunities, to ensure that no one becomes too rich at the expense of their neighbours, to prevent excessive poverty, and to ensure that lesser degrees of poverty do not continue for long periods. It encourages people to serve others, to place their neighbours' interests above their own, to be as generous as possible, to refrain from ill will, and to be long suffering in the face of adversity. Retribution, in the sense of human revenge, plays no part in the New Testament understanding of justice. Vengeance belongs to God alone. How does this compare with Roman and Greek ideas of justice?

Roman Law

Roman Law, in its early forms, could be quite brutal. *The Twelve Tables* is the earliest existing code of Roman law.[35] Table 3 deals with the issue of debt. When a debt had been acknowledged, or judgement had been given, the debtor had 30 days to pay up. If he did not, or could not pay, his creditor could arrest him and bind him in fetters for 60 days, during which time the debtor had the right to be fed, and to try to negotiate a compromise. The debtor was brought before the consul's court in the market place on the last three market days of his captivity (there were normally eight days between markets). If by the third occasion he had still not paid, or otherwise arranged his release, he could be sold as a slave or executed. If there were several creditors, they could divide the body (*partis secanto*) between themselves.[36]

Table 4 explains that a son could only be freed from his father's power once he had been offered for sale and manumitted three times. Finally, table 9 states that there can be no personal exception to the laws: nobody can escape the penalty for breaches of the law because of their social status. The only restriction placed by the *Twelve Tables* on the father, as head of the household, was that he could not order

---

34 Dunn (1988), pp. 374–87.

35 Scott (2001), volume 1, pp. 57–77.

36 There are difficulties of interpretation here: 'partis secanto', translates as 'they shall cut pieces'. According to Warmington (1938, p. 440), the earliest writers interpreted this as 'cut up the debtor's body', but often the debtor's estate was divided. Warmington suggests that the law laid down division of the body, while custom ordained division of his estate. Scott (2001, volume 1, p. 64, footnote 1) acknowledges that the debtor's life was often at the mercy of his creditors.

the execution of anyone unless the courts had first convicted them of a crime.[37] Restrained only by this restriction, the father had almost absolute power over his household. He could exact retribution whenever and however he saw fit. The clear aim of early Roman Law, then, was to give people personal vengeance over those who had wronged them. Over time, the praetors tempered the severity of Roman Law, by introducing exceptions to counteract the damaging effects of strict adherence to the laws. This developed into the concept of equity. Laws could be promulgated either by the praetors, on a case by case basis, or by the public will as expressed in a plebiscite. The patricians at first argued that such laws did not apply to them, as they were not plebeians and therefore not parties to the vote, but by the later republic the authority of plebiscites was unchallenged. Personal vengeance now played less part in proceedings, but there was still a great emphasis on power over others and absolute ownership of property in Roman Law.

In *De Officiis*, Marcus Tullius Cicero (1913), writing around 45 BC, takes a rather different view of the law. He believes that we owe certain duties even to those who have wronged us. He argues that retribution and punishment should be designed to bring offenders to repentance, to prevent re-offending, and deter others from doing wrong.[38] In Cicero's view, justice has two aims: 'to keep one man from doing harm to another, unless provoked by wrong' and 'to lead men to use common possessions for the common interests, private property for their own'.[39] Each should seek the common good, even when it hurts one's own interests to do so. This principle, he believes, is established both by natural law (reason applied to nature, and equity), and by civil statutes. Cicero was a philosopher, not a jurist. As such, he seems to be almost a lone voice for distributive justice among Romans – and as we have seen, his idea of justice, while strikingly similar to Judaeo-Christian ideas in places, diverges sharply from them elsewhere. Mainstream Roman opinion was clearly in favour of retributive justice.

Gaius, who was active in the second century AD, gave his view that exceptions 'have been introduced for the purpose of defending those against whom actions have been brought; for it often happens that a party is liable by the Civil Law, when it would be unjust for a judgment to be rendered against him'.[40] These exceptions applied to situations, not to individuals, in keeping with the *Twelve Tables*, generally where someone would be penalised twice, were the law to be applied strictly. In some cases, these exceptions could be overridden, so a system of checks and balances developed. One glaring example of the inequity exceptions were created to remedy is the treatment of mortgages. Ownership, in early law, was absolute. Loans, in the sense we understand them, were not possible, since possession of the money, unless

---

37 See Salvian (1962), pp. 231–2.

38 Cicero (1913), pp. 35–7.

39 Ibid., p. 23. Compare *De Finibus* (Cicero, 1931, p. 469), in which justice is linked with dutiful affection, kindness, liberality, goodwill, courtesy and the other graces of the same kind.

40 From section 116 of the fourth commentary. Scott (2001), volume 1, p. 206.

it was stolen, entailed its ownership. While the *Twelve Tables* did allow for hire, both of people and property, payment had to be made in full before the person's labour or use of the property was secured. The hirer was effectively buying the goods or labour for a limited time.

If someone wanted to borrow money, in the sense of a modern mortgage, and had a field to offer as security, the creditor would not part with ownership of his/her money without receiving another ownership in return. Generally, the title in the field passed from debtor to creditor at the time the mortgage was agreed. Under early Roman Law, the creditor was not obliged to allow the debtor to use the field, even if farming it was the debtor's only hope of repaying the mortgage. This was a matter for negotiation. If the debtor repaid the loan on the due date, he or she regained ownership. If not, the creditor did not have to return the field and could, in some circumstances, still pursue the debtor for the debt.[41]

By the time of Gaius, the exceptions made this impossible. If the creditor sued, the court had to decide in favour of the debtor. Nevertheless, if someone wanted to take out a mortgage, even under later law, he or she would have to transfer ownership of the collateral to the creditor for the duration of the loan, even if he or she retained the right of use. Security in the sense we understand it was unknown to Roman Law. Despite this legal softening, Kagan sees the whole development of Roman Law as based on notions of power, dominion and status – all principles contrary to equality. Consequently, he thinks, Roman Law became rigid and inflexible – the letter of the law was all that mattered, the spirit of the law was irrelevant.[42] This view fits well with what we have seen of early Roman Law, although the introduction of equity softened the harshness of early law. As we have seen, the New Testament view of justice is very different. Roman Law was based on what the Bible might call the world's idea of justice – it placed a great deal of emphasis on personal vengeance and power. It had little if any sense of corporate action. Within it, equity was seen as a corrective: a means to re-establish some form of equality when a strict application of the law failed to produce a just outcome. The concept that all are equal before the law simply did not apply – Roman citizens had more rights than Latins, and slaves had no rights at all.

We have not yet established a link between early Roman Law and later Canon Law of the Western Church, although, as we shall see in the next chapter, this influence was widespread and profound. Roman Law was not the only such influence: Germanic Law and Greek thought also had their influence, and I shall argue that political pressures also had significant effects. We have explored the authoritarian model of justice. We now turn to the other extreme, which I believe contributed to the growth of democracy in the Church.

---

41 Kagan (1955), pp. 62 and 144.
42 Ibid., p. 63.

Greek Philosophy[43]

I believe, as I said earlier, that the growth of democracy in the Church owes a great deal to Greek philosophy. Tracing this idea back from the Reformers is not as straightforward as it might seem. None of the major Reformers was particularly keen on Greek philosophy, and their successors did not always cite their non–Biblical sources. All three of the major Reformers were familiar with, and influenced by, Aristotle. Luther was a monk, and Zwingli and Calvin were classical scholars. The Protestant emphasis on freedom of conscience was, I shall later suggest, largely the result of Zwingli's work. Not all of the philosophers we will discuss were Greek: Seneca was Roman, but his views are generally typical of the Stoic school, and so I shall use him as their representative. Seneca was no supporter of personal freedom – in fact, like almost all the Stoics, he was a determinist.[44] While the Church has never accepted determinism *per se*, I shall argue that Stoicism, with a few modifications, formed a natural receptacle for the Church's doctrine. Plato was also a major influence on the Church, particularly through Augustine and his successors. We shall therefore consider the views of Plato, Aristotle and Seneca.

We begin with Plato, who discusses justice as it relates to people: by asking 'What is a just man?', rather than by treating justice as a concept, as I have done earlier in this chapter.[45] Seneca and Aristotle treat justice as both a virtue and a concept. Plato's main works on justice are *The Republic* (1987) and *The Laws* (1970). The *Republic* sets out Plato's vision of the ideal constitution of a city, The *Laws*, which is less prescriptive and more pragmatic, tries to flesh out how to achieve this in practice. The first thing to say is that Plato would be horrified by individualism. It is his view that the universe is structured hierarchically, and therefore that every citizen has a specific rôle in society: one should perform that, and only that, rôle for which one is best suited. In so doing, one should work for the common good. Plato sees the ultimate justice in a society in which everyone knows his or her place, does the duties society assigns them, and generally conforms. His ideal society is a small city-state with ruling, military and working classes. Children, he believes, should be assigned to the appropriate class according to their natural abilities, not their parentage. Once an individual had been given a position in society, however, Plato expected him or her to obey the governing classes without question. Only the rulers would be taught philosophy, and therefore be able to administer society for the common good. He did not believe that anyone unable to fulfil a specific rôle in society could have a life worth living, and therefore argued that those incapable, through illness or age, of contributing to society should die.

Plato spells out his ideas about how this state could be built in practice in the *Laws*. These broadly follow his earlier ideas of a small state, with no large discrepancies

---

43 My treatment of Plato and Aristotle here is indebted to Morrison (1997), chapter 2. The interpretation is mine, but I have found his analysis helpful.

44 See Long and Sedley (1987), pp. 333–43 and 386–94.

45 The word translated 'justice' is '*dikaiosunē*' in both Plato and Aristotle.

of wealth or status, but are shot through with a streak of pragmatism, notably absent from his earlier work. It was Plato's hope that in such a society, laws would be obeyed because the citizens believed they were right, out of rational obedience, rather than through fear of punishment. While Plato is being less idealistic[46] here, it is clear that his idealism has not vanished completely. He seems to think that once people know the right thing to do, they will instinctively do it. Plato's view on punishment is noticeably different from the early Roman approach, with which his views are roughly contemporary. He believes that 'the cardinal rule should be that in every case the sum is to vary in proportion to the damage done, so that the loss is made good. And each offender is to pay an additional penalty appropriate to his crime, to encourage him to reform'.[47] This rule sits well with Numbers 5:6. Plato's idea of justice, then, shares some ideas with Jewish Law, and has distributive elements – unlike Roman Law it is not principally concerned with retribution – while in other areas it is authoritarian almost to the point of totalitarianism.

Aristotle defines justice as 'the virtue through which each group of men retain their own things, in conformity with the law'.[48] For him, liberty is the way to achieve virtue, and therefore happiness, the ultimate aim and supreme good of human life. Society can only be just if it strives to achieve happiness for all its citizens. Aristotle recognised that in tyrannies, oligarchies and the like, most people were unhappy most of the time. For Aristotle, therefore, while a single elected ruler was his preferred option in theory, democracy was often the least harmful form of government in practice, because even elected monarchs tended to become tyrants in time. In a democracy, everyone contributed to the governing of society and could therefore ensure their interests were represented. Aristotle's idea of democracy is rather different from ours, but the cornerstone of both ideas is personal freedom, which for him can only exist in a democratic state. In such a state, all rule and are ruled in turn, 'whence it follows that the majority must be supreme, and that whatever the majority approve must be the end and the just'.[49]

Aristotle is also concerned about equality: 'All men think justice to be a sort of equality, and to a certain extent they agree with what we have said in our philosophical works about ethics',[50] namely that what is neither equal nor proportionate is unjust. Justice in its general sense is not a part of virtue: it is virtue. General justice is related to particular justice in the way that illegal is related to unfair. While general justice consists in keeping the law, particular justice entails giving others their due.[51] Aristotle does accept, however, that there can be bad law, which people are not bound to follow, and that equity (*epieikeia*) can correct its deficiencies.[52] Aristotle

---

46 I use 'idealistic' and 'idealism' in their common, rather than philosophical, senses.

47 Plato (1970), p. 481.

48 Aristotle (1991), p. 105.

49 Aristotle (1996), pp. 154–5. Compare pp. 83–5 and 106–9, and Aristotle (1976), p. 275.

50 Ibid., p. 79.

51 Aristotle (1976), pp. 171–9.

52 Ibid., pp. 198–200.

defines *epieikeia* as 'right going beyond the written law'.[53] Bauer translates *epieikeia* as 'clemency, gentleness, graciousness', referring this use of the word back to books 5 and 14 of the *Ethics*, in addition to its use in the Acts of the Apostles.[54] This, then, is different from the concept of equity in Roman Law. It balances, counteracts or completes the law, wherever necessary, when strict application of the law would produce imperfect justice or simple injustice. 'Justice for all can be achieved only through the subtle and judicious dialectics of imposing the law in most cases and letting *epieikeia* prevail in some'.[55]

Aristotle understands distributive justice in a slightly different sense to ours,[56] but his idea of particular justice fits well within our definition of distributive justice. He values conformity almost as much as Plato. He sees the constitutions of many cities as chaotic. He believes that the happiness of the individual is the same as the happiness of the state. 'There can be no doubt', he tells us, 'no one denies they are the same'.[57] Unfortunately, Aristotle also shared his tutor's view that those who could not contribute to society should be excluded from it. He argued that those of low intelligence should be enslaved because they were not naturally fitted to freedom, and that severely handicapped children should be left to die. Unlike Plato, however, Aristotle believed that people could find their own position in society. He thought they should choose a job for which they had the ability. He also saw great wickedness in humanity, and did not accept that people would always do what they should, even if they knew what was right. He was far less idealistic than Plato. Aristotle argued that freedom is good for humanity, but that an orderly society must place limits on that freedom. He valued freedom more than conformity, but he did not believe that total freedom was compatible with order. This is much closer to modern ideas of freedom than Plato's view.

It seems to me that Aristotle has improved on several deficiencies in Plato, but from a Biblical perspective, he is not immune from criticism himself. Firstly, his views seem to reflect a lack of compassion for his fellow humans, particularly the marginalised. He apparently sees no injustice in advocating that those who do not fit into his pattern for society should at best be enslaved, and at worst left to die. Secondly, his assertion that whatever the majority approves must be the end, and must be just, is particularly problematic. This places the will of the people above the will of God, and is in direct conflict with the Biblical view that humans have fallen from their original state of complete communion with God. He was not, however, the

---

53 Aristotle (1991), p. 127.

54 Acts 24:4. Tertullus asked Felix to hear his case against Paul 'with your customary graciousness (*tē sē epieikeia*)'.

55 Örsy (1992), p. 44, italics as original.

56 He considered that distributive justice governed the distribution of public assets among members of the community, rather than providing equal opportunities, and contrasted it with rectificatory (or commutative) justice, which could rectify injustices which took place during transactions between two parties. Both come under his heading of particular justice. See Aristotle (1976), pp. 174–7 and 198–200.

57 Aristotle (1996), p. 168.

only philosopher to advance this view. The Stoic Seneca also saw public acceptance as evidence for truth. He believed that if everyone accepted an idea, this provided strong evidence that it was true.

Edwyn Bevan (1913), explains that the Stoics taught that happiness came from living in agreement with nature, which in turn meant living virtuously: in other words, by aligning one's will with the will of God. 'I am happy, when I do not want things to be any other than they are. Among the things present to my consciousness may be a painful sensation, but it is not an evil for me, if it is what I myself will'.[58] They argued that the whole universe was rational, and driven by rational principles. They drew a distinction between God and the creation, but maintained that they were closely linked. The universe was one substance, namely reason; and that reason was God. Thus, God was everywhere. Everything was, in its ultimate origin, God. Humans lived, moved and had their being in God. The Stoics saw God as a transcendent, rational, intelligent and immortal animal, the creator of all, perfectly happy, all pervasive, and perfectly good.[59]

This view has a much more Eastern perspective than Aristotle, and is strikingly similar to Christianity. There are, however, two major differences. Firstly, the Stoics were determinist. Long and Sedley (1987) argue that Zeno[60] and Cleanthes, the first two heads of the Stoic school, were compatibilists, who believed that determinism was compatible with humans bearing responsibility for their actions. They acknowledge, however, that later Stoics accepted full-blown determinism.[61] In Seneca, it verges at times on fatalism. In general, the Church's doctrine of providence has not embraced determinism, although some Calvinist views of predestination have come fairly close to doing so. The other major contrast was that the Stoics cultivated indifference to their fate. Since they were convinced they could neither change nor avoid it, the best way to avoid worrying about the future was to resign themselves to it. They sought to avoid emotional entanglements with others, so that they would remain calm and untroubled were the other to become ill, to suffer misfortune, torture or slavery, or to die suddenly. Seneca was quite clear on this point: 'The question has often been raised whether it is better to have moderate emotions, or none at all. Philosophers of our school reject the emotions'.[62] This view is noticeably different from the Christian way of love, which calls everyone to sacrifice themselves for the benefit of others. Nevertheless, Christianity and Stoicism overlap considerably, and it would not be surprising if the Stoics had influenced the Church. We shall explore how they interacted shortly. First, we must set out Seneca's views on justice.

---

58 Bevan (1913), p. 28.

59 Long and Sedley (1987), p. 323.

60 Zeno of Citium (c334–c262 BC), the founder of Stoicism, should not be confused with Zeno of Elea (c490–c430 BC), the Eleatic philosopher whose paradoxes of motion exercised Aristotle, Zeno of Sidon (c155–c75 BC), who was Epicurean, or Zeno of Tarsus, who was the fourth head of the Stoic school.

61 Ibid., pp. 392–4.

62 Seneca (1925), p. 333.

The supreme good, according to Seneca, is virtue. 'Man's highest good is attained if he has fulfilled the good for which nature designed him at birth ... to live in accordance with his own nature'.[63] In this way, humans can avoid conflict with the forces surrounding them, and thus can avoid the unhappiness that comes with conflict. Only a virtuous soul can achieve consistency in the whole of life. The way to this virtue is philosophy, whose sole function is to discover the truth. Religion, duty, justice, and all the other parts of virtue, are linked in close–united fellowship. The four main parts of virtue are justice, prudence, self–control and bravery. To be just means to give every person his/her due. Unfortunately, Seneca never spells out what this means in any detail, and we have to extract his views of justice from a variety of unconnected references. Seneca believes that justice is a certain attitude, state, and power of the soul. It entails fair play, which is desirable in itself – it should take neither fear nor hope of reward to compel us to be fair. If it does, we are not acting justly. No one can become happy through another's unhappiness. The idea that one can is the opposite of wisdom, from which the only escape is a return to living in accord with one's nature and the will of the gods, and a restoration to our condition before humans fell into error. Seneca agreed with Posidonius' assessment of justice in the golden age, in which only the wise ruled. They protected the weak from the strong, gave good advice, provided for their people and considered ruling a form of service.[64]

The parallels with Plato's ideas about philosopher-kings and the Christian idea of leadership as service are obvious. Armed with these ideas about Seneca's view of justice, we now need to consider what giving each his/her due means. This depends on whether or not everyone is equal. Seneca discusses this in his letters about death. 'An equal law consists, not of that which all have experienced, but that which has been laid down for all. Be sure to prescribe for your mind this sense of equity; we should all pay without complaint the tax of our mortality'.[65] 'Death has its fixed rule, – equitable and unavoidable. Who can complain when he is governed by terms which include everyone? The chief part of equity, however, is equality'.[66]

Equity, for Seneca, is the idea that everyone becomes equal when facing death. It does not, however, seem to play a major part in his idea of justice for the living. He does not see it as a corrective to the law, since as a determinist he thinks blind fate is supreme. He does believe that we should do what fate allows us to do to make our own lives, and the lives of our fellow humans, as happy as possible. We should not, however, become emotionally involved with them in the process. Seneca's idea of justice has no place for retribution. It is distributive in character. It seeks the advantage of others. Seneca's justice, however, unlike Biblical justice, is surrendered to fate and sees no way to change the natural order.

---

63 Seneca (1917), pp. 277–9.
64 Seneca (1920), pp. 397–9. Posidonius' original text is lost.
65 Seneca (1925), p. 227.
66 Seneca (1920), p. 217.

We have seen, then, that while our philosophers agreed that justice entailed giving each his/her due, they did not agree on what this meant. Plato and Aristotle thought that some were due more than others. Seneca implied, but does not seem to have said overtly, that everyone was due the same. Plato saw conformity as the way to happiness, for Aristotle it was freedom, for Seneca it was resignation to the divine will. What can we draw from this? Firstly, that from a Biblical perspective, they all leave something to be desired. Plato and Aristotle both took up positions which followed from their assumptions, but which left some outside the scope of justice. This does not fit with the Biblical view that justice is due to all.[67] Seneca encouraged his readers to become indifferent to suffering – both their own and the suffering of others. This is incompatible with loving one's neighbours.[68] Secondly, they all have something to commend them: Plato sought a society in which everyone had fulfilling work. Aristotle believed everyone should be free. Seneca thought everyone should follow the divine will. We shall shortly see that elements of Greek thought have been imported into the Church. Where their views were compatible with Christianity, we should not expect them to have caused problems. We should, however, examine whether any of the more questionable elements of their work have survived, and if so, what effect they have had on the subsequent development of doctrine. We begin by looking at the effects of Roman Law and Greek philosophy on the New Testament.

Roman and Greek Influence on the New Testament[69]

Roman Law

The first point of contact between Roman legal theory and the New Testament concerns debt. In Matthew 5:25–26, Jesus teaches the crowd to keep short accounts. If someone sues you, we are told, come to terms with him before you get to court, because if the judge decides against you, you will be thrown into prison until you have paid all you owe. There seems to be a consensus among the commentators I have consulted that debtors were not imprisoned under Jewish Law, so these passages must refer to some other law.[70] As we can see, Roman Law is the prime candidate. The parable of the unmerciful slave (Matthew 18:23–35), is even clearer. This slave was forgiven a huge debt of 10,000 talents, but he refused to forgive a fellow-slave the much smaller debt of 100 denarii. When his master found out, he ordered the torture of the unmerciful slave until the debt was paid in full.[71] Again,

---

67 Deuteronomy 10:17–19.
68 Leviticus 19:18.
69 I am indebted to Hicks (1896), for raising the issues I discuss in this section.
70 Davies and Allison (1988), p. 520, Luz (1989), pp. 281 and 290.
71 This is not strictly in accordance with Roman Law. Once the debt had been cancelled it could not be reinstated, although the master would still have been entitled to torture his slave for ingratitude.

the punishment here seems to point to a non-Jewish environment, as Jews rarely employed torture.

We should also examine the parable of the untrustworthy slave in Matthew 24:45–51 and Luke 12:41–48. This slave was placed at the head of the household, but instead of running it well, he bullied the other slaves and spent time drinking with his friends. The parable concludes that when the master returns, he will cut the slave into pieces (*dichotomēsei auton*) and throw him out with the hypocrites. C.F. Evans (1990, p. 537) and Joseph Fitzmyer (1985, p. 986) have great difficulty in interpreting Luke's version of this passage. Both agree that this is unusually savage punishment, which they cannot easily fit into a Hebrew context. Davies and Allison (1997), commenting on Matthew's account, argue that while the Jewish tradition does include accounts of offenders cut in two, most have speculated that this parable is figurative, and that it may refer either to a beating, or to expulsion from the community of Israel.[72] Given the similarity of the language here to the provisions of the *Twelve Tables*, however, there is another alternative: these passages may refer to Roman Debt Law. The Vulgate translates this clause in both Matthew's and Luke's accounts as *et dividet eum partemque*,[73] which, while not quite *partis secanto* is close enough to suggest a similar line of thought. There is also an obvious parallel with the petition in the Lord's Prayer, which reads 'forgive us our debts (*opheilēmata* in Matthew 6:12, rendered *hamartias* [sins] in Luke 11:4) as we forgive those indebted to us'. In this instance, however, the commentators agree that the thought here is Hebrew, not Roman.[74]

It might also appear that there is Roman imagery relating to inheritance law in Revelation 5:1–3, which speaks of a search in heaven to find someone worthy to open a scroll with writing on both sides and seven seals. When Rome introduced written wills, they had to be sealed by seven witnesses. Earlier verbal wills also had to be made in the presence of seven witnesses. The seals and witnesses were guarantees that the will was genuine, and the surviving witnesses were expected to testify to that effect in court when the beneficiaries claimed their inheritances. The parallel is obvious, but there are problems. Firstly, Revelation does not refer to the opening and reading of the book after the undoing of the seventh seal, which on this view would be the most important part of the unsealing. Secondly, there is no surviving example of a will from the ancient world with writing on both sides of the scroll. Since the contents of such a document would be open to all, there would also be no need to unseal it. David Aune (1997) suggests that this scroll is modelled on the scroll in Ezekiel 2:9–10, which was written with 'dirges and laments and

72 Davies and Allison (1997), pp. 390–1.

73 Both Greek and Latin clauses are identical in Matthew 24:51 and Luke 24:16. Mounce (1993), also suggests that the meaning of both is 'inflict a severe punishment', rather than 'cut up', but Bauer (1979), while agreeing that this reading is possible, finds no exact linguistic parallels for it.

74 Davies and Allison (1988), pp. 610–2, Luz (1989), p. 384, C.F. Evans (1990), pp. 482–3 and Fitzmyer (1985), p. 906.

words of woe', in other words, with Ezekiel's message of divine judgement. Aune further suggests that the author's use of this image may suggest that he thinks that Revelation 5 reveals Ezekiel's true meaning.[75]

Finally, we consider adoption (*huiothesia*). Bauer (1979) understands this as a spiritual change, in which God accepts converts as His sons. This relationship will be completed only when the time of fulfilment releases them from their earthly bodies. This represents a new relationship introduced by justification. While the Torah required kinsmen-redeemers to redeem their families from debt or slavery if necessary,[76] Rupert Davies (Richardson and Bowden, 1983) points out that there was no legal procedure for adoption in ancient Israel. Adoptions in the Old Testament took the form of extending the protection of the family to its new member, and seemed to have no further legal consequences.[77] Roman Law, however, regulated adoption in much more detail. Roman adoption left one in a state close to captivity. We have seen that the only way a son could gain freedom from his father's power was by being sold and manumitted three times. The ceremony of adoption differed from the ceremony for buying a slave by only one word: *filius*, or its appropriate declension, was substituted for *servus*.[78] Again, seven witnesses were required to testify to the adoption when the son claimed his inheritance. Adoption was effectively the end of one life and the beginning of another. Legally, one became a different person after adoption. It seems that Paul uses adoption in the stronger Roman sense in Galatians 4:1–7, and particularly in Romans 8:14–17, in which Paul tells us that all who are led by the spirit of God have become His sons, and that they have received a spirit of adoption (*huiothesias*), not slavery. The Spirit of God affirms to those so adopted that they are children of God.[79] Note that the Holy Spirit bears witness, fulfilling the requirement for a testimony about the adoption, with the testimony of God counting for more than the testimony of men. The *Dictionary of New Testament Background* (Evans and Porter, 2000) states that Paul made good use of the Roman law of adoption to illustrate theological principles.[80] Both Jews and Christians are seen as adopted by God, giving God paternal rights over both: all that believers have and are belongs to God. If we interpret this passage in this sense, we get a much more vivid idea of the eternal union between the believer and God. Those who are heirs of God, and fellow-heirs with Christ, have a full share in both the costs and benefits of being God's children.

---

75 Aune (1997), pp. 345–6.

76 Leviticus 25:25, 28 and 48–49.

77 Richardson and Bowden (1983), p. 5. Compare Sanday and Headlam (1908), p. 203.

78 Ball (1891), pp. 281–2, cited in Hicks (1896), p. 172. Ball does not state his source and I have been unable to find it, but Gaius confirms that adoptions involved ceremonies, which normally took place before governors (*Institutes*, 1.100. Scott, 2001, volume 1, p. 96).

79 Both Sanday and Headlam (1908, p. 203) and Burton (1921, p. 220) accept that the sense of *huiothesia* is the reception of humans as God's sons and daughters. All three authors emphasise the spiritual aspects of adoption, and none of them thinks the thought behind it is Jewish.

80 Evans and Porter (2000), pp. 990–991.

The influence of Roman Law on the New Testament, then, seems to have produced some vivid imagery which expresses a stronger sense of God's grace and mercy than might have been available from a purely Jewish account. The New Testament, however, consistently emphasises the spiritual aspects of the Christian life above the juridical, which it sees as distinctly secondary, if not wholly unimportant. Consequently, Roman Law and the imagery associated with it do not seem to have had a substantive effect on the content of Biblical ideas of justice.

Greek Philosophy

We have already seen the parallels between Christianity and Stoicism, particularly in the work of Seneca. We must now consider to what extent the writers of the New Testament, and Paul in particular, were influenced by Stoicism. Christianity and Stoicism have totally different aims and suppositions. Stoics are determinists and have tended to be fatalists. They are also materialists, who deny or at least doubt the existence of anything beyond the material. Christians look to the redemption of the world and acknowledge the existence of the spiritual realm. Stoicism was well established in Tarsus when Paul was growing up. Tarsus produced a head for the Stoic school in Athens, probably in the early second century BC.[81] Evans and Porter find many similarities between Stoic terminology and the language of the New Testament, particularly in Acts 17 and in the letters of Paul. This Stoic influence also extended to writers of the Patristic period: Tertullian, for example, regarded Seneca as a kindred spirit.[82]

Luke describes Paul's visit to Athens in Acts 17:16–34. Paul had fled from Thessalonica and Berea, and had sought safety in Athens. He was outraged by the number of idols in the city. Nevertheless, he made use of the Greek fondness for natural theology, and an altar to an unknown God (*Agnōstō theō*), to illustrate God's nature and the place of Jesus in his theology when talking with Stoics and Epicureans in the Areopagus. We can see several parallels between Paul's testimony and Stoic philosophy. First, Paul told them, God created everything. He does not live in shrines made by humans. We should not suppose that He is like any humanly designed image. He accepts service from humans not because He lacks anything, indeed He is the universal giver of life and breath, but because He wants us to find Him. In Him we live, move, and have our being. Indeed, we are His offspring. He has fixed a day on which He will have the world judged justly by a man He has designated, and He has given assurance of this by raising this man from the dead.

The Stoics believed that God was intelligent, designing fire, methodically creating the world. He encompassed all the seminal principles by which fate brought things about. He was breath pervading the world, taking different names as he altered the

---

81 This was Zeno of Tarsus. See footnote 60 above.

82 Ibid, p. 1141. Compare *A Treatise on the Soul*, chapter 20 (Roberts and Donaldson, 1999, volume 3, p. 200), in which Tertullian describes Seneca as 'so often on our side (*saepe noster*)'.

matter through which he passed.[83] God was cause, and he moulded the matter that made up the universe.[84] They also believed that God indwelt the creation. Seneca tells us that 'We do not need to uplift our hands towards heaven, or to beg the keeper of a temple to approach his idol's ear, as if in this way our prayers were more likely to be heard. God is near you, he is with you, he is within you'.[85] This, however, is not Christianity. Seneca adds that we do not know which god indwells each good man.[86] The Stoics also believed that God could be found by reason – that they could produce arguments that proved God's existence. They did not seem to have any idea of a final consummation at the end of time, but it is not difficult to see how they could fit the idea into their determinist view of the universe. The main difficulty for the Stoics, therefore, was the resurrection of the dead, for which Stoicism had no parallel. Not surprisingly, this caused a vigorous debate.

Troels Engberg-Pedersen (1994) argues that Paul successfully fused Stoic ideas into his thought without causing friction with Christianity. He argues that in Philippians, Paul uses Stoic motifs to illustrate his idea of judgement on the Day of the Lord, relying on the fact that Paul exhorts the Philippians to work out their salvation with fear and trembling.[87] This is similar to the Stoic concept of virtue: that one should strive to live in accordance with nature. Christians should look to each other's interests, not merely their own,[88] Thus, there is a close similarity between Paul's thought and Stoicism.[89] However, Engberg-Pedersen does not identify anything in his analysis of Philippians that is distinctively Stoic and could not also have been said by an orthodox Christian of the first century. He does, however, identify distinctively Christian elements that are not found in Stoicism, including the calling of God and the belief that the ideal community will be realised at some future time. He also identifies the major, defining difference between Christian thought and Stoicism, namely the lordship of Christ. Stoicism has nothing to compare with Christ, and therefore, for all the harmony between Stoic ethics and Paul's thought, Stoicism falls short of the glory of God.[90]

The influence of Greek philosophy, particularly Stoicism, bears many similarities to the influence of Roman Law. Philosophy provided Paul and others with analogies they could use to communicate with Gentiles, and gave them the chance to write more vividly. It does not appear that the New Testament writers based their theology on Greek ethical ideas, although they often used such ideas to illustrate their theology.[91] While Christians and Stoics had many similar ideas, it seems that the two streams of

---

83 Long and Sedley (1987), section 46A, pp. 274–5.
84 Seneca (1917), p. 445.
85 Ibid., p. 273.
86 Ibid. Seneca quotes from section 8.352 of Virgil's *Aeneid* (1958, p. 211).
87 Philippians 2:12.
88 Philippians 2:4.
89 Engberg–Pedersen (1994), p. 256.
90 Ibid., p. 290.
91 Neusner and Chilton (1997, p. 9) offer a similar argument about the Mishnah and Talmuds.

thought remained separate due to their different assumptions. Our conclusion from this is that the New Testament idea of justice was untouched by the ideas of the Romans and the Greeks. The writers used illustrations from both sources for their preaching, but there is no evidence that they adopted pagan ideas when forming their model of justice.

Conclusion

We have examined four different systems of justice. Jewish Law, in its Old Testament form, aimed for equality of opportunity for all. In the New Testament, justice incorporated all this, and added the concept of generosity. Roman Law was authoritarian in its early forms, and aimed to give successful plaintiffs power over their opponents. Greek philosophers agreed that justice meant giving each his/her due, but differed over how much each was due, and how justice should be administered. For our purposes, we should note two things. Firstly, all four agree that justice is no respecter of persons. In the Bible, everyone, whether Jew or Gentile, is entitled to at least some justice, although different authors disagree over who has what rights.

While under the Old Testament, Jews could apparently enslave Gentiles or charge them interest, things they could not do to other Jews, the New enjoins generosity, and places more emphasis than the Old on loving one's neighbour as oneself. While the Old Testament sometimes places Jews above Gentiles, the New treats all as equal before God. Both, however, share the view that certain rights are held by everyone, although the New Testament offers more rights to Gentiles than the Old. The principle that all people are entitled to a hearing also applies in Roman Law. The *Twelve Tables*, for all their brutality, do not permit personal exceptions. Praetorian and popular exceptions applied to situations, not to people. Equally, the Greek principle that justice meant giving each his due entails that everyone is entitled to some redress when wronged.

When it comes to the aims of justice, however, the differences become apparent. The Bible sees justice as a way to ensure no one is excluded from society through poverty or slavery, and a means to give everyone the same opportunities. It is also linked with righteousness: the aim of justice should be to bring people into a right relationship with God. Roman Law saw justice as a way for those wronged to take revenge on those who had wronged them. Equality of opportunity was not really an issue: the Romans were much more interested in power and dominion. Greek philosophy saw justice as virtue, or a part of virtue: a way to achieve happiness. One became virtuous, or just, as much for one's own sake as for the sake of others. If others benefited from this, that was fine, but the aim of much philosophy was the attainment of personal happiness. True, our philosophers identified the good of the community with the good of the individual, but it is easy to see how later authors could have overlooked the corporate dimension of this happiness. In conclusion, then, we can see highly developed authoritarian elements in Roman Law and libertarian elements in Greek philosophy. We have seen that early Christianity encountered these systems of thought, and that early Christians made use of them to illustrate the New Testament. We must now go on to explore how Roman and Greek ideas developed within the Church, and to show what effect they had on later Christian doctrine.

Chapter 4

Roman Canon Law, Power and Justice

Introduction

The Roman Catholic Church and the Church of England exercise their authority through the bishops under Canon Law. Canon Law has developed gradually over the centuries, since Paul used the word *kanoni* in Galatians 6:16 to describe his rules that circumcision is nothing, and that new creation is everything. Elsewhere in the New Testament, law is denoted by *nomos*. Walter Bauer (1979) explains that *kanōn* meant 'straight rod' in the New Testament, and came to stand for revealed truth or a rule of faith in the second-century Church.[1] Canon Law began with the declarations of Councils, which were codified in due course, and grew into a Corpus of regulations by which the Church governed itself. Since 1917, Rome has organised its Canon Law into a Code. There have been two versions of this Code, in 1917 and 1983. We shall refer to both Codes in both Latin and English. For the 1917 Code, we shall use the English text by Peters (2001), and the original Latin text (Benedict XV, 1949). For the 1983 Code we shall use the English text by the Canon Law Society of Great Britain and Ireland (1997), and the original Latin text (John Paul II, 1983). For clarity, throughout this study, I shall refer to Latin codes (both civil and Canonical) with the word 'Codex', and I shall refer to their English translations as 'Code'. Both Codes abrogate all previous Canons they do not restate.[2]

I shall, when we discuss Canon Law in the twentieth century, refer mainly to the 1983 Code, as amended by the Apostolic Letter *Ad Tuendam Fidem* (John Paul II, 1998a). This is a single, concise, up-to-date, statement of Roman Canon Law, with which we can compare the testimony of earlier witnesses. We shall first examine the early witnesses, to identify their ideas of justice and power. We shall then try to see how these ideas have developed through the ages, and try to identify some of the influences that have contributed to these changes. Canon Law is an immensely complex subject. It is not my aim to give a full history of Canon Law – that would take us far beyond the scope of this study. Rather, I intend to try to isolate particular influences on Roman Canon Law that in my view have contributed to an authoritarian and centralised understanding of Church government.

Unfortunately, English Canon Law is not so tidy. There is no complete reference work of English Canon Law, as, like English Civil Law it is drawn from many sources. English Canon Law is based on a mixture of Canons passed by General Synod and its

---

1 Bauer (1979), p. 403. For a fuller exposition see Kittel (1965), pp. 596–602.
2 Canon 6 §1 in each Code.

predecessors, Case Law as established by Consistory Court, and Measures passed by Synod and approved by Parliament. Further, unlike Roman Canon Law, which has no force outside the Church, English Canon Law can indirectly have the same force as Civil Law in England, through measures such as the blasphemy laws. General Synod and its predecessors, rather than other bodies, have generally decided how the bishops and clergy should relate to lay Christians. It therefore seems reasonable to concentrate largely on the Canons produced by Synod, and to refer to other material where appropriate. Since the sources of English Canon Law differ from Roman sources, we should expect to find different influences in post-Reformation England from those we find in Rome, and therefore different emphases. We shall restrict ourselves in this chapter to Roman Canon Law. We shall deal with English Canon Law in chapter 5.

Roman Canon Law

A Brief History

James A. Coriden, in his *Introduction to Canon Law* (2004), defines Roman Canon Law as 'the rules that govern the public order of the Roman Catholic Church ... ecclesiastical regulations'.[3] He then gives an overview of the history of Canon Law. Yves Congar (Todd, 1962) has produced the standard Roman Catholic account of the history of authority in the Church, and while his treatment goes beyond the limits of this work, parts of it are also relevant for us. Coriden begins with the Didache, written about AD 100, which is among the earliest important Canonical documents. It became the pattern for other collections of customs in particular Churches, issued without formal authority, and distributed to other Churches for mutual support and encouragement. The early bishops, such as Clement of Rome, Ignatius of Antioch, and Polycarp, also wrote to each other, to encourage, to resolve conflicts, and to advise.

In due course, local synods of bishops began to meet together to discuss problems and seek consensus on disciplinary or doctrinal matters. These synods, patterned on the Synod of Jerusalem described in Acts 15, eventually gave rise to the Ecumenical Councils, which were to play such a large part in the development of Canon Law. Before Constantine, the Church was free to develop its own structures and regulations. Since its members were regulated by Roman Civil Law, however, when the Church needed new structures, it adopted the most convenient ones then in use. At this stage, the Canons were statements of custom, and decisions were made by Councils. After Constantine embraced Christianity, the Canons began to gain the status of law. This, at first, caused tension between Church and state. In the fourth century, several emperors tried to dominate the Church, often supporting heretical

---

3   Coriden (2004), p. 4. This seems a good description of how Roman Canon Law works, so I shall accept it.

factions and persecuting the orthodox. Eventually, this relationship became closer. Ambrose and Theodosius I agreed that the Church would recognise the emperor's civil and political supremacy, and the emperor would recognise the Church's supremacy in faith, discipline, and liturgy. Each was entitled to the support of the other. The Church, in other words, became the state religion.[4]

The influence of Roman Law began, and both Theodosius II and Justinian I made laws, some of their own invention, on behalf of the Church. Since there were now definite advantages in being a Christian, Church membership mushroomed. Not surprisingly, however, preparation and commitment were often lacking among the new Christians. Consequently, Coriden tells us, the bishops began to appoint presbyters to act as their deputies to lead remote Churches, and therefore it became impossible for them to know all the Christians in their dioceses personally. Congar points out that at the same time, bishops gained secular power, which effectively gave them the same rank as senators, and perhaps left them inclined to govern the Church as they governed the populace.[5] Congar states that the ancient Latin rite of ordination places emphasis on service (*ministerium*) rather than power (*dominium* or *potestas*), and that it presents 'an essentially moral idea of authority'.[6] He concedes, however, that not all popes have followed this course. The practice, in other words, did not always follow the theory.

Rome also began to play an important part in maintaining communion between Churches separated by great distances, by acting as a depository of the orthodox faith. Coriden identifies the connections with Peter and Paul, and Rome's status as the imperial capital as the major causes of this. By the third century, bishops often referred disputed questions to Rome for settlement. By the time of Pope Leo I, the Bishop of Rome was generally accepted as the Patriarch of the West. Leo also vigorously promoted the idea that the Bishops of Rome are the heirs of Peter. From the fourth century, popes issued decretals, which, in due course, were placed, alongside the earlier collections of Canons. The most important collection of Canons produced was the Dionysiana. Adrian I gave an expanded version of this collection to Charlemagne in AD 774 (the Dionysiana Hadriana), which the emperor tried to enforce throughout his realm. When this period of reform was concluded, Pope Leo III crowned him as Holy Roman Emperor on Christmas Day 800.[7]

The Feudal period, which followed, introduced vassals, patrons and benefices. The local lord was entitled to give priests the revenue from some land in exchange for the priest's work in the parish. Since the lord owned this land, he could give its income to whoever he chose. He often chose a priest with whom he was comfortable, sometimes without regard for the priest's qualifications or pastoral skill. The same happened to bishops and monks whose cathedrals and monasteries did not own the

---

4   Ibid., pp. 10–13. The diocese and province, for example, were adopted from the Roman Empire.

5   Todd (1962), pp. 128–32.

6   Ibid., p. 131.

7   Coriden (2004), pp. 13–15.

land on which they were built: the clergy ended up in service to secular rulers. This led to the Lay Investiture Controversy, during which popes Leo IX and Gregory VII tried to regain control of ecclesiastical offices and appointments.[8] It took 50 years of conflict, military as well as theological, before the influence of the patrons was reduced to a veto on appointments at the Synod of Worms in 1122. During this period, the Canonical tradition underwent strong Germanic influence. The concept of the parish as benefice, the oath of fidelity, the right of patronage and the ceremony of promising reverence and obedience to the bishop (a replica of the Feudal act of vassal homage), were among the results.[9] While there seems to be more emphasis on individual fealty than on communal obedience here, it also appears that Germanic influences had more influence on who held authority than how such authority was understood. During the Lay Investiture Controversy, Congar tells us, Leo IX and Gregory VII vigorously tried to purify the Church by ridding it of its identification with secular political society. Instead, Gregory in particular claimed complete autonomy and sovereignty for the Church by divine institution. He also asked churchmen (beginning with Peter Damian) to find juridical texts supporting his position. This led to the production of some new collections of Canons, which we shall now consider.[10]

The twelfth and thirteenth centuries were the Classical Period of Canon Law. It became the subject of academic study, and several collections of Canons were published. Canon Law, Coriden tells us, was again influenced by Roman Law, which was studied alongside it. The two systems were regarded as complementary – where Canon Law lacked provision, Canonists usually sought a solution in Roman Law.[11] Congar explains that Canonists of this period became interested in divine justice, expressed in Church Law and particularly in the rights of the pontiff. He tells us that, for example, Jeremiah 1:10 became understood as an assertion of the divine right of the pope and of his right to depose kings.[12] Nevertheless, while Congar accepts that the Church began to formulate its authority on the basis of legal principles, and submit 'certain themes and certain texts to a legalistic interpretation,'[13] he maintains that the dominant aspect of authority at the time was spiritual. While this may be true in theory, it appears that practice was rather different. The 1302 Bull, *Unam Sanctam* (Bettenson, 1943), for example, declares, 'we declare, state, define and pronounce that it is altogether necessary to salvation for every human creature to be subject to

---

8   Hugh Lawrence (in Hoose, 2002, pp. 43–4) and Paul Avis (2001, p. 41) argue that the Gregorian reforms were the start of the process leading to the centralisation of episcopal appointments and Church government. The most influential mediaeval treatise supporting this position was Giles of Rome's *On Ecclesiastical Power* (Dyson, 2004).

9   Ibid., pp. 15–17.

10   Todd (1962), pp. 136–7.

11   Coriden (2004), pp. 18–20.

12   Todd (1962), p. 138. Congar also offers contemporary reinterpretations of 1 Corinthians 2:15 (no one can judge the pope), and 6:3 (the pope has the right to judge secular powers).

13   Ibid., p. 138.

the Roman pontiff".[14] Boniface VIII makes it clear that this power is both spiritual and temporal.[15]

Then three crises arose in quick succession: the Great Western Schism with the Avignon Papacy, and then the arrival of the Black Death, in 1347, caused great turmoil in the fourteenth century. In the fifteenth, the Reformation began. These events caused increasing centralisation in the Church, as Rome began to reserve appointments to the Holy See. Most Canonical work in this period concerned schism, heresy, benefices, elections and taxes.[16] The 1500 edition of Gratian's *Decretum*, an attempt to harmonise seemingly conflicting Canons, and its 1582 revision, which became the standard edition, were the most significant works of this period. The Canon Law that Luther rejected was largely unchanged from the mid–fourteenth century. Centralisation continued after Trent, reaching its peak at Vatican I. The last major development in Canon Law was codification, with the first Codex being issued in 1917, and the second in 1983, following the reforms introduced by Vatican II.

Ladislas Örsy (1992) divides the history of Canon Law into four periods.[17] He argues that from the beginning to the time of Gratian, the Church used a non–critical and non–scientific approach. Canon Law during this period, he tells us, was the distillation of the practical wisdom of the community. It was neither organised nor evaluated. The Church was motivated largely by pastoral need. From Gratian to Trent, however, Örsy argues, the critical approach was used. Gratian's attempt to assess the relative importance of Canons began the process leading to organised collections of Canons. Between Trent and Vatican II, however, this critical spirit was lost. This, Örsy argues, was due to two factors. First, Canon Law was seen as a defence against enemies, both within and outside the Church – it ceased to develop and became static. Interpretation tended to become narrowly literal. The second factor was the influence of the mediaeval view that both Church and state were perfect societies. Consequently, the secular model 'was uncritically applied to the church'.[18] Örsy explains in a footnote that the perfect society view was debatable anyway, and that when the perfect society as it applied to the state was used as a model for the Church, it became fatally flawed, facilitating the importation of secular ideas into the Church.[19]

Since Vatican II, Örsy argues, Rome has been restructuring itself to respond to the challenges of recognising that the Church extends beyond the Roman Catholic Church, and reforming its institutions accordingly. For Örsy, then, the period most relevant to our enquiry is post–Tridentine. However, we have seen indications that

---

14 Bettenson (1943), p. 161. Compare Denzinger (1932), p. 220.

15 'Both are in the power of the Church'. Ibid., p. 160. Compare Denzinger (1932), p. 219.

16 Coriden (2004), pp. 20–25.

17 Örsy (1992), pp. 24–5, Compare Gerosa (2002), pp. 60–61.

18 Ibid., p. 25.

19 Ibid., footnote 10. He also suggests that Church law needs some de-secularisation to make the truth and beauty of the Church more visible to all, a position with which I have some sympathy.

authority was expressed most clearly in terms of power when Canon Law was most influenced by Roman Law, and when the Church faced opposition. The periods between the Apostolic Canons, probably of the late third century, and the coronation of the first Holy Roman Emperor, between the First and Fourth Lateran Councils, and around Trent and the two Vatican Councils are also likely to be particularly significant. We shall therefore examine Canonical documents from these periods, and compare them with other law of the time, particularly with the ecclesiastical law of the Christian Roman emperors.

From the Apostolic Constitutions to Constantinople IV

We begin with the Apostolic Constitutions. This document, apparently signed by Clement of Rome (Pope Clement I, c90–c99), is generally regarded as late third or early fourth century. Its tone is generally of exhortation; it encourages the faithful to adhere to certain norms of behaviour. At the end of the document are 85 Canons. Four of these are commands, but a reason is always given: either by a charge of disorder or by a Scriptural text. A few Canons will give a flavour of the document. Canon 10 explains that those who enter Churches and hear the Scriptures read, but leave before the prayers and the Communion 'must be suspended, as causing disorder in the church'.[20] Canon 35 instructs bishops not to make important decisions without consulting the chief bishop, but even for smaller decisions, he must not 'do anything without the consent of all; for it is by this means there will be unanimity, and God will be glorified by Christ, in the Holy Spirit'.[21] Finally, Canon 53 states that clergy fasting or not receiving Communion on feast days must be 'deprived, as 'having a seared conscience,' and 'becoming a cause of scandal to many'.[22] In each case, behaviour is commended or a penalty is prescribed, and a reason is given: 'causing disorder', 'God will be glorified', 'scandal to many'. The motivation here is order and decency: these are distillations of practical wisdom learnt during the early period of the Church.

By the time of the First Nicene Council in 325, however, the tone of the Canons had changed altogether. Canon 2, for example, which prohibits the ordination of the recently baptised, ends with a statement that anyone contravening these regulations may lose his clerical status for defying 'this great synod (*tē megalē sunodō*)'.[23] Similarly, in Canon 3 'This great synod absolutely forbids (*apēgoreuse chatholu hē megalē sunodos*)'[24] a cleric to keep a woman who is not his mother, sister or aunt, or who is not above suspicion, in his house. Again, no reason is given, although we might reasonably presume it is to avoid a scandal. Canon 14 declares that 'this holy and great synod decrees (*edoxe tē hagia kai megalē sunodō*)' that lapsed catechumens

---

20 Roberts and Donaldson (1999), volume 7, p. 501.
21 Ibid., p. 502.
22 Ibid., p. 503.
23 Tanner (1990), p. *7.
24 Ibid.

must spend three years as hearers before being allowed to pray with catechumens who have not lapsed.[25] Finally, Canon 15 states that clerics must not transfer from one city to another, because this might cause factions and disturbance. It concludes that any attempt to make such a transfer after the decision of 'this holy and great synod (*tēs hagias kai megalēs sunodou*)'[26] will be null and void. One cannot help noticing the Council's willingness to assert and elevate its own authority rather than to explain itself to the faithful; its use of decree rather than persuasion, a line that would have been untenable before Constantine's conversion.[27] Nevertheless, the word 'decree' occurs only five times in the 20 Canons. Four of these occurrences are translations of *dokeō*. The stronger word, *horidzō* occurs only once, in Canon 8, and there it refers to and reaffirms the existing decrees of the Church.

The Canons of the Council of Constantinople (381) largely restate those of Nicaea I, in addition to anathematising some heresies that had arisen in the meantime. Constantinople's main innovation was the insertion of the Bishop of Constantinople into the second highest place of honour, behind the Bishop of Rome.[28] Nevertheless, Canon 6, which deals with accusations against bishops and clergy, seems partially to have reverted to the earlier pattern of the Apostolic Canons, in that it tells those who attempt to bypass the disciplinary procedures of the Church by accusing bishops before secular authorities that their accusations will not be heard, because they have 'made a mockery of the canons and violated the good order of the church'.[29] Note that the reason for this prohibition has reappeared: it is to maintain good order in the Church. The verb 'to decree' (*horidzō* in Greek, and *decerno* in Latin)[30] appears only once here, in Canon 2, where it is used to describe the decisions of the First Nicene Council. There is less evidence here of the authoritarian element apparently introduced at Nicaea I.

The Council of Ephesus (431) dealt mainly with Nestorianism, and did not produce any new Canons. The next Ecumenical Council, Chalcedon (451), however, did result in Canonical development. Fourteen of its 30 Canons are presented as decrees, on a variety of subjects from cohabitation to commendatory letters for the poor to matters of ordination. Clerics or monks who break Canon 3, for example, (by meddling in other people's business) 'must be subject to ecclesiastical penalties'.[31] Monks who disobey their bishops must 'be excommunicated, lest God's name be blasphemed'.[32] In general, these Canons follow the spirit of the Apostolic Canons

---

25 Ibid., p. *13. 'Has decided' might be a better translation of *edoxe/placuit*.

26 Ibid.

27 Chilton and Neusner (1999, pp. 155 and 170) see continuity between the Council of Jerusalem and the later Councils of the Church, but think that Eusebius' comparison of Constantine with Christ shaped the way that Nicaea I and its successors operated.

28 Canon 3. Tanner (1990), p. 32.

29 Ibid., p. *34.

30 'Decree' henceforth is a translation of a part of *horidzō* unless otherwise specified.

31 Ibid., p. *89.

32 Canon 4. Ibid.

in exhorting obedience and explaining why this is beneficial, even though they are presented as decrees.

Other Canons, however, do not allow this interpretation. Canon 10, for example, forbids the appointment of clerics to Churches in two cities, adding that anyone defying 'this great and universal synod (*tēs megalēs kai oikomenikēs tautēs sunodou*)'[33] will lose their personal rank. Canon 12 uses similar language. It prohibits the division of provinces by civil authorities at the behest of bishops hoping to become metropolitans in the process. The Canon states that 'The sacred synod therefore decrees (*Ōrise toinun hē hagia sunodos*)'[34] that no bishop should dare to do so in future, and provides that any who become metropolitans in this way may retain the title as a mark of honour, but may not prejudice the rights of the established metropolitan. In these Canons, the authoritarian element begun at Nicaea I appears to continue. Finally, Canon 23 of Chalcedon, which instructs the public attorney first to direct those causing disruption in Churches to leave Constantinople, and if they do not comply, to expel them forcibly, introduces the first suggestion of the state being encouraged to enforce Church Law.[35]

Constantinople II and III (553 and 680–1) neither debated ecclesiastical discipline nor issued any Canons, so we pass on to Nicaea II (787). The first thing one notices about the Canons of Nicaea II is that they are full of quotations from Scripture, in a way not found in previous Canons. The first Canon, a joyful reaffirmation of all the Canons that have gone before, contains seven quotations from the Bible in nine sentences. Canon 4 contains another six Biblical references, and Scripture also appears in Canons 2, 5, 6, 7, 13, 15, 16 and 22. In all, Nicaea II issued 22 Canons, of which six are presented as decrees. Of these, three decrees are derived directly from Biblical quotations, one is derived indirectly from Scripture, one from the writings of Basil, and only one stands on its own merits. We seem to have reverted to the older pattern, in which things are commanded or prohibited because of their inherent goodness or otherwise. Nicaea II comes across as far less authoritarian than Nicaea I, although the potential for authoritarianism remains in the structure of the later Canons. We should note that the Latin translation of *horidzō* has changed from *decerno* [decree] to *definio* [define].

Finally, we turn to the Fourth Council of Constantinople (869–870). This Council was not received in the East, and was only acknowledged as an Ecumenical Council in the West from the eleventh century onwards. We have seen the developments leading to the beginning of the Holy Roman Empire in 800, and we might therefore expect to see their effects in the Canons of this Council. Canon 1, as we might expect, reaffirms the Canons of the previous Councils, but for the first time, it describes them as definitions (*definitiones*), rather than as rules (*regulae/kanones*).[36] This places a

---

33   Ibid.

34   Ibid., p. *93.

35   Ibid., pp. *97–8.

36   Ibid., p. 166. Tanner tells us that the Council considered and esteemed the Canons 'as a second word of God, in accordance with the great and most wise Denis ...' This, however,

high priority on the observance of the Canons, and is noticeably stronger than the declarations of Constantinople I, Chalcedon and Nicaea II. The monarchical theory of the papacy, as extended to include the bishops, makes its first explicit appearance in the documents of an Ecumenical Council at the start of Canon 2:

> Obey your leaders and submit to them; for they are keeping watch over your souls, as persons who will have to give account, commands Paul, the great apostle. So, having both the most blessed pope Nicholas as the instrument of the Holy Spirit and his successor, the most holy pope Hadrian, we declare and order that everything which has been expounded and promulgated by them in a synod at various times ... should be maintained and observed together with the canons there set forth, unchanged and unaltered, and no bishop, priest or deacon or anyone from the ranks of the clergy should dare to overturn or reject any of these things.[37]

There seem to be two new claims here: first, that Ecumenical Synods act as agents of the pope, and second, that the popes are the instruments of the Holy Spirit, a claim similar to that entailed by the later papal title 'Vicar of Christ'. Canon 21, which is entitled 'The pope of Rome or any other patriarch must not be treated with disrespect by anyone', contains the first reference to the pope as the supreme pontiff and chief pastor of the Catholic Church in a Canon of an Ecumenical Council. Canon 22 decrees that during the election of a bishop, every ruler and lay person should 'be silent and mind his own business (*silere ac attendere sibi)*'[38] until the election was complete, unless invited by the Church to intervene. All 27 Canons from Constantinople IV are presented as decrees, and the tone is authoritarian throughout. This time, however, the pope, not the Council, seems to be the source of the authoritarian claims.

We have seen, then, how the Canons of the Church in the third century were a distillation of practical wisdom, and were exhortations to beneficial behaviour. We have seen that at Nicaea I they became authoritarian, and that the Council was seen as the source of that authority. We have seen that the authoritarianism gradually diminished in the period to Nicaea II, at which Scriptural passages made their most prominent appearances in the Canons. Finally, we have seen the return of authoritarian Canons at Constantinople IV, but that this time the pope was the source of authority. We must now try to establish what influences contributed to these shifts of emphasis.

---

seems to rest on a misreading of Pseudo–Dionysius the Areopagite, who appears to refer to a respectful awe for the liturgy, rather than Canon Law. See *The Ecclesiastical Hierarchy*, 1:4 (Luibheid, 1987, pp. 198–9).

37   Ibid., p. *167.

38   Ibid., p. *183.

Secular Law

Constantine

Eusebius, in his *Life of Constantine* (Cameron and Hall, 1999) paints a glowing
picture of the emperor's influence on the Church. While it is clear that Eusebius
wrote a hagiography making liberal use of his rose-tinted spectacles, the *Life*
seems to reflect the regard in which Constantine was held in the early Church,
and it certainly contains information useful to us. While it would be wise to be
sceptical about Eusebius' interpretation of the facts, he quotes a number of original
Constantinian texts. These texts seem, in general, to be genuine.[39] It is instructive
to examine Constantine's view of the relationship between Church and state. In
book 4, chapter 24 of the *Life*, Eusebius reports that Constantine, while entertaining
a company of bishops, informed them that he too was a bishop, informing them
in Eusebius' hearing that 'I am perhaps a bishop, appointed by God over those
outside'.[40] Eusebius then explains how Constantine's acts matched his words: 'he
exercised a bishop's supervision over all his subjects, and pressed them all, as far as
lay in his power, to lead the Godly life'.[41] He added his sanction to the decisions of
episcopal synods, and forbade provincial governors to annul any synodical decrees.
He was devoted to God, and was 'fair to all and impartial in his benefits'.[42]

Constantine's laws are, as we might expect, very favourable towards the Church,
but he was still willing to let other religious practices go on, albeit with extra
restrictions.[43] His authoritarian approach is also visible in his legislation, which
continued to influence both Roman Law and Ecclesiastical Law long after his death.
Book 2, title 1, section 1 of the *Theodosian Code* expresses Constantine's will that
for those caught breaking the law should be sent to prison, where 'tortures shall tear
them in pieces, [and] the avenging sword shall destroy them'.[44] Book 4, title 10,
section 1 added that if ungrateful freedmen became proud or offended their patrons
or former masters, they could be re–enslaved at will. While this law may have been
seen as fair at the time, it cannot, by any stretch of the imagination, be described as
'impartial in [its] benefits'. In fact, it bears all the hallmarks of the view that the aim
of justice is to give those who have been wronged revenge upon their adversaries.[45]

---

39   Cameron and Hall (1999), pp. 18–19. Compare Baynes (1972), pp. 5–7.

40   Ibid., p. 161.

41   Ibid. Neusner and Chilton (1997, p. 152) comment that Eusebius' treatment of
Constantine follows the old Stoic idea that the devout emperor's rule corresponds to God's
rule, and in particular that as Constantine obeyed Christ, he imitated Christ's glory.

42   Ibid., p. 163.

43   Pharr (1952), book 16, title 10, pp. 472–6. In sections 1 and 3 respectively, Constantine
authorised soothsayers to remain in the palace, and allowed temples outside the city walls to
stay open.

44   Ibid., p. 37.

45   Ibid., pp. 91–2. Book 4, title 12, section 1, for example, provides that if a woman is
injured by a slave 'she shall be avenged by the due severity of the law'. Similarly, book 9,

I have already argued that this view is typical of early Roman Law, and is far from what I would regard as a Biblical view of justice.[46] Constantine was also the author of another law with far–reaching implications:

> To insist upon the ancient customs is the discipline of future times. Therefore, when nothing that is in the public interest interferes, practices which have long been observed shall remain valid.[47]

This principle, which we shall shortly see restated in a slightly different form in Justinian's *Institutes*, in due course entered Canon Law as the principle of desuetude. If the people did not wish to receive a particular new Canon, they could annul it by setting up and maintaining a contrary custom. Alternatively, if the Canon required a particular action, they could simply ignore it and continue their existing practice as if nothing had happened. After a suitable period, normally 40 years, the Canon lost its force and it was abrogated.[48]

The Theodosian Code

The *Theodosian Code* was in general a codification of existing law, rather than new legislation. The major section of new material, in book 16 of the *Code*, deals with Ecclesiastical Law. It defines Catholic Christianity as the faith transmitted by Peter to the Romans, and followed by the Pontiff Damasus and Peter, bishop of Alexandria. This definition, promulgated by Gratian, Valentinian II and Theodosius I, states that 'we shall believe in the single deity of the Father, the Son and the Holy Spirit, under the concept of equal majesty and of the Holy Trinity'.[49] Those who did not so believe, they judged 'demented and insane'.[50] Unbelievers could expect to be 'smitten first by divine vengeance and secondly by the retribution of Our own initiative, which we shall assume in accordance with the divine judgement'.[51] One cannot escape the impression here that while the emperors might have believed that vengeance belongs to the Lord, they wanted to share in this work themselves.

The *Code* refers repeatedly to tax exemptions and exemptions from public service for clerics, which were introduced by Constantine and reaffirmed by his successors,

---

title 1, section 4 (p. 224) provides that if a Provincial were charged with a crime, Constantine would investigate himself, and if the case were proven, 'I Myself will avenge Myself'.

46   Above, Chapter 4.

47   Book 5, title 20. Ibid., p. 117.

48   The principle of desuetude in Canon Law is, of course, one application of the consensus fidelem. It is, however, rather surprising to find this principle being derived from Roman Civil Law.

49   Book 16, title 1, section 2. Ibid., p 440.

50   Ibid.

51   Ibid.

despite occasional abuse of these laws by some wealthy plebeians.[52] Honorius and Theodosius II expected Church courts to enforce Canon Law. They commanded, in 421, 'that the ancient practice and the pristine ecclesiastical canons which have been in force up to the present shall be observed throughout all the provinces of Illyricum and that all innovations shall cease'.[53] This may have had some influence on Canon 23 of the Council of Chalcedon, which, as we saw earlier, urged the secular authorities to act against those who violated Canon Law.

The laws against heresy and schism were especially severe. Gratian, Valentinian II and Theodosius I made their laws confiscating the property of heretics retroactive, contrary to general Roman jurisprudence, and they encouraged the use of informants, who were normally executed, by allowing them to report heresy with impunity.[54] Heretics were forbidden from holding assemblies, and if any were found working in the imperial service, under Arcadius and Honorius, they could expect dismissal and expulsion from the city. In some cases, they could also lose their citizenship, their property, and their inheritances, but not, at this stage, their lives.

Theodosius II and Valentinian III defined heretics as those who were not in communion with the pope. Those who refused to return to communion with him within 20 days of being identified as a heretic or schismatic incurred the full penalty of the law. Similar penalties applied to apostates. Arcadius and Honorius, however, reserved their severest treatment for the sacrilegious. Book 16, title 2, section 31 introduced execution for anyone who should 'break forth into such sacrilege that he should invade the Catholic churches and should inflict any outrage on the priests and ministers, or on the worship itself and on the place of worship'.[55] This is, as far as I know, unprecedented in early Church Law. It seems that the emperors legislated on this matter on behalf of the Church, but based their laws on purely secular principles, without regard to the Canonical tradition of the Church.

Apart from this, it seems that the *Theodosian Code* introduced two other major innovations to Church Law. First, by legislating on behalf of the Church, the emperors brought Church and state closer together. Consequently, Canon Law, which until Constantine had been seen as guidance based on the accumulated wisdom of the Church, became elevated to the status of Ecclesiastical Law. It became as binding on the faithful, and, in some cases, everyone else, as the Civil Law was on the population as a whole. We have already seen this effect in Canon 23 of Chalcedon. The second innovation was the definition that heretics and schismatics were those who were not in communion with the pope. This fits well with the view we explored earlier that Rome was the depository of the orthodox faith, although the emphasis by now was

---

52   See book 16, title 2, sections 17 and 19. Ibid., p. 443. Clerical service exempted them from tax and public service.

53   Section 45. Ibid., p. 449.

54   Book 10, title 10. Ibid., pp. 273–9. By the Middle Ages, informants no longer faced automatic execution, but if their accusations proved to be false, they suffered the penalty the accused would have received, had they been convicted. Compare Deuteronomy 19:15–21.

55   Ibid., p. 445.

shifting from the Roman Church to the Roman Bishop as the source of orthodoxy. There seems as yet, however, no sign of the Petrine primacy in either Ecclesiastical or Civil Law.

Justinian

Justinian sets out the principles of his law in the *Institutes* (Scott, 2001), which are then fleshed out in detail in the *Digest* and the *Code*. 'Justice is the constant and perpetual desire to give to each one that to which he is entitled ... Jurisprudence is the knowledge of matters divine and human, and the comprehension of what is just and what is unjust ... The following are the precepts of the law: to live honestly, not to injure one another, and to give to each one that which belongs to him'.[56] This law is both written and unwritten. 'The unwritten law is that which usage has confirmed, for customs long observed and sanctioned by the consent of those who employ them, resemble law'.[57] Once again, we have the familiar definition of justice. Note, however, that the definition of unwritten law has changed. Now there is a requirement for the consent of those who observe the customs. This seems to be much closer to the Canonical theory of desuetude than Constantine's view of custom as law.

Justinian's Ecclesiastical Law is set out in titles 1–13 of book 1 of the *Code of Civil Law*, and in various places in the *Novels*. We shall discuss only the new material. It begins in title 1, with a letter from Pope John II to Justinian. In this letter, John claims that Justinian has 'preserved reverence for the See of Rome, and has subjected all things to its authority, and has given it unity'.[58] This clearly echoes the view that the popes are the successors of Peter. John continues: 'This see is indeed the head of all churches, as the rules of the Fathers and the decrees of Emperors assert, and the words of your most reverend piety testify'.[59] This illustrates the increasingly close relationship between Church and state. This relationship was strengthened by the emperor Frederick, in around 455, when he ordered that all customs opposed to the liberty of the Church and its ministers, or contrary to Canon or Imperial Law, 'shall be null and void'.[60] In these two statements, we see how the emperors began to adjust civil law to bring it in line with the practice of the Church. They also legislated in favour of the Church. Following a decree of Emperor Leo I in 470, the Church began to hold its property in perpetuity. It largely lost the power to dispose of land or goods it no longer needed, and was protected against gifts of worthless land. This

---

56   Book 1, title 1. Scott (2001), volume 2, p. 5. *The Digest* (p. 211) reveals that this comes from the *Rules of Ulpianus*, book 1. This has become a standard definition of justice.

57   Book 1, title 2. Ibid., p. 7. The *Digest* (p. 225) reveals that this comes from the *Digest of Julianus*, book 94. The full text includes the statement that unwritten laws are abrogated 'not only by the vote of the legislator, but also through disuse by the silent consent of all'.

58   Ibid., p. 11.

59   Ibid.

60   Ibid., p. 18.

idea seems unprecedented in Church Law, and may well have been an invention of
the emperors.

When Justinian began to frame new laws, he seems to have seen himself as acting
on behalf of God. Title 3 of the first collection of the *Novels* set limits on the number
of clerics in Constantinople, in an attempt to ensure that the Churches had adequate
means to support them. This might seem like sanctified common sense, but Justinian
informed the stewards of the Church that those who did not comply 'will be subjected
to Divine punishment, as well as be compelled to indemnify the Holy Church out
of their own property'.[61] Similarly, in title 5, which regulated monasteries, Justinian
told the Patriarchs that 'the most severe punishment shall be inflicted upon those
who disobey the present [Justinian's] law (We refer to celestial penalties which it is
necessary to impose upon those who show contempt for the rules of their spiritual
guides)'.[62] Both these examples suggest that Justinian believed that he was entitled
to legislate for the Church on his authority as emperor. The most startling example
of this view appears in title 4 of the second collection, in which Justinian claims the
right to legislate for both Church and state, in the same way as the emperors of old,
who held the title of Pontifex Maximus before it was taken over by the popes.

Justinian then prohibited exceptions to laws affecting the Churches for 100 years
after promulgation. For other laws, this period was 30 years. The Church, in other
words, was protected for a lifetime instead of a generation. This also seems to have
been Justinian's invention. Further, he changed the law on clerical celibacy. Canon
27 of the Apostolic Canons prohibited clergy above the rank of reader from marrying
if they were single when ordained. This Canon did not, however, prevent men who
were married becoming bishops, provided they were married before they were
ordained. The Church had always favoured priestly continence, and had required
married men to refrain from intercourse with their wives after ordination since at
least the fourth century. Justinian, however, extended this ban, requiring married
bishops to separate from their wives, and insisting that henceforth, only single men
could become bishops. In doing so, he explicitly stated that he was extending the law
concerning bishops, in order that 'the sacred canons shall be observed hereafter',
despite the fact that Canon 6 of the Apostolic Canons prohibited clergy from
separating from their wives. This reform did not succeed immediately, and Justinian
felt it necessary to restate the ban in his 22nd and 137th new constitutions.[63]

He was also willing to transfer some of his powers to the bishops. In title 6 of
the second collection, he promoted Catollianus, a provincial bishop, to the post of
archbishop of the First Justinianian, giving him the superior privileges, power, and

---

61   Ibid., p. 21.

62   Ibid., p. 30. The implication seems to be that Justinian is himself among the spiritual
guides.

63   Scott (2001), volume 16, pp. 31 and 133, and volume 17, pp. 152–7. When Gregory
VII began to enforce clerical celibacy following a Lent Synod at the Lateran in 1074, he seems
to have done so out of a similar desire for the purity of the clergy. Compare Bowden (1840),
volume 2, p. 10.

authority that this title confers over other clerics. Catollianus was also to enjoy the first sacerdotal dignity and the highest honours of the priesthood. He became the supreme judge and head of the Church in his province, and was freed entirely from the authority of the bishop of Thessalonica. He was invested with 'supreme power, unlimited sacerdotal supervision and the right of appointment'.[64] Here we see the view of the archbishop as viceroy, in addition to his episcopal duties as a servant of the local Church. These rôles do not sit easily together. The relationship between Church and state is now at its closest. We shall examine this passage again when we discuss the 1983 Code of Canon Law.

Unfortunately, we have no convenient Ecumenical Council with which to compare this legislation, since the Ecumenical Councils of the sixth and seventh centuries (Constantinople II and III) issued declarations of faith and anathemas, not legislation. Nicaea II, which took place in AD 787, was two and a half centuries later, by which time we might reasonably expect that any effects of Justinian's *Code* would be heavily diluted by later material. We can, however, note that Justinian brought together the ideas of emperor as legislator and bishop as legislator, in the process apparently introducing the idea that the bishop, as opposed to Councils, could produce binding legislation, although it was binding only within his diocese. This idea survives in the current Code of Canon Law, where bishops, within their dioceses, are identified as the sole legislators for the Church.[65]

Charlemagne

Roman Law was the major, but not the only influence on Canon Law. From the ninth century, Germanic Law began to be an influence. Germanic Law, unlike Roman Law, was not territorial, was generally based on tribal custom, rather than royal decree, was often unwritten, and applied only to the members of one tribe.[66] The main Germanic influence on Roman Canon Law, however, began with the Capitulary of Charlemagne (Henderson, 1965), king of the Franks and the first Holy Roman Emperor. In section 5, he declares himself protector and defender of the Church, and decrees that no one should presume to injure the Church through fraud or plunder. In section 10, he orders that bishops and priests should live by the Canons and teach others to do so. This closely follows the Roman tradition. The new material is in section 11, which urges bishops, abbots and abbesses that they should 'surpass in veneration and diligence those subject to them ... not oppress them with severe and tyrannous rule ... carefully guard the flock committed to them, with simple love, with mercy and charity, and by the example of good works'.[67]

---

64   Ibid., p. 69.
65   See Canon 466.
66   See Foster (1993), pp. 6–7. Kings sometimes added provisions that did not conflict with tribal customs.
67   Henderson (1965), p. 192.

This seems to be the first reference to the idea of authority as service in a document of Ecclesiastical Law for around 700 years. As we have seen, Constantinople IV, 60 years later, took a rather different view of the bishop's rôle. Nevertheless, Charlemagne's view survives in a different form in the current Code of Canon Law, at least as far as it concerns Religious communities. Canon 618 states that religious superiors must use their authority in a spirit of service, being docile to the will of God and promoting voluntary co-operation and obedience, 'without prejudice however to their authority to decide and to command what is to be done'.[68]

Charlemagne saw the empire as both a monarchy and a theocracy, with himself at the top as protector and defender of both Church and state. It seems that he wanted to preserve the unity of Church and state, but to reduce the authority of the bishops who, under Justinian, were equal partners with the emperor. This, more than anything else, seems to have caused the Church to reject his theory of Ecclesiastical Law and to revert to a more Justinianian position after his death. It is sadly a truism, even in the Church, that few give up power willingly. It seems that the bishops were happy to go along with the emperors while the power of the Church was increasing and its position was improving. When Charlemagne tried to apply the brakes, however, they resisted him, and ultimately ignored him. We can see, then, that between Constantine and Charlemagne the power of the bishops increased, and the popes began to assert their claims to supremacy over the whole Church. The emperors encouraged this process, and no doubt found it more convenient to manage ecclesiastical affairs through a single person than through a council of bishops. The bishops became the counterparts of secular princes, and adopted models of government proposed by secular emperors. Ecclesiastical rule thus became difficult to distinguish from secular rule: both were authoritarian, and at times absolutist.[69]

While we have examined political influences on the development of the ecclesiastical hierarchy in the Roman Catholic Church, it is clear that Plato exercised considerable influence over the early Church, and we should also consider the possibility that there was some Platonic influence involved in the hierarchical development of Church structures. The First Letter of Clement states that there is a diversity of functions in the Church, with the bishop leading, and others performing their allotted functions according to his will. This order, he tells us, was appointed by the Apostles according to God's will.[70] Similarly, Ignatius of Antioch is keen to stress the authority of the bishop and the clergy, arguing repeatedly that the Church should 'follow the bishop as Christ follows the Father, and the presbytery as if it were the

---

68   Canon Law Society (1997), p. 143. This Canon also shows clear signs of the influence of Roman Law in the way it talks of subjects and commands. There is no such provision concerning bishops in the Code.

69   Hugh Lawrence (in Hoose, 2002, pp. 44–7) argues that as the Church became the spiritual arm of the Empire, it effectively turned itself into a state, with Canon Law performing the function of Civil Law.

70   1 Clement 61–62. Lake (1912), pp. 79–81.

Apostles. And reverence the deacons as the command of God'.[71] Ignatius insists that he says this not because of any human knowledge, but because of the preaching of the Holy Spirit.[72] Origen, one of the first Christian Neoplatonists, argues in book 1, chapter 8 of *De Principiis* that there is a hierarchy in heaven, which is based on the spiritual merit of the angels.[73] When he applies a similar structure to the Church in his second homily on Numbers, he is quite clear that those in priestly ministry are not necessarily at the top of this hierarchy.[74] Augustine, in book XI of *The City of God* (1984), argues that the universe is hierarchical, with angels above men, the sentient above the non–sentient, the intelligent above the unthinking, the immortal above the mortal, and the good above the bad. He also tells us that the heavenly and earthly cities are interwoven and intermingled with each other. Unfortunately, Augustine does not appear to elaborate on this in detail.[75] Eugène Portalié (1960) does not believe that Augustine's motivation for this was Platonic; rather, he thinks Augustine was merely justifying ancient practice.[76] Pseudo-Dionysius the Areopagite, however, does offer a Neoplatonic argument that the universe is hierarchical, and that the ecclesiastical hierarchy is a reflection of the celestial hierarchy.[77] The lack of detail on this issue in Augustine may have made it possible for those who thought Pseudo–Dionysius wrote earlier than Augustine to read back a Neoplatonic hierarchy into Augustine's doctrine of the Church. It is far from clear, however, that the earliest people to argue for an episcopal hierarchy did so for Platonic reasons. Thus, the development of the episcopal hierarchy does not seem to be rooted in Neoplatonism.[78]

Having examined and discarded this possibility, we can also now offer an explanation for the development of Canonical theory through the Ecumenical Councils that we have discussed. At first, it seems, the Canons of Nicaea I became authoritarian because Constantine tried to impose his authority on the Church, and obtained its sanction through his control of the Council. As the power of the bishops increased, there was less need for the Councils to make such emphatic statements. Consequently, the authoritarian tone diminished, and Scriptural quotations became more prominent, possibly as an alternative source of justification for the Canons. Finally, following Charlemagne, the Western Church in particular sought to emphasise the power of the pope against the power of the emperor, and so the authoritarian tone returned, to ensure the compliance of the faithful. This may account, in part, for

---

71 Letter to Smyrna 8.1. Compare Letters to Ephesus 5, Magnesia 2–3 and 6–7, and Trallia 2. Ibid., pp. 179, 199–203, 213–4 and 261.

72 Letter to Philadelphia 7.2. Compare Letter to Trallia 2. Ibid., pp. 213–5 and 247.

73 Roberts and Donaldson (1999), volume 4, pp. 264–7.

74 Tollinton (1929), pp. 128–30.

75 Augustine (1984), pp. 429–30 and 447–8.

76 Portalié (1960), pp. 236–7.

77 See in particular chapter 3 of *The Celestial Hierarchy* and chapter 5 of *The Ecclesiastical Hierarchy*. Luibheid (1987), pp. 143–259.

78 Chilton and Neusner (1999, pp. 112 and 119) argue that the development of episcopal authority around the doctrine of apostolic succession was nevertheless a move away from New Testament thought. Compare von Campenhausen (1997), pp. 234–6.

the fact that Constantinople IV was never received in the East. It seems, then, that the mediaeval Western Church inherited an authoritarian view of the papacy and of bishops that was quite foreign to the view of the early Church. This authoritarian approach was largely the result of undue influence by Roman emperors trying to apply secular models to Church government, and the uncritical acquiescence of bishops in this process. We must now consider how this model developed during the High Middle Ages.

Gratian

Gratian was a scholar and teacher active in Bologna in the second half of the twelfth century. Other authors were citing his major work, the *Harmony of Discordant Canons*, otherwise known as the *Decretum*, by 1170. This work was built upon, extended and modified by Gratian's successors, and many commentaries were written about it. The *Decretum* begins with 101 distinctions, with which to resolve apparent contradictions between Canons, before describing 36 fictional cases to illustrate these distinctions. In the process, it refers to around 3800 texts. There is currently no authoritative twelfth-century edition of the *Decretum*,[79] so we shall use the text that became the standard version of the *Decretum*, the 1582 edition with the *Ordinary Gloss*. We shall largely restrict our analysis to the first 20 distinctions, which became known as the *Treatise on Law*.[80]

Distinction 3 sets out the definition that a Canon is a rule, which leads people to behave correctly, presents a norm, or sets straight what is twisted or bent. It states that some Canons are decrees of pontiffs, while others are statutes of Councils held under the authority of the pope, or a patriarch, primate or metropolitan.[81] Distinction 10 explains that secular law does not supersede Ecclesiastical Law. Gratian cites Pope Nicholas I (858–867) who stated that 'Imperial ordinances are not to be followed in any ecclesiastical dispute, especially since they sometimes contradict an evangelical or canonical sanction'.[82] In general, Gratian argues, the Church should follow Civil Law, except when it clashes with Canon Law. Distinction 11 states that custom should yield to ordinances. Gratian cites the view of Nicholas I that Canons ordained by popes should not be overturned by contrary customs, yet Gratian argues that custom should be preserved undisturbed when it does not conflict with either human law or reason. It seems that desuetude, at this period, was strictly restricted. Distinction 17 holds that Councils cannot lawfully be held without the authority

---

79   The authorship and dating of several sections is also disputed. Anders Winroth (2000) has argued that this edition is a second recension by a subsequent editor, and that four manuscripts that have until recently been seen as abridged versions of the *Decretum* may, in fact, contain the original text.

80   Gratian (1993), pp. vii–xiv.

81   Ibid., pp. 10–11.

82   Ibid., p. 33. While Nicholas was pope, the emperors were gaining power at the expense of the bishops.

of the Holy See, and that a Council not so convoked is not valid. Both of these statements, however, come from the forged decretals of Pseudo–Isidore,[83] which Gratian evidently held to be genuine. As we have seen, they do not reflect the actual practice of the Church in late antiquity. Finally, Gratian argues in distinction 19 that the decretals have the same legal force as Canons.

Gratian does not define new law. He tries to synthesise and arrange existing legislation. He argues that Canon Law supersedes Civil Law, that law overrides custom, that decretals and Canons have equal force, and that the popes are the source of all authority. He does, however, seem to have had an agenda of his own. Stanley Chodorow (1972) argues that Gratian set out to prove that the popes held absolute sovereignty over Church Law.[84] Indeed, Gratian tried to apply to Church Law the Roman maxim that the prince is loosed from the laws.[85] This power, Chodorow tells us, was balanced by mercy, and only applied to the pope when he was making laws.[86] As we have seen, Gratian argues that the pope holds the important legislative power in the Church. Only popes could summon Councils, which could only legislate with papal approval. The pope, on the other hand, could legislate without consulting anyone else, provided his decrees did not contradict Divine Law, and were just, practical and convenient. This is a very Roman outlook. We can therefore see that the popes, bolstered by Gratian's support, were asserting their authority over the Councils, and that the forged decretals were being accepted as evidence that this had always been so. The popes had also managed to raise the status of their own decrees, which had gained the same standing as Canon Law, enabling them to legislate without holding a Council. They had restricted the scope for others to overturn their legislation by establishing contrary customs, and they had asserted their independence from secular rulers.

Thomas Aquinas

Aquinas never wrote a treatise on Canon Law as such, although he sometimes used the Canons to support his position, but he did write extensively on law and justice, and his work laid the foundation for subsequent Catholic theology. We must therefore consider his views. His relevant comments on justice and equity are in the *Summa Contra Gentiles* (hereafter SCG), book 1 (1975a), chapter 93 and book 3, part 2 (1975d), chapter 128, and in the *Summa Theologica* (1981, hereafter ST), part 1, question 21 and part 2, section 2, questions 57–61, 80 and 120. In the ST, Thomas

---

83   See endnotes 284 and 285 to Gratian. Ibid., p. 106.

84   Chodorow (1972), p. 133. Compare Gallagher (2002), pp. 127–8.

85   Gratian adds that only the Roman Church, which no one may judge, can deliver judgement on any matter. See Decreti, Secunda Pars, Causa IX, Questio III, C.9. (CIC, volume 1, column 609) and Gallagher (2002), p. 130. Chadwick (1967, pp. 245–6) traces this claim back to a dispute between Symmachus and Laurentius, who both claimed the Papacy between 498 and 506.

86   Ibid., p. 136.

refers both to Aristotle and to Cicero as sources of legal theory. We might therefore expect to find a mixture of Greek and Roman jurisprudence underlying his ideas.

Thomas begins with Aristotle's distinction between commutative and distributive justice, arguing that commutative justice, which seeks to rectify injustices in commercial transactions, does not apply to God, while distributive justice, whereby a ruler gives to each what his rank deserves, does.[87] God exercises justice when He gives each thing its due according to its nature and condition, 'since what is due to each thing is due to it as ordered to it according to the divine wisdom'.[88] This justice is God's essence. Thomas then considers human justice, which governs people's dealings with each other. Justice involves balance, equity, equality and rightness. He defines justice as 'a habit whereby a man renders to each one his due by a constant and perpetual will'.[89] This is very similar to Aristotle's definition of particular justice. He agrees with Cicero that justice must 'keep men together in society and mutual intercourse',[90] and concludes that divine justice is distributive, but also commutative. Since the Old Testament tells us that divine judgement involves retribution, it is reasonable that human justice should do the same where appropriate.[91]

Equity (*epieikeia*) exists to prevent injustices where situations not foreseen by legislators arose. It was against the law to refuse to return a madman's sword to him, or to refuse to return money on deposit when its owner intended to use it to rebel against the authorities, but in such situations complying with the letter of the law could lead to disaster. Equity permitted those entrusted with the sword or the cash to refuse to return it to its owner without penalty. Thus understood, equity did not set aside justice; it set aside the letter of the law when following it would have led to an injustice.[92] This understanding of equity, however, is Roman. The Greek meaning of *epieikeia*, as we discussed in chapter 4, is 'clemency, gentleness, graciousness,' as opposed to evenness or fairness. It seems that Thomas has subtly changed Aristotle's meaning here. Thus, justice comprises giving each his due, as ordered by divine wisdom, including punishment when appropriate, and holding society together in peace. This understanding draws on Hebrew, Roman and Greek ideas of justice, but draws a distinction between justice and equity, and therefore is not wholly Biblical. The major difference between Thomas' definition of justice and the definitions of Aristotle, Cicero and Ulpian, however, is that Thomas roots his concept of justice

---

87   Ia.21.1.

88   Ia.21.1, ad 3. Compare SCG (1975a), chapter 93, section 6, p. 286.

89   IaIIae.58.1. Compare SCG (1975b), chapters 28 and 29, pp. 79–85, and Ulpian's view that justice is 'the perpetual and constant will to render to each one his right'. Scott (2001), volume 2, p. 211.

90   IaIIae.58.2, citing Cicero (1913), 1, 7. Compare SCG (1975a), chapter 93, section 11, p. 288.

91   IaIIae.61.4. Compare IaIIae.801, ad 1, which states that the revenge taken by authority of a public power, in accordance with a judge's sentence, belongs to commutative justice, while the revenge taken upon oneself, or sought from a judge, though not justice itself, can also be a virtue.

92   IaIIae.120.1, ad 1. Thomas equates *epieikeia* with *aequitas*.

in his doctrine of God: the others seem to arrive at their definitions using reason alone.

Thomas holds that law 'is a rule and measure of acts, whereby man is induced to act or is restrained from acting',[93] and that it is ordained for the common good. All good law comes ultimately from God, and ranges from Divine Law to human custom. It aims to make people act virtuously under reason. In his treatment of human law in itself,[94] Thomas raises several objections to Isidore's division of human laws. Unusually, Thomas does not rebut these objections; instead, he states that the authority of Isidore is sufficient to overturn them. Pseudo–Isidore, we may recall, greatly influenced Gratian's *Decretum*, which as we have seen became the standard Canonical text for several centuries. In consequence, both Isidore's genuine work and the forgeries attributed to him gained authority. Where his sources disagree, Thomas sometimes uses the authority of particular writers to determine the case.[95] Most, but not all, of the authors he cites are Christians. He twice uses Aristotle alone to settle a case. Each time Aristotle's authority suffices, it decides the question against other pagan authors. Thomas rarely opposes Aristotle to Biblical or Christian writers. Where he does so, he rejects Aristotle, he argues against what he sees as a misinterpretation of the Christian source, or he uses Aristotle to illustrate his reasons for preferring one Christian source to another. Indeed, Thomas explicitly refuses to place philosophy above revelation:

> This science [Sacred Doctrine] can in a sense depend on the philosophical sciences, not as though it stood in need of them, but only in order to make its teachings clearer. For it accepts its principles not from other sciences; but immediately from God by revelation.[96]

The SCG has a different structure to the ST, but it seems that every time Thomas holds up Aristotle alongside Scripture in the SCG, it is to show how well Aristotle agrees with the Bible.[97]

Thomas sees a blend of monarchy, aristocracy, oligarchy and democracy as the ideal system of government.[98] He believes that this system gives rise to law as Isidore

---

93   IaIIae.90.1.

94   IaIIae.95.4.

95   He does this 42 times in ST. Compare Jordan (1992), pp. 26–30. Jordan concludes that when Thomas uses Aristotle as an authority, Aristotle is not the main authority, and his arguments are conditioned by the structure of Thomas' own inquiry.

96   Ia.1.5, ad 2. Jordan (pp. 6–7 and 32–41) argues that Thomas was happy to use philosophy as a source of knowledge once its errors had been purged, but that he both honoured Aristotle, by naming him as the greatest philosopher, and judged him, by setting him below the least of believers.

97   Thomas does this many times in SCG. On no occasion in this work does Thomas contrast Aristotle with Scripture in order to show that the Philosopher is wrong. Arvin Vos (1985, p. 111) states that while in the ST Thomas uses reason to explain what is believed, he uses it in the SCG to show that belief is not unreasonable.

98   ST, IaIIae.95.4, compare IaIIae.105.1. This contrasts with Thomas' earlier view that monarchy is the ideal form of government. Compare *On Princely Government*, chapter 2, in

understood it, namely as rules established by both the plebeians and those of higher birth.[99] We should note, however, that mixed forms of government occurred more often in Greece than in Rome. Thomas also believes that while everyone is subject to the law, not everyone is subject to the same law, since the citizens of one city are not subject to the law of another.[100] This looks like a statement of Germanic, not Roman Law. Under the emperors, everyone in Rome was subject to Roman Law, whatever their nationality. This passage suggests that (say) Frankish citizens in Rome would be subject to Frankish, not Roman Law. This is a marked shift from the situation of late antiquity. Thomas reaffirms the earlier Roman tradition that custom can acquire the force of law, yet he does so without reference to early Roman Law. He quotes Augustine, in a passage taken from Gratian and Isidore, yet does not refer to either the Theodosian or Justinianian Codes. This suggests that he gave theological arguments more precedence than legal positions. It seems, then, that he drew on Roman, German and Greek legal theory for the ST, but did not commit himself to any of them, despite the strong Roman and Germanic influences on Canon Law and his own fondness of Aristotle.[101] He retains a distinction between justice and equity, but seems less Aristotelian than one might expect.[102]

Thomas refers twice to Church authority in the ST. When discussing disbelief in general, he emphasises that even doctors of the Church must give way to the custom and authority of the Church, from which they derive their authority. He adds that questions of faith should be referred to Peter, 'against whose authority neither Jerome nor Augustine nor any of the holy doctors defended their opinion'.[103] Thomas was promoting the accepted view here, but this statement is simply not true. Cyprian expressed outrage when Pope Stephen I proposed that the Church should follow 'the examples of heretics, that, for the celebration of the heavenly sacraments, light should borrow discipline from darkness and Christians do what antichrists do'[104] by accepting that baptism administered by Novatians was valid. This shows that Cyprian thought Stephen's teaching was both authoritative and wrong. Henry Chadwick (1967) states that the dispute continued until the death of Stephen in 256 and the martyrdom of Cyprian in 258, and even then it took another 55 years for the bishops of Carthage to abandon Cyprian's position.[105] Thomas, then, reaffirms the

---

Aquinas (1987). Thomas states here that the authority of Isidore has settled the issue.

99   See Gratian (1993), distinction 2, C1, p. 8.

100 IaIIae.96.5.

101 In fact, Thomas seems to have tried to harmonise Augustine and Aristotle, but in general, Augustine seems to take precedence.

102 O'Connor (1967, p. 4) states that Thomas takes Aristotle's system as the skeleton for his thinking, but believes that other mediaeval authors owe more to Aristotle. Thomas, he thinks, refocuses Aristotle and changes the emphasis of Aristotle's thought to accommodate thirteenth-century Christian ideas.

103 IaIIae.11.2, ad 3. This is from the *Decretum*, secunda pars, causa xxiv, questio 1, c. XII, *Quotiens* (CIC, volume 1, column 970).

104 Cyprian (1964), p. 288.

105 Chadwick (1967), p. 121.

Church's position of the time without including much Greek or Roman legal theory in his concept of justice, in marked contrast to many Canonists active at the time. His theory of justice does, however, show some Germanic influence, which we might expect to be well established by that time. He reaffirms the power and authority of the popes, without seeking to justify it with arguments from antiquity. He uses Canon Law as source material to support his theology, without exploring its underlying jurisprudence. Neither Gratian nor Thomas seems to have added anything radically new. Both supported, and in Gratian's case encouraged, existing and developing practice in the Church. We must now consider the effects of all this on the General Councils of Western Church during this period.

The Mediaeval Lateran Councils

The first four Lateran Councils were concerned with a mixture of the reform of abuses and the relationship between Church and state. Unlike earlier Councils, the Lateran Councils speak in the name of the pope, not the Council Fathers. Lateran I (1123) was the first Western general Council after the Lay Investiture Controversy was resolved in 1122. Its mantra seems to be 'we absolutely forbid' (*prohibemus/interdicimus*). Its prohibitions include selling benefices, ordaining without episcopal consent, cohabitation with priests, managing Churches and harassing Crusaders. Canon 15, however, states that the Council confirms papal decrees 'with the authority of the Holy Spirit'.[106] If this Canon has been recorded correctly,[107] it seems to be the first time a Council has claimed that the pope acts on behalf of the Holy Spirit. It may show that the idea that the pope is the Vicar of Christ[108] was gaining acceptance. Our main interest in Lateran II centres on a single Canon, namely Canon 20:

> As is right, we do not deny to kings and princes the right to dispense justice, in consultation with the archbishops and bishops.[109]

This statement is quite astonishing for two reasons. Firstly, the assertion that kings could only pass judgement on their subjects in consultation with archbishops and bishops was, as far as I know, unprecedented when proposed at the Council of Claremont in 1130. While the view that the bishops should be consulted about matters of justice received limited acceptance in Germanic countries, it had no parallel in Roman Law. Secondly, it is difficult to see how the Church or the pope could stop kings and princes from dispensing justice even if they didn't consult the

---

106 Tanner (1990), p. *193.

107 It is missing from some manuscripts of the Council, and has a totally different form in some others.

108 Paul Collins (MacEoin, 1998, p. 24) points out that this term came into widespread usage during the pontificate of Innocent III (1198–1216). Compare Southern (1970), pp. 104–5.

109 Ibid., p. *202.

bishops. This seems to show the continuing attempts of the popes to increase their influence. In Lateran III, Germanic influences came to the fore again, but the Council added little new Canon Law.

In many ways, Lateran IV (1215) was a new start. It begins with a new creed, promulgated by Innocent III, describing the Trinity in much more detail than the Niceno–Constantinopolitan creed had done. It also introduces the perpetual virginity of Mary, and states that only a priest properly ordained according to the Church's key can bring about the transformation of the elements in the Eucharist. Constitution 18 forbids subdeacons, deacons and priests from duelling, from commanding mercenaries and from practising the art of surgery.[110] Many of the Council's constitutions contain new material, but the links with the past are equally evident. The third constitution provides that heretics should be handed over to the state for punishment. Those who sheltered heretics, or allowed heretics to remain on their land, were declared excommunicate for up to a year. Landowners refusing to expel them within the year lost their land.[111]

Constitution 12, on general chapters of monks, states that referral to the Holy See is required if a bishop refuses to remove a superior judged unsuitable by the chapter, or if there are matters on which the chapter cannot agree. It also contrasts superiors, whose rights need to be preserved, with their subjects (*inferiores*, not yet *subditos*), who need to be protected from injustice.[112] Constitution 26 requires all bishops in Italy to present themselves personally to the Roman pontiff for confirmation of their office, and provides the possibility of a pontifical blessing for bishops outside Italy 'for the time being'.[113] Constitution 29 prohibits clerics from holding more than one benefice, except for 'exalted and lettered persons,' who may do so with a papal dispensation.[114] Constitution 30 suspends the powers of appointment of those who repeatedly appoint unworthy men to Churches. Only one of the five Patriarchs could relax this suspension. Centralisation of power in the Church was clearly under way by this stage. Constitution 44 informs lay people that their lot is to obey, not to be in command. While this provision was aimed at preventing princes from disposing of Church property, it illustrates the increasing separation between the clerics and the laity in the Church. Constitution 51 informs those who invent malicious impediments to prevent legitimate weddings that they 'will not escape the church's vengeance'.[115]

Constitution 62 restricts the duration of indulgences to a year on the dedication of a basilica, and 40 days on its anniversary, since this is the practice of the pope,

---

110 Ibid., p. *244. This is a revised version of the ancient prohibition on priests shedding blood. It does not, however, portray the lower clergy of the time in a particularly flattering light.

111 Ibid., pp. *233–4.

112 Ibid., p. *241.

113 *Quod interim*. Ibid., pp. *247–8.

114 *Sublimes tamen et litteras personas*. Ibid., pp. *248–9. There is an evident clash between this provision and James 2:1–7.

115 *Ecclesiasticam non effugiet ultionem*. Ibid., p. *258.

'who possesses the plenitude of power'.[116] The Council also insisted that Jews and Saracens should dress differently from Christians, prohibited Jews who converted to Christianity either from retaining their old rites or from holding public office. We can see, then, the continuing trend of centralisation of power in the hands of the popes. Rome continued to reserve powers to the Holy See, and became, at least in theory, the source of all authority in the Church. Within the Church, the popes were claiming similar powers to the civil powers of the Roman and Holy Roman emperors. The idea of vengeance against one's enemies, which I have argued is characteristic of early Roman legal theory, and the idea that the Jews should be suppressed, which is a more Germanic theory, although reflected to a lesser extent in the Codes of Theodosius and Justinian, were beginning to appear in the documents of Western General Councils.

The major development of this period, then is that systematic treatments of justice and law had begun to appear, such as Gratian's *Decretum*. Under the influence of Scholasticism, things were beginning to be categorised. Canon Law, in other words, had ceased to be a random collection of custom, papal decretals (genuine and forged), and pronouncements of Councils, and had instead become an organised body of law. It was later to be expanded by Gregory IX in his *Liber Extra* of 1234, which dealt with papal decretals between the *Decretum* and that date. These documents technically remained in force until the first Code of Canon Law came into force on 19 May 1918, although Canon Law continued to develop in the meantime, and Canons of the Council of Trent superseded some earlier material. Where problems arose for which Canon Law made no provision, Canonists continued to look to Justinian's *Corpus Iuris Civilis* for answers. This was the situation when the Reformation began. Until this stage, Anglicans had been part of the Roman Catholic Church, and therefore all that has gone before fed into English Canon Law, which we shall examine in the next chapter. The rest of this chapter applies only to Rome. We now consider the Roman Catholic response to the Reformation, the Council of Trent.

The Council of Trent

The documents of the Council of Trent (1545–63) are second in length only to those of Vatican II. Trent established a large body of Canon Law on a variety of subjects, most of which are not relevant to this enquiry. Some of this law was new, some restated older material. Much Tridentine material was later incorporated into the 1917 Code of Canon Law, and sections of this survive, in modified form, in the 1983 Code. Unlike earlier Councils, Trent did not organise its Canons into a single body at the end. Instead, the Canons were arranged by subject, and inserted at the appropriate point in the documents for each session. In some cases, there is more than one list of Canons within a session. I shall therefore refer to the Canons by session, subject and number.

---

116 *Qui plenitudinem obtinet potestatis.* Ibid., p. *264.

In session 14, the Council discusses penance and last anointing. In Canon 3, on penance, the Council anathematises those who say that the authority in John 20:22–23 to bind and loose sins refers only to the authority to preach the Gospel, rather than conferring the authority to forgive and retain sins 'as the catholic church has from the beginning understood them'.[117] Canon 9 of the same section anathematises those who deny that sacramental absolution by a priest is a judicial act, holding instead that it is a declaration that the penitent's sins are forgiven if he or she believes they are forgiven. Canon 10 anathematises those who extend the authority to bind and loose to all believers, rather than only the priests. Canon 15 anathematises those who say that the Church has the power to loose, but not to bind.[118] The Council is clearly trying to establish that exercising the keys is an act of justice open to all priests, and only to priests. With the keys, the priest can declare that God has forgiven the penitents, or has not forgiven them, rather than just asking God's forgiveness on them. The Council believes that the priests have Scriptural authority to perform this act. This view also presupposes that the priests' concept of justice is the same as God's concept, a position disputed by the Reformers but supported indirectly by Canons 10 and 11 on justification in session 6.[119] These Canons state that the faithful are justified (*iustificari*)[120] through the justice of Christ, by which He obtained merit for us, and through the grace and charity of the Holy Spirit. It seems to follow from this that since Christ has brought them back into a right relationship with God, and they have the Holy Spirit, they can make just assessments in the Spirit's power.[121] Exercising the keys, however, is not the only function of priestly authority. Canon 10 of the decree on reform in session 24 states that in order that bishops 'may more easily keep the people they govern in dutiful obedience',[122] they have the right and power (*ius et potestatem*) to do anything they consider necessary for the correction of their subjects (*subditorum*) or the good of their diocese.

By this stage, the Church had begun to use the language of power, justice and subjection still used in the current Code of Canon Law. The Council makes it clear that when the bishops exercise this authority, they do so as delegates of the Holy See. This theme runs throughout the Council, and it appears in many of its Canons. It is, however, stated more explicitly and more often in the Council of Trent than it was in earlier Councils. Finally, the Council states in its 25th and final session that it believes it has spelt out its position with total clarity:

---

117 Ibid., p. *711.

118 Ibid., pp. *712–3.

119 Ibid., p. *679.

120 The New Testament word is *dikaioō* [make righteous].

121 I am aware that my argument here can equally well be applied to the laity. My point, however, is that the argument can be made on behalf of the clergy. Entering the debate about lay people pronouncing absolution or presiding at the Eucharist would take us too far from our subject.

122 *Aptius quem regunt populum in possint in officio atque obedientia continere.* Ibid., p. *765.

If any difficulty arises over the reception of these decrees, or any matters are raised as needing clarification (which the council does not believe to be the case) or definition, the council is confident that, in addition to other remedies it has put in hand, the pope will ensure that the needs of the provinces are met for the glory of God and the peace of the Church.[123]

This, when combined with Lateran V's prohibition on glosses,[124] seems to have quelled further debate. The next General Council of the Latin Church was not held until 1869, 303 years after the end of the Council of Trent. In Trent, then, we see the culmination of a millennium and a half of thought on the nature of justice and authority on the Church. The Council held that all authority was vested in the pope, and that he delegated some of his authority to the clergy, who acted in his name. It emphasised that the forgiveness or otherwise of sins, through the power of the keys given to Peter and handed on to the popes, his successors, was a major function of ecclesiastical justice. It thought its position clear and complete, and did not encourage debate of, or commentary on, its provisions. This position, which was amplified and strengthened by Vatican I, did not significantly change until Canon Law was codified in 1917 and 1983.

Vatican I

Vatican I restated the faith in an attempt to counter the effects of the Enlightenment, and claimed that the pope had power in certain circumstances to make *ex cathedra* statements binding on all Christians. The Orthodox Churches, Anglicans, Protestants, and a small group of Catholic Churches, notably in Germany, The Netherlands and Austria, vigorously rejected the Council's conclusion that he could so act. This Council, therefore, is probably the most discussed and debated of them all. It added little new Canon Law, but it significantly changed the way the Church understood and presented its authority.

In chapter 3 of the dogmatic constitution on the Catholic faith, the Council requires belief in the Word of God, as contained in Scripture and the tradition of the Church, and in things proposed by the church to be believed as divine revelation, whether by solemn judgements or through the normal use of authority.[125] In chapter 4, the Council states that God's revealed doctrine is to be faithfully protected and put forth infallibly as a divine deposit of faith, rather than as a philosophical discovery subject to later revision.[126] This is all brought together in the constitution *Pastor Aeternus*, which spells out this doctrine in great detail.

---

123 Ibid., p. *798.

124 We forbid each and all of Christ's faithful, under penalty of immediate excommunication, to presume to interpret or gloss what has been produced and carried out in the present Council without our permission and that of the apostolic see. Ibid., p. *654.

125 Ibid., p. *807.

126 Ibid., p. *809.

Its first chapter anathematises those who say that Peter was not appointed by Christ as the prince of the apostles and the visible head of the whole church, or that his primacy was of honour only, and not of true and proper jurisdiction given directly and immediately to him by Jesus Christ.[127] Chapter 2 anathematises those who say that the Petrine Primacy was not instituted by Christ, or that the popes are not the successors of Peter in this primacy.[128] Chapter 3 anathematises those who say that the Roman pontiff merely supervises and guides, rather than exercising full, supreme, ordinary and immediate power and jurisdiction over all Christians in matters of Church government and discipline, as well as in matters of faith and morals.[129] This explication of the doctrine of infallibility concludes with the famous definition at the end of chapter 4 that *ex cathedra* statements of the pope are 'of themselves, and not by the consent of the church, irreformable'.[130] While the Council acknowledges that bishops receive their power and authority directly from their consecration, it is clear that they can only exercise it under papal supervision.

Paul Collins (1997) argues that before Vatican I, those running the Church supervised three activities: teaching, the celebration of the sacraments, and Church government. He argues that Vatican I combined the first and the third, subordinating teaching and doctrine to Church government, and placed control of all three in the hands of the pope. This, he argues, led to a reduction in the theological diversity in the Church to the point where the agenda of the pope of the time became identified with the doctrine of the Church.[131] Patrick Granfield (1980) feels that Vatican I portrayed the Church 'more as a legal corporation than as a worshipping community directed by the Spirit'.[132] He argues that the 1917 Code of Canon Law was designed to provide the legal structure within which to implement the pope's supreme authority. He also argues that many in the Church assumed that because the pope could teach infallibly, he must always do so. Consequently, 'the papal magisterium became inflated and

---

127 Ibid., p. *812. Ambrose, writing on the primacy in 381, took precisely the view condemned here: he explained that Peter's primacy was one of confession, not of honour, 'a primacy of faith, not of rank' (Giles, 1952, p. 144). We should note that Ambrose thought that honour came from sacrifice and was the source of authority. Since Rome was the seat of the martyrdom of Peter and Paul, who were least in the eyes of the great, it gained great honour from their ultimate sacrifice, and thus a greater authority than other Churches. This, however, did not give it primacy of rank, or the right to rule over Christians elsewhere.

128 Ibid., p. *813.

129 Ibid., p. *815. Again, Ambrose falls foul of this anathema, as does Bernard of Clairvaux.

130 Ibid. p. *816.

131 Collins (1997), pp. 63–4.

132 Granfield (1980), p. 50. This is perhaps not surprising given that Pius IX was a Canonist, not a theologian. Hill (1988, p. 95) argues that 'the influence of canon lawyers on theology … has always been incalculably disastrous', sentiments with which I have some sympathy.

the bishops were expected only to communicate papal teaching faithfully to their flocks'.[133]

It seems that Vatican I turned the papacy from an ecclesiastical office of supervision, guidance and correction, albeit an office with considerable power attached to it, into an absolute monarchy. This seems to stand in marked contrast to the Biblical view of leadership as service. We shall shortly see that this concern was later to be echoed by a twentieth century pope, namely Paul VI. This idea of leadership, however was not enshrined in Canon Law until 1983. Finally, we turn our attention to the last major development in Canon Law, namely codification.

The Twentieth Century

The Code of Benedict XV: 1917[134]

The 1917 Codex is set out in the form of a collection of Roman Law. It begins with general norms. It then considers persons, first clerics, then Religious, then the laity. It then moves on to things.[135] It deals with sacraments, sacred places and times, and worship, describes the teaching office of the Church, and regulates benefices and Church property. Next, it considers procedures, such as trials and canonisations. Finally, it deals with crime and penalties. The important sections for our enquiry concern clerics and the hierarchy, the governance of Religious communities, and the teaching authority of the Church. We shall survey this Code, before making a more thorough examination of the 1983 Code.

We begin with the Canons concerning clerics and the hierarchy. Canon 108 §3 states that the sacred hierarchy of bishops, priests and deacons is of divine institution, with the supreme pontificate and the subordinate bishops.[136] Canons 218 and 219 explain that the pope, as successor of Peter, has supreme and full power of jurisdiction over the universal Church, not just a primacy of honour. This power includes matters of Church government and discipline, as well as matters of faith and morals. If legitimately elected, he obtains this full and supreme power of jurisdiction by Divine Law. This is a restatement of the position taken by Vatican I. Only the pope can summon an Ecumenical Council, and only he can confirm its decrees. While an Ecumenical Council holds supreme power over the universal Church, it cannot hear appeals against the pope.[137] The pope also has the sole right to appoint metropolitans and bishops, who have jurisdiction in their own right, and are the ordinary and

---

133 Ibid., p. 60.

134 I am indebted to Bouscaren, Ellis, and Korth (1963) for guiding me through the 1917 Codex before the translation by Peters (2001) was published.

135 The title of section II is *De Rebus*.

136 Peters (2001), p. 61. In the 1917 Code, the word 'minister' is used instead of 'deacon'.

137 Canons 222–8.

immediate pastors in their dioceses, but serve under papal authority.[138] While the pope
holds his authority by Divine Law, other clerics, including archbishops and bishops,
obtain their jurisdiction through Canonical mission (*canonica missione*), given by a
competent ecclesiastical authority, not through the consent or call of the people or
secular power.[139] This gives the impression that the archbishops and bishops act as
vicars of the pope, while parish priests and other clergy act as vicars of the bishop.
This ecclesiastical authority has been exercised through sacred congregations since
the Council of Trent.

Collins (1997) points out that the most important of these congregations, the
congregation of the Holy Office, holds the guardianship of faith and morals. The
pope, as president of this congregation, can appoint whoever he chooses to it, and
as chairman he can control its agenda. These provisions effectively allow him to
take absolute power over the Church in matters of faith and morals.[140] Further,
Canon 1324 conflates heresy and error, which had previously been distinct.[141] These
changes, Collins argues, were introduced 'in a purely canonical context, without
reference to theology'.[142] One has to agree with Collins' assessment. Ecclesiastical
jurisdiction is reserved to the ordained, whose orders allow them to administer the
sacraments, including penance, in which they exercise the keys. With ordination
comes the requirement to obey the bishop in all things under his jurisdiction. Clerics
can only exercise jurisdiction directly upon their subjects (*subditos*).[143] For bishops,
these are in general the clergy and the lay faithful in the diocese, although others
might be affected indirectly by their activities. Superiors of Religious communities
share some episcopal responsibilities, in that they govern their communities. All
Religious are subject to the pope, as their supreme superior, both as members of
the Church, and through their vow of obedience.[144] The Sacred Congregation of
Religious administers this supervision. Religious are also subject, in varying degrees,
to the authority of their local bishop,[145] but superiors have the power of mastery, or
sovereignty (*dominativam*) over their subjects (*subditos*). This, however, is not full
power and jurisdiction; it is limited by the Holy See.[146] Within the limits of their
authority, however, abbots and priors have extensive influence over the lives of the
members of their institutes.

---

138 Canons 329–34.
139 Canon 109.
140 Collins (1997), pp. 67–8. See Canons 246–7.
141 Ibid. This conflation is not evident in Canon 754 of the 1983 Code, which replaced
this provision.
142 Ibid., p. 68.
143 Canons 119, 201 §1 and 127.
144 Canon 499 §1.
145 Bouscaren, Ellis and Korth (1963, pp. 241–2) explain that in exempt institutes,
which are under direct papal authority, the bishop's supervision is limited to certain situations
expressly defined by Canon Law. In non-exempt institutes the members are subject to the
bishop as clerics or laity, but not as Religious. See Canons 500 and 618.
146 Canon 501.

The Code refers to justice and equity on several occasions. Canon 888 §1 reminds the priest that, when hearing confession, he is both judge (*iudicis*) and physician (*medici*), and that he must therefore dispense both divine justice and divine mercy (*divinae iustitiae simul et misericordiae ministrum*) to penitents. Throughout the section on processes,[147] judges are urged to promote justice (*iustitia*). Where Canon Law has no provision for a particular situation, Canon 20 instructs judges to seek a solution in laws enacted in similar situations, taking into account Canonical equity (*aequitate canonica*), the practice of the Roman Curia, and the common and constant opinions of the doctors. Canon 643 §2 obliges Religious Superiors to provide for women leaving communities they have entered without a dowry 'in accordance with natural equity' (*naturali aequitate servata*).

We can see, then, that the Code takes account of both divine justice and natural equity, and urges judges to do the same when exercising their office. However, there has been a subtle change of emphasis. Canon 18 states that the Canons are to be interpreted according to their plain meaning, and if there is any lack of clarity, reference should be made to parallel provisions in the Code, to the purposes and circumstances of the law and to the mind of the legislator. Canon Law has therefore changed from being an expression of Godly reason to being the manifestation of the will of the legislator, an indication of increasing centralisation within the Church.[148] The Code restates the doctrine of Vatican I on the teaching office of the Church: the Church has the right and the duty to preach the Gospel and teach all nations the evangelical doctrine. This Divine and Catholic Faith is contained in the written Scriptures and tradition. The Church can also define doctrine, either through an Ecumenical Council, or through *ex cathedra* pronouncements of the pope. These definitions are to be received as infallible. Bishops, who do not teach infallibly, are nevertheless authentic teachers of the faith when they teach under papal authority.[149]

This model of authority is wholly top-down. All authority derives from the pope, as successor of Peter and Vicar of Christ. The pope delegates elements of his authority to bishops and Religious supervisors, who in turn delegate elements of their authority to clerics under their supervision. This structure seems very similar to that of Imperial Rome, with the pope in the place of the emperor.[150] Nevertheless, there is a detectable change of emphasis here. I have argued that early Roman Law saw justice as retribution. The Codex gives the impression that it sees justice as law: rather than giving those wronged the chance to avenge themselves, it seems designed to keep everyone in order. At this stage, lay people played no part in decision-making beyond receiving the decisions with a grateful heart, unless they happened to be

---

147 Canons 1552–2194.

148 Compare Mannion, Gaillardetz, Kerkhofs and Wilson (2003), p. 355, Örsy (1992), p. 47 and Canon 17 of the 1983 Code.

149 See Canons 1322–6. Conversely, 'by divine law, all are bound to embrace the Church of God and rightly to heed her truth'.

150 Compare Southern (1970), pp. 24–6.

theologians or Canonists invited to aid the bishops in their deliberations. We should note that there is some quite strong language, possibly borrowed from Vatican I, used in the 1917 Codex to describe the power of the bishops. All this would change in the wake of the Second Vatican Council, and the new Code of Canon Law to which it led.

Vatican II

Vatican II had an immense effect on the Roman Catholic Church and on its relationship with the rest of the world. For the first time, Rome recognised that the Church extended beyond the Churches in communion with the Holy See, recognised the existence of other Churches and ecclesial bodies, and began to encourage ecumenism. The Council reformed the rôle of bishops and Religious. It discussed education, priestly formation and relationships with non-Christian religions. It discussed missionary activity and the place of the Church in the world. Most importantly for our purposes, it discussed the doctrine of the Church, religious freedom and the role of the laity. *Lumen Gentium* deals with the hierarchical constitution of the Church. In chapter 3, it states that the clergy are at the service of their brothers and sisters.[151] It then restates and amplifies Vatican I's doctrines of the Petrine primacy and papal infallibility. Vatican II, however, reinterprets this doctrine. It ties papal pronouncements more closely to the authority of the bishops, the magisterium, and, indeed, urges the pope to consult them. The collegial power of the bishops means that when they act in concert with the pope, they can also teach infallibly when they exercise the supreme teaching office with the pope.[152]

Another change in Vatican II is the description of the bishops as shepherds (*pastores*) of their flocks (*gregem electi*), rather than as rulers of their subjects.[153] The Council still emphasises the power of the bishops, but it seems to do so in a gentler and more pastorally sensitive way. Vatican II also devotes some effort to developing a theology of the laity. While the Council is clear that the Church is governed by the bishops, it states that lay people have the right to receive abundant help (*abundanter accipiendi*) from the clergy, and that they should make their needs known. It continues: 'In accordance with the knowledge, competence or authority they possess, they have the right and indeed sometimes the duty to make known their opinion on matters which concern the good of the church'.[154]

They should do this through established channels with respect for the truth, with courage and with prudence. Pastors are encouraged to make use of this counsel, and

---

151 *Ministri enim, qui sacra potestate pollunt, fratribus suis inserviunt.* Tanner (1990), p. *862.

152 Ibid., p. *870.

153 See, for example, *Lumen Gentium*, sections 21 and 28. Ibid., p. 865, line 7 and p. 874, line 4.

154 *Pro scienta, competentia et praestantia quibus pollent, facultatem, immo aliquando et officium habent suam sententiam de iis quae bonum ecclesiae respiciunt declarandi.* Ibid., p. *879. *Praestantia* would be better translated as 'excellence,' not 'authority'.

give those who offer it freedom and space to act.[155] The Council states, in the decree on the apostolate of the laity, that the norms it proposes are to be taken as norms for the reform of Canon Law.[156] Chapter 1 states that lay people share in the Prophetic, Priestly and Kingly offices of Christ, exercising their mission by working towards evangelising and sanctifying others, thereby taking the spirit of the gospel out into the temporal order, and so perfecting it.[157] Their office comes from their union with Christ, in Whom they are consecrated as a royal priesthood and a holy people.[158] This office is exercised in co-operation with the bishops, who foster this work, set out its principles, provide spiritual help and direct its efforts to the common good and the preservation of doctrine and good order.[159] When discussing religious freedom, the Council declares that everyone is entitled to freedom from religious coercion. No one should be forced to act against his conscience, or be prevented from acting in accordance with it. This right should not be curtailed 'as long as due public order is preserved'.[160] The principle is that the people should have the maximum amount of liberty and the minimum of restraint. It does not extend to allowing people to reject all control and discount every duty of obedience.[161]

Vatican II, then, attempts to redefine the relationship between the pope and the bishops, and tries to anchor infallibility more in the magisterium than the pope. This move does not seem to have been entirely successful, and the relationship between pope and bishops has yet to be satisfactorily resolved. The Council also seems, possibly for the first time, to recognise the need for lay participation in the work of the Church, and set out a framework in which it could happen. We shall shortly discuss how fully these ideas have been implemented, but it is clear that the Council produced a significant change in the Roman Catholic Church's approach to the rest of the world. Since this new approach was not reflected in the 1917 Code of Canon Law, which was thoroughly imbued with the values of Vatican I and, I have argued, with Roman legal theory, a revision was needed. During the course of this revision, Pope Paul VI observed, in an address to the Holy Roman Rota on 28 January 1971:

> It cannot be denied that the Church, in the course of her history, has taken from other cultures (Roman Law is a well-known example but it is not the only one) certain norms for the exercise of her judicial power. It is unfortunately true that the Church, in the exercise of her power, whether judicial (procedural) or coercive (penal), has in the course of the

---

155 Ibid., p. *879.

156 Ibid., p. *982.

157 *Rerum temporalium ordinem spiritu evangelico perfundendum ac perficiendum.* Ibid.

158 Ibid. See 1 Peter 2:4–10. Gerosa (2002, p. 46) argues that Vatican II intended Canon Law to become a means of realising ecclesial communion, rather than a way of ensuring its well-being.

159 Ibid., p. *996.

160 *Dummodo iustus ordo publicus servetur.* Ibid., p. *1003.

161 Ibid., p. *1006.

centuries borrowed from civil legislations certain serious imperfections, even methods which were unjust in the true and proper sense, at least objectively speaking.[162]

Paul VI clearly had something like this in mind when, in 1965, he told the commission revising the code that they should not only implement the reforms of Vatican II, they should apply to the new Code a new habit of mind (*novus habitus mentis*). He gave them ten principles for their revision. These concerned the protection of the rights of the faithful, harmony between public governance and the governance of conscience, the fostering of pastoral care, episcopal rights to dispense from the general laws of the Church, subsidiarity, authority as service, and the administration of the new Code.[163] It only remains for us to consider how successfully the commission performed its function.

The Code of John Paul II: 1983

The revised Code has a very different order from its predecessor. It begins, as before, with general norms. It then deals with the people of God, the teaching office of the Church, its sanctifying office, its temporal goods, sanctions in the Church, and finally processes. This organisation is in itself a sign that the commission has taken on board some of the reforms of Vatican II. When one looks at the Canons, however, one is struck by the frequency of use of the language of power and subjection, by the comparative scarcity of references to justice and equity, and by the often authoritarian tone of the Code's references to authority and power. Vatican II saw the bishops as shepherds, supervising the flock of the faithful, rather than masters ruling over their subjects. There are two Latin words that would seem to describe this rôle aptly: *minister* [servant] and *pastor* [shepherd]. While *minister* appears frequently in the Codex, on no occasion is it used to describe the authority of bishops (in fact, ministry is generally contrasted with authority). *Pastor* also appears frequently in the Codex, often closely associated with *minister*. On only one occasion, however, in Canon 375, is governance described as part of the pastoral duty of a bishop. This seems surprising, given that the subject of governance and authority features in 368 Canons. The word *grex* [flock] never appears at all, although lay people are often described as *christifidelibus*. This gives the impression that both the language and thought of the Codex are more deeply rooted in Vatican I than Vatican II. It is not obvious that this is a desirable situation. It seems that Paul VI's attempt to ensure that authority was understood as service in the revised Codex has only been partially successful. With this in mind, we now consider the Code in more detail.

We first consider justice. Throughout the Code, the interpretation of justice is left open to courts and legislators. All ten references to justice in the section on general norms allow exceptions to these norms for a 'just impediment' or 'just reason'. The closest the Code comes to defining justice is Canon 19, which states

---

162　Cited in Morrisey (1978), p. 7.
163　Coriden (2004), pp. 39–40.

that for non-penal matters for which there is no express provision, 'the question is to be decided by taking into account laws enacted in similar matters, the general principles of law observed with canonical equity, the jurisprudence and practice of the Roman Curia, and the common and constant opinion of learned authors'. The guiding principle behind Canonical interpretation, it seems, is tradition, aided where necessary by Roman Law, observed in the way that brings the maximum theological benefit. This is amplified by Canon 221, which gives the faithful the right to be judged 'according to the principles of law, to be applied with equity'.[164] The Code speaks of a just freedom to research, with due submission to the magisterium,[165] just freedom to investigate the truth,[166] promoting social justice,[167] the restoration of justice and reparation (in the case of scandal),[168] and provision for separated spouses 'in accordance with the norms of justice, christian charity and natural equity'.[169] It appears that this concept of justice balances law against the needs of the people, and aims to produce the greatest good for the most people.[170] It is theologically informed, and, while it maintains a distinction between justice and equity, it sits well with both the Biblical view of justice I have identified, and the stated intentions of the Second Vatican Council.

It seems to me that the principle of justice behind the Code, while not perfect, is praiseworthy, and, when compared with Vatican I and the 1917 Codex, represents a large step in the right direction. When we look at the way the 1983 Code implements this principle, however, a different picture emerges. Most of the occurrences of authority in the Code (*auctoritate* and its parts in the Codex) refer to the office or person who enables the faithful to act (the competent ecclesiastical authority), not an attribute of the bishops by which they guide and govern the faithful. There are, however, several exceptions. Canon 334 states that the bishops, cardinals and others assist the pope in the performance of his office 'in his name and by his authority, for the good of all the Churches, in accordance with the norms determined by

---

164 *Iudicentur servatis iuris praescriptis, cum aequitate applicandis.* Gerosa (2002, p. 77) believes that the relationship between *aequitatus canonica* and Canon Law is analogous to that between *epieikeia* and *nomos*. Compare Beal, Coriden and Green (2000), pp. 78–9 and 281.

165 Canon 218. Beal, Coriden and Green (2000, p. 275) emphasise that scholarship is not an end in itself, but should serve the community and clarify the faith.

166 Canon 386 §2.

167 Canons 222 §2 and 528 §1.

168 Canon 695 §1.

169 *Iuxta normas iustitiae, christianae caritatis et naturalis aequitatis.* Canon 1148 §3. This Canon applies to converts who have polygamous marriages, but the principle has wider applications.

170 Gerosa (2002, p. 56) argues that unlike the 1917 Code, in which the clergy were the main subject, the 1983 Code is aimed principally at the lay faithful.

law'.[171] The same is true of the Roman Curia.[172] Canon 344 states that the Synod of Bishops is directly under the authority of the pope. Canons 375 and 435 explain that metropolitans and bishops have immediate and ordinary authority within their jurisdictions, but that they can only exercise this authority in hierarchical communion with the pope and the other members of the College of Bishops. Canon 432 §1 states that 'The provincial council and the Metropolitan have authority over the ecclesiastical province, in accordance with the law'. Canon 406 §2 allows a Diocesan Bishop to appoint vicars general or episcopal vicars 'solely on his authority'. Only the bishop can publish the decrees of his Diocesan Synod, and the moderator of the diocesan curia, the financial administrator, the pastoral council, and parish priest can only act under his authority.

This use of *auctoritas*, however, is much closer to the sense of the word most used to describe episcopal government: *potestas* [power].[173] *Potestas* appears 123 times in the Codex. Most of the time, it is translated as 'power', but on 18 occasions, it is translated 'authority'. Interestingly, out of 13 uses of *potestas* in the section on Religious communities, ten are translated authority. In no other section does this happen more than twice. We may recall that in the 1917 Codex, superiors had the power of mastery (*dominativam*) over their communities. The position has been rather different since 1983. Canon 618 explains that

> the authority which Superiors receive from God through the ministry of the Church is to be exercised by them in a spirit of service (*servitii*). In fulfilling their office they are to be docile to the will of God, and are to govern those subject to them as children of God ... without prejudice however to their authority to decide and to command what is to be done (*firma tamen ipsorum auctoritate decernendi et praecipiendi quae agenda sunt*).

The Religious Superior, who in the 1917 Codex seemingly had more power over the community than the bishop had over the laity, is now expected to act as servant, rather than master, except when there are decisions to be made. Interestingly, the 1983 Code contains no such injunction to the bishops, who are merely enjoined to be 'solicitous for all Christ's faithful'.[174] While more in accord with the declarations of Vatican II than the relationship of ruler and subjects, this still does not really meet the Council's intentions. We should note, however, that while the Code has accepted the principle of leadership as service, it still refers to Religious Superiors, who share some of the rights of bishops, as ruling over their subjects (*ipsi subditos regant*). This seems to be the result of poor and inconsistent editing, a feature that bedevils the 1983 Codex.

---

171 Beal, Coriden and Green (2000, p. 442) note the absence of Ecumenical Councils from this list, and believe this ecclesiologically appropriate 'since they do not act in the name and under the authority of the pope'. Instead, pope and bishops exercise their authority together in such Councils.
172 Canon 360.
173 Compare ibid., pp. 183–9.
174 Canon 383 §1.

Power, in the 1983 Codex as in the 1917, begins at the top. The pope has supreme, full, immediate and universal ordinary power in the Church.[175] This, we may recall, is very similar to the power given by Justinian I to Catollianus, who acquired supreme power, unlimited sacerdotal supervision and the right of appointment. The pope's power extends to the College of Bishops, when acting in union with their head, and bishops have 'ordinary, proper and immediate power' within their dioceses.[176] This, they delegate within the parish to parish priests.[177] There is, however, a change of emphasis here. Beal, Coriden and Green (2000) point out that Canon 336, which describes the rôle of the bishops, is a product of Vatican II, and has no Canonical antecedents. The 1917 Code dealt with Ecumenical Councils in a separate chapter following the chapter on the pope.[178] In the 1983 Code they are part of the article on the College of Bishops.[179] The 1917 Code emphasises the supreme power of an Ecumenical Council. The 1983 Code speaks of the power of the College of Bishops, although the Code places more emphasis on the supremacy of the pope than Vatican II does.[180] Power seems to have moved from the pope alone to the pope and the bishops acting as a college.

Canon 118 of the 1917 Code states that only clerics (*clerici*) can obtain powers, whether of orders or of jurisdiction. Canon 108 §1 defines clerics as 'those who are taken into divine ministries at least by the reception of first tonsure'. This definition includes some who are not ordained. Canon 129 of the 1983 Code states that those in sacred orders are capable of the power of governance,[181] and that lay people can co–operate in the exercise of this power.[182] This has led to two schools of thought on the jurisdiction of the laity. The Roman school holds that Vatican II spoke of the powers of bishops and emphasised the oneness of their authority, without considering or intending to consider the role of lay people in authority or their exercise of jurisdiction. Thus, since lay people have exercised jurisdiction in the past, they can continue to do so. The German (or Munich) school, on the other hand, holds that since power is indivisible, and comes only through ordination, lay people cannot exercise jurisdiction.[183] In practice, however, lay people are unable to

---

175 Canon 331.

176 *Potestas ordinaria, propria et immediata.* Canon 381 §1.

177 Canon 515 §1.

178 Canons 222–9. Peters (2001), pp. 94–6.

179 Canons 336–41.

180 Beal, Coriden and Green (2000), p. 444. Compare *Lumen Gentium*, sections 20, 22 and 23 (Tanner, 1990, pp. 863–8). Beal, Coriden and Green (p. 446) point out that only three Canons describe the position of the pope within the College of Bishops, as proposed by Vatican II, rather than dealing with the pope first and then with the bishops, following the earlier order.

181 Canon 266 states that one becomes a cleric by reception of the diaconate.

182 Norman Doe (1996, p. 57) states that 'lay members of the faithful may co–operate in the exercise of this power, but they do not possess it'.

183 Beal, Coriden and Green (2000), pp. 184–5. I am more inclined to accept the Roman view as representing the wishes of the Council, while those compiling the Code may have

exercise jurisdiction in more places in England than they are able to do so. Those with suitable character or knowledge, however, can discharge certain ecclesiastical functions, or act as expert advisors to the councils in the Church.[184] While this is a greater role for the laity than that envisaged by the 1917 Codex, it still falls some way short of the full participation in the Prophetic, Priestly and Kingly ministry of Christ advocated by Vatican II.[185] While lay people may perform these functions largely unimpeded towards those outside the Church, it seems that within the Church their opportunities are still limited.

Finally, we should note that despite the efforts of Vatican II, several references to subjection (*subdo/subicio*) remain in the 1983 Code. It is not at all clear that this is a helpful way to describe the relationship between different sections of the People of God. It seems, then, that the decrees of Vatican II have been partially, if inconsistently, applied in the current Code of Canon Law. It appears, however, that the ethos of the current Code is that of Vatican I, not Vatican II. The Code's underlying concept of justice, which is clearly informed by Vatican II not Vatican I, has much to commend it, but as we have seen, this concept has neither been fully nor consistently implemented. Further revision seems necessary to achieve this. The changes made since 1917 seem to be moving the Church towards the vision of Vatican II, but these changes do not, as yet, seem to have been incorporated sufficiently in Canon Law.

Conclusion

We have seen that Canon Law developed over the centuries from a collection of accumulated wisdom to a system of Ecclesiastical Law. We have further seen that a variety of influences have shaped the way Canon Law developed. I have argued that some of these influences have been at best unhelpful, and at worst in conflict with the principles of Christianity. I agree with Örsy that removing secular influences from Canonical Jurisprudence would leave the Church with a more effective tool for governance, and it appears that since Vatican II, the Roman Catholic Church has made tentative steps in this direction. We have seen that emphatic Canonical pronouncements began when Christianity was established as the imperial religion. We have seen how the growth of the power of bishops and Councils was accompanied by a gradual reduction in the strength of language of the Canons. We have seen how it increased again when the popes found their power waning in the Holy Roman Empire, and how the Canons again became strident in the face of opposition from the Reformers at the Council of Trent, and from the Gallicans at Vatican I. We have identified secular influences which may have contributed to these changes. Finally, we have seen the change in approach caused by Vatican II and traced its effects on

---

leaned more towards the German view.

184 Canon 228. While these functions may give them authority over other lay people, it is not authority in the same sense as the authority of the bishops. They cannot, in general, make decisions without the consent of the clergy, to whom jurisdiction is reserved.

185 David McLoughlin makes a similar point in Hoose (2002), p. 187.

the current Code of Canon Law. While Roman Law has clearly played its part in this development – it is difficult to see how this trend could have gone so far without the concept of *paterfamilias* or something like it – opposition would appear to be the key here. The Church seems to have made its most emphatic statements when it has faced the greatest opposition, whether from pagans, secular rulers, Reformers, or factions within the Church.[186] In times of what we might call 'normality', official pronouncements seem to have been much milder in tone.

Thus, we have Nicaea I emphasising the authority of the Church following Constantine's adoption of Christianity as the official religion of the empire in the teeth of opposition from pagans. We have Constantinople IV declaring the power of the pope in response to the attempts of Holy Roman Emperors to reduce the power of the bishops. We have Trent vigorously rejecting what it saw as the errors of the Reformers. Finally, we have Vatican I emphatically asserting the power of the pope under opposition from the Gallicans and under pressure from Italian troops approaching the Papal States. Councils were never called without conflict, of course, but in slightly less turbulent times we have Nicaea II issuing Canons based at least as much on the authority of Scripture as on episcopal authority, we have Lateran IV reforming the Church and restoring spiritual discipline, and supremely we have Vatican II reforming the Church, and trying to introduce a new habit of mind into Roman Catholic thought. It seems that since Vatican II, the Roman Catholic Church has begun to remove some of the more harmful secular influences I have identified from its system of Church government. This process, while welcome, still has a considerable way to go. It is likely that a further revised Code of Canon Law will be necessary if the decisions of Vatican II are to be implemented fully. We must now turn our attention to the activities of the Church of England, as we go on to examine English Canon Law.

---

186 Hugh Lawrence expresses a similar view in Hoose (2002), p. 53.

Chapter 5

English Canon Law Since the Reformation

Introduction

Since the Reformation, the Church of England has taken a different approach to Canon Law. Henry VIII, when he severed the link with Rome, became head of the English Church in place of the pope. This meant that the Church was subject to royal authority, rather than papal authority. In due course, as the struggle between monarch and parliament developed, this changed from direct accountability to the sovereign to accountability to the sovereign in parliament. Consequently, Canon Law became subject to Parliamentary Law and English Common Law.[1]

Gerald Bray (1998) identifies three sources of English Canon Law: Scripture, tradition, and reason.[2] I shall argue that reason has been the most influential of the three in establishing an English Anglican view of Canon Law distinct from that of Rome. Bray tells us that a series of upheavals in the Church of England led to the introduction of several different sets of Canons before stability was reached. Henry VIII's Canons of 1529 were greatly modified in 1556 by the Legatine Constitutions of Cardinal Pole, who was trying to restore England to Roman obedience during the reign of Mary I. Elizabeth I was responsible for further attempts at reform in 1566, 1571, 1576, 1585 and 1597,[3] but these reforms did not last. The Canons did not reach a stable form until 1604, and then remained in force until 1969, receiving their first revision of any sort in 1865.[4] The process leading to the general revision of the 1604 Canons began in 1939, resulting in a report and set of proposed Canons in 1947 (Archbishops' Commission, 1947). This report is wide-ranging and thorough, exploring the history of Canon Law back to the New Testament, and explaining how and why certain Canons had fallen into disuse. It became the foundation for the revised Canons promulgated in 1964 and 1969, and still in force.

---

1   By Canon Law, I mean the law made by Convocations and General Synod for the internal governance of the Church. I use Ecclesiastical Law to describe the whole body of law affecting the Church.

2   Bray (1998), pp. xxix–xxxiv.

3   Ibid., pp. xxxiv–liv. The Canons of 1576, 1585 and 1597 were all approved in the previous year. I shall date these documents from when they received royal assent, not when Convocation passed them.

4   Ibid., p. lxi. Unsuccessful attempts were made to modify the 1604 Canons in 1606, 1640, 1875 and 1879.

It seems, therefore, that we need to examine the Canons of 1604, the proposed Canons of 1947, and the Canons of 1964 onwards in detail. We shall also consider the views of Richard Hooker, the most prominent Anglican Divine of the seventeenth century, whose views seem to reflect quite closely those of the compilers of the 1604 Canons. Since the Church of England Assembly (Powers) Act of 1919 (hereafter 'The Enabling Act'), the Church Assembly has had the power to legislate by Measure, a power it transferred to General Synod through the Synodical Government Measure, 1969 (hereafter 'SGM'). There is now a considerable body of Measures, to which we shall have to refer in due course. These are at least as important as Canon Law in Church government. When we discuss the post-1969 situation, we shall refer to several Measures in addition to our discussion of Canon Law. We begin with Richard Hooker.

Richard Hooker

Hooker's major work is *Of the Lawes of Ecclesiasticall Politie*. This defends the episcopacy against the arguments of Presbyterian Puritans. It presents the Church of England as both Catholic and Reformed, having kept the best of Roman practice where it was not seen to conflict with Scripture, and changed things where it seemed Rome had erred. The preface and books 1–4 were published in 1593, book 5 in 1597, books 6 and 8 in 1648, and book 7 in 1662. While sales were slow at first, by the early seventeenth century the *Lawes* had become a contemporary classic.[5] The status of Hooker's work in 1603, however, is unclear. I shall argue that Hooker's ideas in books 1 to 5 are so similar to those underlying the 1604 Canons that if they did not directly influence those Canons, they at least illustrate the thinking behind them.[6] Hooker's posthumous work contains more development of his views of justice and authority, and we shall need to consider these as well.

Hooker's first book, *Concerning Lawes and their severall kindes in generall*, sets out his views of law and justice. God is the source of both, and His law is eternal. The law that applies to the creation Hooker calls natural law. This, he tells us, is 'a law *cœlestiall* and heavenly: the law of reason that which bindeth creatures reasonable in this world, and with which by reason they may most plainly perceive themselves bound; that which bindeth them, and is not knowen but by a speciall revelation from God.'[7] Hooker draws a close parallel between human reason and Divine Law. He calls reason a second eternal law, which, even when it is repugnant to Divine Law, is in some sense conformable to the first eternal law, namely the law as it is in the bosom of God. This is similar to Gratian's use of natural law in the first distinction in the *Decretum* (1993) which is there contrasted with custom.[8] Hooker

---

5   Hooker (1977a), pp. xvi–xxiv.

6   Richard Helmholz (Doe, Hill and Ombres, 1998, p. 28) sees Hooker as the closest one could hope to get to a representative voice and spokesman for the Elizabethan Church.

7   Ibid., p. 63. Italics Hooker's.

8   Gratian (1993), pp. 3–8, Hooker (1977a), p. 119.

therefore founds his doctrine of justice in the attributes of God, and views human theories of law as developments and applications of divine justice to everyday life. In book 2 of the *Lawes*, Hooker addresses the Puritan objections that Scripture is the sole authority in the Church, and that it sets out a single Church order, which the Church of England had not followed.

The most interesting objection here is Thomas Cartwright's claim that, in doctrinal matters, Scriptural authority is everything, and human authority is worthless. Hooker's reply is that if we are to learn from Scripture, humans must expound it, and that therefore human authority must prevail, especially with those who deny its worth, 'as far as equity requireth,'[9] and no further. Hooker thought the Puritans were making the opposite error to Rome, which, he argued, was claiming that Scripture was insufficient. Instead, he tells us, they claimed that to do anything by a law not found in Scripture was sinful.[10]

Hooker did not define equity in detail here, but he did believe that any human authority must be exercised within the bounds of reason. In book 5, chapter 9, he tells us that equity is applied

> not to turne the edge of justice, or to make voyde at certaine tymes and in certaine men through meere voluntarie grace or benevolence that which continewallie and universallie should be of force (as some understand it) but in verie truth to practise generall lawes accordinge to theire right meaninge.'[11]

Equity, he tells us, is not against the law, but above it; binding men's consciences in areas the law cannot reach. He believes that even the laws of Christ must be 'construed and understood according to the rules of naturall equitie.'[12] Hooker's clearest definition of equity comes in his autograph notes to the posthumous books, and was therefore not publicly known in 1603: 'I understand by this that the letter of the law should be departed from when reason persuades.'[13] This statement does not, in itself, conflict with the views of equity we have already discussed.[14] Hooker's view, however, places much more emphasis on reason, and his claim that reason must govern the interpretation of even God's law comes close to an assertion that justice and reason are inseparable. In chapter 1 of book 5, Hooker seems to take this line of argument even further, arguing that 'So naturall is the union of Religion with Justice, that wee may boldlie denie there is either, where both are not.'[15] We have already seen how closely Hooker identifies justice with reason, and this suggests

---

9   Hooker (1997a), p. 181. See Cartwright (1575), pp. 17–23. On p. 21, Cartwright cites an impressive list of Church Fathers in support of his case.

10   Ibid., p. 191.

11   Hooker (1977b), p. 44.

12   Ibid., p. 258.

13   Hooker (1981), p. 514.

14   See above, chapter 3.

15   Hooker (1977b), p. 17.

that he might also have been prepared to deny that religion and reason could exist separately unless they were both present together.

For Hooker, then, reason was a central element of justice, and was an essential element of Christianity. Even in the early decades of the Church of England, the concern for reason, which was to become so important in Anglicanism, was evident. The last three books of Hooker's work were published posthumously. They concerned the assertions that the Church's ecclesiastical jurisdiction was corrupt and repugnant to Scripture, that the Church should not have bishops endued with the authority and honour it did have, and that no civil prince should have ecclesiastical jurisdiction. While these matters do not relate directly to the concepts of justice we have been discussing, and nor could they have affected the 1604 Canons, Hooker's comments on authority are relevant to our enquiry, and we shall now consider them. Hooker describes spiritual authority, which he equates with spiritual jurisdiction and spiritual power, as 'a power, which Christ hath given to bee used over them, which are subject unto it, for the eternall good of their soules, according to his owne most sacred lawes, and the wholesome positive constitutions of his Church.'[16] Hooker tells us that Christ, in Matthew 16:19, gave the Apostles and the bishops who followed them the duty to guide, command, judge and correct his family. Those entrusted with this job, he tells us, would have to render a strict account before the throne of grace. They were not given this power for their own financial gain, but to use it for the good of those 'whome *Jesus Christ* hath most deerely bought.'[17] This power extended to both doctrinal and disciplinary measures.

The aim of this discipline was to 'heale mens consciences, to cure theyr sinnes, to reclayme offendors from iniquitie, and to make them by repentance just.'[18] This, Hooker thinks, placed the Church of England at a doctrinal distance from Rome, in that the Church of England did not, in general, require external works of penance. Rather, Anglicans concentrated on the inward conversion of the heart. Hooker acknowledged that Roman priests did have genuine authority to remit sins, but claimed that they did so without regard to two restraints: they proceeded without due order and they extended themselves beyond due bounds. Jesus may have given priests the power to bind and loose, but He did not give them that authority to the extent that no sin could be forgiven except by a priest: in His sovereignty He retained the right and the power to bind or loose sinners in their absence. When it came to the absolution, Hooker believed, the priest did not himself forgive: he merely pronounced what God had already done, and loosed the chains the Church had placed on the offender.[19] In the context of the debate at the time over the place of works in the economy of salvation, this represents a distinctly Protestant emphasis:

---

16 Hooker (1981), p. 5.

17 Ibid., p. 14. Italics Hooker's.

18 Ibid., p. 15. This implies that Church discipline, and presumably by extension Church authority, should aim to make sinners right with God. As we have seen, all the Churches we consider here have expressed an awareness of this need. See above, chapter 3.

19 Ibid., pp. 70–82.

that faith alone could save and that works, while desirable as a mark of conversion of heart, were not essential.

We saw in the last chapter that a Roman bishop is the sole legislator within his diocese. I have argued that governance is one of his major functions. This is not, however, how Hooker sees the rôle of Anglican bishops. When answering the charge that prelacy does no good, Hooker argues that authority is a constraining power. It is not sufficient for the head of a household to give tasks to labourers unless he also appoints a chief workman to make sure they do the work. In the same way, 'Constitutions and Canons made for the ordering of Church affairs, are dead Taskmasters. The due execution of Laws spiritual dependeth most on the vigilant care of the chiefest spiritual Governors, whose charge is to see that such Laws be kept by the Clergy and people under them.'[20] For Hooker, therefore, the task of an Anglican bishop is not to rule, it is to supervise: the bishops are set to watch over the flock, correcting them when necessary. The touchstone for this supervision and guidance is reason, which, as a gift of God, enables the bishops to lead wisely and to judge justly. It is unlikely that Hooker was the first person to believe this. There is evidence that Henry VIII held a similar view when presented with the Canons of the Convocation of 1529. The first Canon, as originally proposed, began as follows:

> Whereas archbishops and bishops ought to be a pattern to the flock, to which their subjects ought to conform, which cannot be done unless they set an example for everyone ...[21]

Henry deleted 'subjects' (*subditi*), which was the word then being used in Roman texts to describe the laity,[22] and replaced it with 'inferiors' (*inferiores*). 'Subjects' never reappeared in English Canon Law, not even in the Legatine Constitutions of Cardinal Pole. Even at this early stage, the Church of England was showing signs of developing a model of episcopacy distinct from the Roman model. With this in mind, we consider the Canons of 1604.

The Canons of 1604

The 1604 Canons were the result of an attempt to iron out the differences between the Puritans in the Church of England on one hand, and the king, bishops and ecclesiastical hierarchy on the other hand. These Canons were intended to form a permanent Corpus. When it became clear that the 1529 Canons were inadequate, Henry VIII set up several commissions in an attempt to produce a satisfactory Corpus. As we have seen, the first seven such attempts were unsuccessful. Presumably Henry was aware of the difficulties: he introduced legislation, in the form of the Submission of the Clergy Act, 1533, to stabilise the situation until the commissions had completed

---

20 Ibid., p. 256.

21 Bray (1998), p. 3. We may notice that this Canon describes the laity as *gregis* [a flock].

22 See above, chapter 4.

their work. This contained a provision that any pre-Reformation Canons not contrary to royal prerogative or general English Law would continue in force until changed by subsequent legislation.[23]

The compilers of the 1604 Corpus decided to arrange the new Canons systematically, dealing first with worship, and then with clergy training and discipline. This was the Church of England's first attempt to arrange its Canons systematically and consistently. Consequently, some material did not fit into the new structure adopted for this Corpus, and was omitted. In line with the Submission of the Clergy Act, the previous set of Canons dealing with this material continued in force: where the 1604 Canons were silent about a particular issue, the 1571 Canons were generally cited.[24] The Convocations of Canterbury and York approved the Canons in 1603, somewhat to the dismay of Parliament, which resented provisions in some of the Canons allowing excommunication for secular crimes, and protested vigorously to the king.

One such offence was impugning the king's supremacy over the Church, for which Canon 2, which we shall shortly discuss, prescribed automatic excommunication, which could only be reversed by the archbishop after public penance. Parliament was outraged, and accordingly refused to accept the Canons. King James I decided to bypass Parliament, and ratified them anyway by letters patent in 1604, once Parliament had been dissolved.[25] This caused a major row, in which Parliament insisted that since it, as the representative of the people, had not ratified the Canons, they had no force on lay people. Parliament eventually won this argument, although its victory was not clearly established for over a century. Nevertheless, the fact that the Canons include provisions on schoolmasters that seem only to apply to the laity[26] clearly shows that the Convocations did not believe that their powers were restricted in this way. Due to pressures of time, the Convocations only adopted the Latin version of these Canons, and so the Latin version became the official text, although the Canons were originally written, and were almost exclusively used, in English. Three main sections are relevant: The first, *Of the Church of England*, begins the Corpus. The second is in a section in the middle, which deals with court proceedings. The third, *Authority of Synods*, is the last section. *Of the Church of England* contains 12 Canons, of which 11 are new. The most contentious of the new Canons is Canon 2:

---

23 25 Henry VIII, c. 19. Section 7 regulates pre–Reformation Canon Law. Gibson (1713), p. *985.

24 Bray (1998), p. lv.

25 Ibid., p. lvi. James was persuaded that the Canons were 'very profitable, not only to our Clergy, but to the whole Church of this our Kingdom, and to all the true Members of it', and commanded clergy and laity alike to observe them. See Gibson (1713), pp. *993–5.

26 Canon 77 requires that teachers have learning and dexterity in teaching, and subscribe to the first and third articles, and the first and second clauses of the second article. The bishop could licence anyone with these qualifications, although Canon 78 required him to give preference to suitably qualified curates.

Whoever shall hereafter affirm that the king's majesty hath not the same authority in causes ecclesiastical that the godly kings had amongst the Jews and Christian emperors of the primitive church; or impeach in any part his regal supremacy in the said causes restored to the crown, and by the laws of this realm therein established; let him be excommunicated ipso facto, and not restored, but only by the archbishop, after his repentance, and public revocation of those his wicked errors.[27]

This Canon makes a presupposition which, to say the least, is theologically contentious: that the Jewish kings could make religious law for the people.[28] I have already argued that this is not true[29] – the Jews did not draw a sharp distinction between secular and religious law, and in both fields, the king was subject to God's law. The prophets could and did hold both kings and people to account. It also neglects early persecution of the Church by the Roman emperors before Constantine. This model of the king as supreme head and governor of the Church of England owes a great deal to the monarchical theory of Church government used by the popes. While Henry VIII and Edward VI seem to have taken this approach, Elizabeth I and James I were generally much more cautious about such things.[30] This Canon was not acceptable to the Puritans, and not surprisingly, it was hotly contested. It is clear that, in Canon 2, the Convocations were claiming that James had full ecclesiastical jurisdiction in the Church. It did not regard his rôle as an interpreter of the law, in the sense we have identified; rather it claimed he held regal supremacy over the Church. It is surprising that James was prepared to ratify this claim: he shared Elizabeth's caution about claiming total jurisdiction over the Church, and was generally very wary of such titles. In effect, he was implicitly endorsing a form of the monarchical theory of the Church, with himself, rather than the pope, at its head. The view of kingship and authority here seems markedly different to the view we have identified in the Old and New Testaments.[31]

The 1604 Canons also regulated the ecclesiastical courts. The archiepiscopal courts deal mainly with matters of probate and marriage, which are now dealt with by civil courts, and are not relevant here. Our main interest is in the ecclesiastical courts under the jurisdiction of bishops and archdeacons. These courts dealt with 'adultery, whoredom, incest, or drunkenness … swearing, ribaldry, usury and any other uncleanness, and wickedness of life.'[32] This section of the Canons sets out the duty of the churchwardens to present such offenders to the bishop for trial at the annual or six-monthly visitation. The wardens were also obliged to present schismatics,

---

27 Ibid., pp. 264–9.

28 Bray states that this was widely believed by both Anglicans and Lutherans. Ibid., p. 264.

29 See above, chapter 3.

30 Elizabeth refused to accept the title 'Head of the Church'. Gibson traces this to a scruple raised by one Lever, a minister at Frankfurt, and to Elizabeth's desire to avoid offending the Popish Party. Ibid., p. 51, footnote o.

31 See above, chapter 4.

32 Canon 109. Ibid., p. 409.

disturbers of divine service, and those who did not receive Communion at Easter. If the churchwardens failed in this duty, through fear, ignorance or negligence, the priest could present sinners instead. He was not, however, obliged to reveal to the bishop anything he heard in the confessional, and indeed was charged not to do so, on pain of irregularity, unless concealing such information could lead to his own execution. His main duty during visitations was to present 'popish recusants', whether they were men, women or children. He also shared the duty of presenting those who did not receive Communion at Easter with the churchwardens. To ensure that, as far as possible, ministers and churchwardens could do this job free of fear, Canon 115 gave them immunity from legal action by aggrieved parishioners: they could not be sued for presenting.[33]

The 1604 Canons are silent on how recalcitrant clergy should be dealt with, but section 5, Canon 9 of the 1571 Canons states that

> if the parson, vicar or curate behave himself otherwise [than mandated by the bishop] in his ministry, or that he read ill, darkly and confusedly, or that he live more loosely and licentiously than is fit for a man of that calling, and thereby great offence be taken; the churchwardens shall speedily present him to the bishop that by and by he may be punished and amendment of his fault may follow.[34]

We can therefore see that the primary responsibility for presenting sinners to the bishop, both lay people and clerics, lay with the churchwardens, who were the representatives of the bishop and the Crown in the parish. The bishop was expected to maintain moral standards within his diocese, but he had to do so within existing legislation: he did not have the power to make law. The position of Anglican bishops here is similar to that of Roman bishops, in that the bishop was the ecclesiastical judge, and that he or his officers pronounced defendants guilty or innocent, and sentenced them where appropriate. Unlike Roman bishops, however, Anglican bishops did not govern as such: they had great influence, but they had no power to legislate.[35] Only the Convocations of Canterbury and York could make Canon Law, and then the proposed Canons did not have legal force on the clergy until they had received Royal Assent.

It seems, therefore, that the Canons of 1604, like Hooker, saw the bishop's rôle as supervision. He had to uphold standards, and had a duty to punish sinners, but

---

33 Canons 110–115. Ibid., pp. 409–15. Wardens could not be compelled to present more than twice a year, although they had the option to do so if they chose.

34 Ibid., p. 197. Section in square brackets mine.

35 See, for example, Canon 10 of the decree on Reform in session 24 of the Council of Trent. This gave bishops the right to do anything they judged necessary to correct their subjects or benefit their diocese 'so that they might more easily keep the people they govern in dutiful obedience.' (*ut aptius quem regunt populum possint in officio atque obedientia continere*). Abuses of episcopal power also led the Council to remind the bishops in session 13 that they should act as shepherds, not oppressors (*pastores, non percussores*). Tanner (1990), pp. 698 and 765.

he could only do so within the law, and he could not know all that happened in his diocese. The churchwardens, who did know what happened in the parish, were obliged to tell him, but might be pressurised not to do so by those with influence. Failure to present could, in these circumstances, be interpreted as an offence. The simplest way to keep the bishop informed was to protect Wardens from legal action arising from presentments, and to allow the minister to present if they felt unable to do so. The influence of reason here is also clear: this seems an admirable example of equity in Hooker's sense. Those who denied that declarations of Synod affected those not present, or affirmed that Synod should be 'despised and contemned' (*reiici ac contemni*) were similarly excommunicated by Canons 140 and 141 respectively.[36] In essence, the aim of these Canons seems to be the maintenance of respect for ecclesiastical authority. Those who refused to accept the teaching or discipline of the Church *ipso facto* placed themselves outside it.

The Canons also referred at times to English Civil Law. Canon 109 informed sinners that they were to be 'punished by the severity of the laws, according to their deserts,'[37] and not re–admitted to Communion until they reformed. Similarly, schismatics were to be 'censured and punished according to such ecclesiastical laws as are prescribed in that behalf.'[38] This clearly illustrates the close relationship between English Ecclesiastical Law and Common Law, and the reason and pragmatism that characterises it. This relationship continues today. We might therefore expect to see reason, shot through with pragmatism, writ large in the Ecclesiastical Law of the twentieth century.

The Proposed Canons of 1947

The Archbishops' Commission charged with revising the 1604 Canons produced a report that Gerald Bray has described as 'far and away the best of its kind ever to have been produced in England.'[39] It begins with a thorough review of Canon Law, starting with the New Testament and explaining how and why the Canons developed. It explains why the 1604 Canons needed an overhaul, and then sets out in detail what effect it believed its changes would have, providing the source material for every Canon it drafted.[40] Many of its Canons are restatements, some modified restatements, of the 1604 Corpus, but other material comes from statute law, court judgements and the Book of Common Prayer. Briden and Hanson (1992) give an apposite account of the situation to which the commission gave its attention:

---

36 Ibid., p. 445.

37 *Ut legem severitate pro meritis possint castigari.* Ibid., p. 409.

38 *Ut poenis et censuris per ecclesiasticas sanctiones irrogatis coerceatur.* Canon 110. Ibid.

39 Bray (1998), p. lxxxvi.

40 Ibid. This review comprises pages 3 to 98 of the commission's report.

The chaotic position in which the reported decisions of the nineteenth century might land us, if they were all taken seriously, can be shown by some almost random examples. It would seem that it is lawful to sing hymns, although no place for them is to be found in the Prayer Book. On the strength of this, the archbishops came to the conclusion (sensibly, but not necessarily correctly) that to sing or say 'Glory be to thee, O God' at the reading of the Gospel and to sing the *Agnus Dei* after the prayer of consecration is lawful. But to give notice during divine worship of the feasts of St Leonard, St Martin, or St Britius (which are not mentioned as holy days in the Prayer Book) has been said to be unlawful, from which (if it is right) it would seem to follow that it would also be unlawful to give notice of a forthcoming church fête. The use of incense during a statutory service is probably unlawful, but, if sanctioned by the bishop in the exercise of the *jus liturgicum*, may perhaps be lawful during other services. The ringing of a bell, however, at the prayer of consecration appears to be unlawful, though why this should be so, while the singing of the *Agnus Dei* is lawful (if it is), passes all reasonable comprehension.[41]

With this in mind, we turn to the Proposed Canons of 1947. Four sections are important: The Church of England; Ministers, their Ordination, Function and Charge; The Ecclesiastical Courts; and The Synods, Assemblies, and Conferences of the Church of England. We begin with the section concerning the Church of England.

Canon 8 restates the Henrician law that any pre-Reformation Canons not contrary to English Law or royal prerogative and not superseded by the 1604 Canons or this code continue in force. It adds the stipulation that the two archbishops, rather than the Church Courts, shall resolve any alleged conflict between Canons. Canon 9, while deferring to the judgement that Canon Law does not, in general, bind the laity, seeks to extend its scope as widely as possible. It states that Canon Law binds the clergy, and those lay people who accept offices within the Church, who serve on Parochial Church Councils or other representative bodies, or who claim 'the benefit of any of the ministrations of the Church.'[42] This move seems perfectly reasonable: it seems only right that those who belong to an organisation, whether Christian or secular, should follow its rules. Concerning ministers, Canon 59 explains that no one can exercise a ministry without the authority of the Diocesan Bishop, or a preaching licence from Oxford or Cambridge University. Canon 71 explains that an archbishop is the superintendent of ecclesiastical matters within his province. Canon 72 explains that bishops have jurisdiction to celebrate the rites of the Church, authorise services, licence alterations in Church buildings, institute clergy, hold visitations and correct those who disobey the Church. The emphasis here is again on the bishop as supervisor and guardian of his diocese, not as its governor.

When it comes to presentments, we see a change in emphasis: while ministers and churchwardens could still present sinners to the bishop, they no longer had to present more than once a year. The presentments became answers to books of articles, about such things as furnishings and fixtures in Church, as well as the conduct of parishioners. Nevertheless, the proviso that ministers should not reveal anything

---

41 Briden and Hanson (1992), p. 97. Emphasis original.
42 Archbishops' Commission (1947), p. 108.

they heard during confession in their presentments was retained, in revised form, in Canon 66, which prohibited ministers from revealing confessions to anyone else.[43] The other provisions in the proposed Canons follow the pattern of 1604.

The Commission added two new provisions to the Canons. It first introduced a requirement not present in the 1604 Corpus, that the Synod could only act with the agreement of both Houses of Clergy, both Houses of Bishops and both archbishops.[44] It then formalised Canonically the Representation of the Laity Measure, 1929, which had introduced a House of Laity to the Church Assembly.[45] The Commission also sought to resolve some of the consequences of the chaotic situation described by Briden and Hanson: Canon 29 gives the minister full responsibility for deciding what music is played, when and on what instruments, during worship. Similarly, Canon 102 gives the minister full discretion on when bells are rung. The apparent aim of the proposed Canons, then, was to bring Canon Law into line with Church practice, and to simplify legislation that had become too cumbersome; in other words its aim was to legalise the actual practice of the Church. It seems to be an attempt to tidy up Church Law, not to make any adjustments to the Church's doctrine or practice.

The Canons of 2000 and General Synod

While the Church Assembly in 1964 and 1969, and General Synod since 1970, have not entirely followed the recommendations of the Commission, they have incorporated many of the Commission's proposals into the current Canons. Section A, concerning the Church of England, follows the pattern of 1604, affirming the practice and theology of the Church of England, and the Royal Supremacy under God, but without excommunicating those who restrict the sovereign's authority.[46] Section B regulates divine service and the administration of the sacraments. Canon B7 gives the minister discretion to give notice of feast days to be observed, whether or not they are in the Prayer Book. Visitations are covered by Canons G5 and G6. The purpose is now to act 'for the edifying and well-governing of Christ's flock, that means may be taken thereby for the supply of things that are lacking and the correction of such things as are amiss.'[47] During such visitations, the minister and churchwardens must make presentments in the form of answers to articles supplied

---

43 Ibid., p. 157. This Canon is a restatement of Canon 21 of Lateran IV, which prescribed perpetual penance in a strict monastery for offenders. See Tanner (1990), p. 245.

44 Canon 126. Ibid., pp. 205–6. The Archbishops' Commission cites pp. 130–138 of *Synodus Anglicana* (Gibson, 1854), which argues that the law providing that civil property of the clergy could not be disposed of without their consent, a matter often discussed in Convocations, developed into an established veto. Thus, neither House could act without the consent of the other, or without the consent of the Archbishops.

45 Canon 130. Ibid., pp. 211–2. In due course, this became the House of Laity of General Synod.

46 Church of England (2005), pp. 3–10.

47 Ibid., p. 164.

by the bishop or archdeacon. These concern parish administration, the state of buildings, arrangements for services and the life and health of the parish, not the naming of sinners.[48] There seems to be a consensus that the disciplinary functions of visitations were taken over by the Ecclesiastical Jurisdiction Measure, 1963. This measure, however, applies only to clergy. The Church effectively abandoned any claim to discipline the laity in 1963.[49]

Canon 8 of 1947, which stated that pre–Reformation Canon Law was, in some circumstances still valid, was not included in the current Canons. We have referred to Parliament's claim that only Canons they approved could bind the laity. We now need to look at the arguments more closely. The 1736 case, *Middleton v Crofts*, established the principle that the 1604 Canons do not, in general, bind the laity.[50] Two subsequent cases expanded upon this statement, and applied it to pre–Reformation Canons. In 1868, Lord Westbury gave judgement in the case of *The Bishop of Exeter v Marshall*, a dispute between the bishop and a patron over who should be placed in a particular benefice.[51] The bishop had refused to institute, citing Canon 13 of the Apostolic Canons, which requires commendatory letters from the sending bishop before any clergyman moving from one city to another can be licensed. Lord Westbury held that

> if it had been pleaded by the bishop to have been the invariable usage of the church from earliest times down to the Reformation, (which would have been evidence of its being a law of the Church,) and that it had been continued and uniformly recognised and acted upon by the bishops of the Anglican Church since the Reformation (which might have shewn it to have been received and adopted as part of the law ecclesiastical recognised by the common law), the fitness of the rule ought not to be questioned.'[52]

Lord Dunboyne expressed this more succinctly when, in 1967, he sat in the Commissary Court of the City and Diocese of Canterbury in *re: St. Mary's, Westwell*:[53]

> The line of cases culminating in *Exeter (Bishop)* v *Marshall* seems to confirm that no directive, rule or usage of pre-Reformation canon law is any longer binding on this court

---

48 Doe (1996), p. 124.

49 The Ecclesiastical Jurisdiction Measure was superseded by the Clergy Discipline Measure 2003.

50 *English Reports* (1903), p. 790 [2 Atkins 654]. In this case, Lord Hardwicke held that Parliament had repeatedly made Ecclesiastical Law that was binding on the laity. Since there could only be one legislature, Convocations could not also perform the same function. He also emphasised that while the Canons did not, of their own force and authority, bind the laity, many provisions in the Canons declared the ancient usage of the Church, which did bind the laity, but this obligation was antecedent to, not arising from, the Canons.

51 *Law Reports* (1868), pp. 17–55.

52 Ibid., pp. 54–5.

53 *Weekly Law Reports* (1968), pp. 513–9.

unless pleaded and proved to be recognised, continued and acted upon in England since the Reformation.[54]

The effect of these two judgements, among others, was to make pre–Reformation Canon Law virtually unenforceable. We saw, when we discussed the 1604 Canons, that section 7 of the Submission of the Clergy Act, 1533, stated that pre-Reformation Canon Law continued to be valid if it had not been superseded and it was consistent with Royal Prerogative and general English Law. Lord Halsbury, in his *Statutes* (1986), however, states that section 7 of this Act was repealed by the Statute Law (Repeals) Act, 1969.[55] Halsbury's *Laws* (1975), states that any pre-Reformation Canons now in force derive their force from post–Reformation instruments, whether Canons, Measures or Acts of Parliament.[56] Where pre-Reformation Canons are still followed, long observance, rather than a pre-Reformation pedigree, gives these customs their force.

Norman Doe (1996), while accepting this provision, states that he often wonders precisely how much ancient case law, and pre-Reformation canon law, is still applicable to and binding on the Church of England. He feels that the need to cite old judicial decisions, 'sometimes with too great a degree of certainty to support what are taken for axiomatic legal propositions'[57] has bedevilled his study. If this is a fair assessment, one can only agree with Doe in lamenting a position that seems very unclear. The minimum solution to this problem would seem to be the formal repeal of all pre-Reformation Canon Law, but perhaps it would be better to repeal all pre-1964 Canons not restated in the current Corpus. This would clear up much of the confusion about which Canons are, or are not, still valid, although some problems of interpretation would still need to be resolved.[58]

The current Canons largely follow the 1604 Canons in matters of authority. Canon C17 states that each archbishop is 'superintendent of all ecclesiastical matters' within his diocese.[59] Similarly, Canon C18 informs bishops that they are the chief pastors in their dioceses, with duties to 'teach and to uphold sound and wholesome doctrine, and to banish and drive away all erroneous and strange opinions.' They must also 'set forward and maintain quietness, love, and peace among all men.'[60] These statements reaffirm the bishops' rôle as supervisors, not legislators.

The Canons affecting Synod concern its membership and structure, not its authority. This subject is covered by the SGM, and by the Standing Orders of General Synod (Church of England, 2000). Schedule 2, section 6 of the SGM states that the functions of General Synod are twofold. First, Synod can consider matters

---

54 Ibid., p. 516.

55 Halsbury (1986), p. 23. For the Act, see Halsbury (2000), pp. 559–61.

56 Halsbury (1975), pp. 140–143.

57 Doe (1996), p. 502.

58 For example, whether the terms of current Canon Law are narrower than those of 1604, and therefore whether the latter affect the interpretation of the former. See ibid.

59 Church of England (2005), p. 102.

60 Ibid., p. 104.

concerning the Church of England and make provision for them by Measure, as prescribed in the Enabling Act, by Canon, or by certain other Acts of Synod. Second, it can express opinions on matters of religious or public interest. Synod motions for most purposes can be carried on a simple majority by show of hands. Final approval for Measures or Canons generally requires a simple majority on a division by houses.[61] Thus, any house can block measures, in the same way that any member of any house can propose them. There is, however, an exception to these rules. Matters concerning doctrine or worship must be submitted to the House of Bishops for approval, and can only be passed 'in terms proposed by the House of Bishops and not otherwise.'[62] Standing Orders 81 to 94 set out how such business proceeds.[63] While it is first debated by the full Synod, before being referred to the House of Bishops,[64] there is currently no requirement for consultation before the amended instrument is sent back for final approval.

This seems rather restrictive. While the bishops, as the guardians of the historic deposit of faith, bear responsibility for defining doctrine, it could be argued that, should the bishops feel it necessary to alter a proposed Measure concerning doctrine or worship, there would be advantages in a period of consultation with lay theologians before such definitions are presented for final approval. Votes on permanent changes to the services of Baptism or Holy Communion or to the Ordinal require a two-thirds majority in all three houses.[65] This reflects the Church's structure of ecclesiastical leadership and synodical government, again emphasising that the bishops' task is supervision not rule: while the bishops have great influence in Synod, and a veto on changes in doctrine or worship, they cannot prescribe Ecclesiastical or Canon Law in the manner of the pope or the Roman bishops.

We can see that the ethos of the 2000 Canons is broadly similar to that of the 1604 Canons: they are designed to regulate the conduct of clergy and certain lay officials according to the established principles of case law, moderation and reason. Over the same period, English Civil Law has undergone a substantial change of ethos, moving from natural justice (the theory that justice is based on moral absolutes, and can approximate to God's justice), through moral justice (which assumes that the prevailing morals of righteous Englishmen can be used as a standard of justice), to individual utility (which is sometimes described as the maximum happiness principle).[66] Theologically, this marks a decline from a view of human law based

---

61 SGM, schedule 2, section 5 (1). Hill (2001), p. 378.

62 Section 7 (1). Ibid.

63 Church of England (2000), pp. 64–73.

64 In the case of a measure the full procedure is followed: first consideration, revision committee, report, further revision (if necessary), and final drafting. The referral to the House of Bishops is an additional stage before final approval. For other matters, only first consideration is required before referral to the House of Bishops. See SO 72–94. Ibid., pp. 56–73.

65 SGM, schedule 2, sections 8 (1 and 1C). Hill (2001), p. 379.

66 Dowrick (1961) explores all three theories in much more detail. The legal principle of individual utility is indelibly associated with Jeremy Bentham (1789), who thought it self-

on notions of divine justice to a system based much more on what is seen, through experience, to work. Ecclesiastical Law, while it has become more pragmatic, has not done so on the grounds of utilitarianism. It therefore largely escaped this decline, and continued to emphasise the close relationship between Divine Law and Church Law.

Conclusion

We can see, then, that the Church of England is led by the bishops, but there is substantially more lay involvement in decision-making than there is in the Roman Catholic Church. Rome is episcopally led and governed. The Church of England is episcopally led and synodically governed, with the bishops taking a leading rôle in decisions of Synod concerning doctrine and worship. In most other circumstances, however, the House of Laity and the House of Clergy have an equal influence over the decisions of the Church, at least in theory. There are both top–down and bottom-up elements in the Church of England's model of government. It is a mix between a hierarchy and a representative democracy. As with all mixed forms of government, there is a balance to be struck: it seems to me that, at the moment, this balance is weighted slightly too far in favour of the bishops. The Church has been influenced by the secular jurisprudence of England, with its emphasis on reason, equity and pragmatism. This seems, in part, to follow from the teaching of Richard Hooker and the Elizabethan Church, and in part from Henry VIII's decision to place Ecclesiastical Law under Civil Law when breaking away from Rome. However, the Church does not seem to have adopted the utilitarianism evident in much secular English Civil Law. It does appear, however, that the Church overemphasises reason. It often seems that English Canon Law aims to keep everyone living together in relative peace and harmony, an objective that does not seem to me to be based on an adequate concept of justice. We have seen that the Churches are concerned, in Hooker's phrase, to use their spiritual jurisdiction to heal consciences, to cure sins, to reclaim offenders from iniquity, and to make them just by repentance.[67] We shall revisit this issue in chapter 9, but first we must examine how the Reformers incorporated liberty into their concepts of justice and authority.

---

evident that the law should seek to make as many people as possible as happy as possible.

67 Hooker (1981), p. 15.

Chapter 6

Liberty, Democracy and Individualism

Introduction

Free Churches, throughout their history, have consistently rejected the use of Canon Law in favour of their views of Christian liberty. In this chapter, we will explore these views, how they were affected by the Reformers' ideas of justice, and how these ideas affected the way the Churches structured themselves. We shall also consider how much these ideas are influenced by the Bible, and how much by ideas from other sources, including such precursors of the Reformation as Marsilius of Padua and John Wyclif. In the next chapter, we will explore whether these Churches have set up structures that perform the same function as Canon Law, and if so how they operate.

I shall argue that Reformed views of liberty went beyond the liberty espoused by Paul, and incorporated elements of Aristotle's thought on democracy. I shall argue that individualism, in the sense that everyone is entitled to freedom of conscience, their beliefs not being subject to examination by others, entered the Reformed Churches through the writing of Zwingli. I believe that Zwingli also contributed to individualism in the sense that he placed more importance on the individual than the community, but I shall concentrate more on the former sense of individualism than the latter. I shall also argue that some of the Reformers took some of their ideas on Church structure from Marsilius, whose ecclesiology is a direct development of his interpretation of Aristotle's writing on secular government.[1] I shall argue that events during the English Commonwealth period introduced further democratic and individualistic elements, foreign to Biblical patterns of Church Government, into Reformed theology. Finally, I shall trace individualism through the writings of eighteenth-century Separatists, and seek to relate their views to those of the earlier Reformers. We begin with the precursors of the Reformation.

---

1   The *Defensor Pacis* is divided into three discourses. The first is an exposition of Aristotle's views on good (secular) government. The second is an application of these views to the Church, and particularly to the papacy of the time. The third is a brief summary of the first two discourses.

Precursors of the Reformation

Joan Lockwood O'Donovan (1991) tells us that while John Wyclif is the pre-eminent forerunner of the Reformation in England, Marsilius of Padua is a background influence of 'certain, if incalculable, significance'.[2] Marsilius' argument against the pope was largely political, while Wyclif's was mainly theological. As we shall see, Marsilius' influence on Wyclif was arguably indirect, through the writings of William of Ockham. There are some important differences in their views. Marsilius argued against Scholasticism, Wyclif argued from within the Scholasticism prevalent at Oxford in the late fourteenth century. We must now examine their views.

Marsilius of Padua

Marsilius opens his first discourse in the *Defensor Pacis* (2001), by explaining the origin and functions of the state, before exploring which is the polity most likely to produce tranquillity. He then applies his ideas at the end of this discourse to 'one singular, and very obscure cause by which the Roman Empire has long been troubled and is still troubled'.[3] Marsilius explores six different polities, all of which are taken directly and explicitly from Aristotle's *Politics*, agreeing with Aristotle that an elected ruler is the best option, and that he should rule according to the law. It is also necessary that the ruler be prudent and just, since the law cannot cover every situation, and therefore the ruler must have some discretion in deciding cases that fall outside its provisions. Rulers must also exhibit equity (*epieikeia*), in its Aristotelian sense of benign moderation of the law where appropriate. Furthermore, rulers must be subject to the law, which receives its force from the approval of those who elect the ruler, and must be punished by the magistrates if they do not comply with it.

While Marsilius accepts that all authority ultimately comes from God, he believes that the people can convey as much power to their ruler as they wish. It seems that Marsilius adopts Aristotle's ideas on justice and on the ideal structure of society in their entirety.[4] Having dealt with human governance, Marsilius then addresses Church government. Christ, he tells us, ordained the apostles as teachers of the Gospel, giving them authority to teach, to administer the sacraments, and to bind and loose sins. These apostles later bestowed their authority upon others, who in turn passed it down through the Apostolic Succession. Some priests also received human authority to direct worship and maintain property in order to avoid scandals

---

2   O'Donovan (1991), p. 11. She also lists William of Ockham as an influence.

3   Namely the situation of the papacy. Marsilius (2001), pp. 4–5. Marsilius addresses his discourses to the Holy Roman Emperor Louis IV. Both were opponents of Pope John XXII. Louis also gave sanctuary to other opponents of John, such as William of Ockham, who in turn was influenced by Marsilius.

4   Marsilius does refer to the Bible and the Fathers in his first discourse, but he refers to Aristotle more than five times as often as Scripture. He often seems to use his Biblical and Patristic references to support Aristotle's position. At one point (p. 38), Marsilius even refers to 'the divine Aristotle'.

in the Church. Ultimately, Peter was given charge of the Church on earth, but no ruling power over those outside the Church, contrary to the claims of some popes, who wished to exercise secular power. Rather, it was the secular powers that should have the authority to decide who exercised which office in the Church.

In Discourse 2, Marsilius distinguishes between three senses of 'judge': anyone who discerns or knows, an expert in law, sometimes called an advocate, and a ruler who passes judgement on his subjects. He argues that those who claim that the pope and his bishops and priests are judges in the third sense, the position he attributes to the papacy of his day, are mistaken. In fact, Marsilius informs us, the human judge, in the third sense, must regulate all human activity that affects others. 'To this coercive judgement all men, lay and clergy, must be subject'.[5] This civil regulation includes limiting the number of clergy, so that they do not disturb the polity of the city or resist the ruler 'by their insolence or freedom from necessary tasks'.[6] While the civil judge must deal with breaches of human law, however, there is only one judge of transgressors of the Divine Law, namely Jesus Christ. He, through His mercy, does not immediately reward or punish those who observe or violate Divine Law. There are, nevertheless, judges who can state what must be done or avoided to gain eternal life, namely the priests. While they have moral authority to command, however, they have no power to coerce: Christ did not force anyone to obey Him, and nor did He authorise anyone else to do so. Marsilius has told us both that Christ has established the priesthood through the Apostolic Succession, and that the state can decide who holds what office in the Church. He tries to resolve this apparent conflict by explaining that the character imprinted on the priest by Christ enables him to administer the sacraments. The power to supervise others, to preach and to order the Church, however, comes from the people. This power is not coercive unless so designated by the state.

This, then, is a model of the Church that is theologically top-down but administratively bottom-up. Alan Gewirth (1951) points out that this model subverts the entire hierarchical structure then in place. It equalises the laity with priests, bishops and pope, and gives entire control of the Church to the people. In the state, he tells us, power flows from the people to the head, which then gains coercive authority over the people. In the Church, there is no such coercive downward authority. The priests are only teachers of the Gospel and dispensers of sacraments: they have no authority to command others.[7] Notice, however, the sources of these models. The administrative model, which is developed in Discourse 1, comes largely from, and on the authority of, Aristotle. In this discourse, Aristotle's views are presented

---

5   Ibid., p. 163. Marsilius points out (p. 186) that Bernard of Clairvaux challenged Pope Eugene III to usurp, if he dared, the lordship if he was an apostle, or the apostolate if he was a lord, because 'you are plainly prohibited from having both. If you wish to have both at once, you shall lose both'. Compare Bernard of Clairvaux (1976), p. 59.

6   Ibid. Marsilius thinks that the state should both approve candidates for ecclesiastical office and appoint them when approved. Compare pp. 263–4.

7   Gewirth (1951), pp. 262–4. Compare O'Donovan (1991), pp. 20–27 and Neuner and Dupuis (1996), p. 281.

more frequently and more forcefully than any others. By contrast, the theological model, as set out in Discourse 2, comes largely from the Bible. Its main argument seems to be that the priests have spiritual government within the Church, but Christ forbids priests to have coercive power.[8] Nevertheless, Marsilius seems to base his ideas about Church Government on his ideas about secular government. Thus, for Marsilius, power in the Church comes from below and is delegated to the clergy by the congregation, to whom they are accountable, even if they have been appointed by the secular authorities. The bottom-up and egalitarian view of the Church at which he arrives, however, bears some similarities to the Free Church views of authority we surveyed in chapter 3.

Rome rejected Marsilius' theory in favour of its preferred theory of the monarchical Episcopate in which the sacred had priority over the secular, and Marsilius was duly excommunicated on 23 October 1327.[9] We must now explore how Marsilius' successors developed his views, and whether there is a link between these views and those of the Reformers.

William of Ockham

Ockham's contribution to this debate came about almost incidentally. Rather than trying to make political or theological points about authority in the Church, his central concern was to win the Franciscan dispute with John XXII over the status of evangelical poverty. John repeatedly condemned the Franciscan position, and the Franciscans appointed Ockham to argue their case. John's unrelenting opposition led Ockham to the conclusion that John was a heretic, and forced him to grapple with issues of ecclesiastical authority.[10]

Ockham argued that Peter received power to rule in the Church, but he received this power only to build up the Church, not to exercise dominion over it.[11] The pope was obliged to provide for the Church, not for himself, in a way that brought honour to God. He had no power to impose on Christians anything not necessary for salvation.[12] He argued, based partly on Canon Law, that secular power came from the people, who delegated their authority to the ruler, while spiritual power came directly from God.[13] He agreed with Marsilius, however, in commending Aristotle's theory of kingship as a model for Church government.[14] Ockham, then, while he took an Aristotelian position on Church government, spiritualised this theory to the extent that his grounds for arguing in favour of a monarchical system of Church

---

8   Compare Matthew 16:16–19, Luke 22:24–26 and O'Donovan (1991), pp. 24–7.

9   For the Bull of Excommunication, see Thatcher and McNeal (1905), p. 324. This is a translation of Denzinger (1932), pp. 226–7.

10   O'Donovan (1991), pp. 13–15.

11   Ockham (1995), pp. 219–21.

12   Ockham (1998), pp. 94–5.

13   Ockham (1992), pp. 111, 113–4 and 159–61, and Ockham (1995), p. 256. Compare McGrade (1974), p. 150 and CIC, volume 1, columns 52–3.

14   Ockham (1995), pp. 127 and 238.

government were based at least in part on Biblical sources. His treatment is not entirely spiritual, however, in that in addition to its debt to Aristotle, it also draws on Roman legal theory.

John Wyclif

For Wyclif, the Bible is the one perfect Word of God, eternal and unchanging, in which all being, truth and law stand revealed, and by which all earthly claims to authority are judged. It follows from this that it is vital that everyone can read God's Word in a language he or she understands. Since the Bible is God's law, it follows that no other law is necessary in the Church. Accordingly, we should reject the pope's laws and all other rules that do not conform to God's law, stand firm against the 'bringinge in of sectis and lawis þat Crist made not … alʒif the fende coloure it'.[15] Unlike Christ, the pope 'wole gladly make a lawe and make þis lawe in more worchip and more drede þan Cristis lawe'.[16] Wyclif clearly has no time for Canon Law.

When it comes to papal power, Wyclif takes a similar line to Marsilius, arguing that the pope is subject to the secular rulers, as Christ was subject to the emperor and his representatives. The way the popes acquired temporal power, far from being the result of holiness and piety, was 'envenymed wiþ sin'.[17] If the pope were superior to secular kings, they would be deprived of their lordship, and each would rule only a small part of his realm. Neither the pope nor the clergy have coercive power, even in the spiritual realm, as Peter had no power over the other apostles, and the jurisdiction of the hierarchy is of secular origin. Unlike Marsilius, however, the later Wyclif denied the pope even the spiritual keys: these, he thinks were passed down from the apostles, first to the priests, and then to all Christians. Each is damned by his own guilt or saved by his own merit, depending on whether he has bound or loosed his own soul.[18]

Wyclif also opposes the ecclesiastical hierarchy. He insists that there can be only one head of the Church on earth, namely Jesus Christ, Who remains the head until the last day. Any attempt to establish a Vicar of Christ on earth denies Christ's power; to do so would be sheer presumption, and would put the devil above Him. On secular power, Wyclif also takes a different line to Marsilius: he believes only those in a state of grace are entitled to dominion. Despite the similarities, however, Wyclif may not have read the *Defensor Pacis*. Workman (1926) tells us that Wyclif does not appear to have heard of Marsilius, since he never refers to the *Defensor*,

---

15   Winn (1929), pp. 137–8, from chapter 10 of *Þe Chirche and hir Membris*. In Middle English, the thorn (þ) is pronounced 'th', and the yogh (ʒ) is pronounced 'ch' or 'y', depending on the context.

16   Ibid., p. 71, from *de Papa*.

17   Ibid., p. 44, from the sermon on the gospel for the 6th Sunday after Easter.

18   Winn (1929), p. 95, from the sermon on *Þe Gospel on þe Chairinge of Seint Petre*.

while scrupulously naming his other sources.[19] There is also no evidence that there was a copy of Marsilius at Oxford at the time. Winn (1929) suggests that William of Ockham was a much more significant influence on Wyclif.[20] It therefore seems that whatever influence Marsilius had on Wyclif, this influence was filtered through Ockham, and therefore spiritualised to some extent. Nevertheless, when Gregory XI issued a bull condemning Wyclif on 31 May 1376, he stated that Wyclif had adopted some of the teachings of Marsilius, 'in changed terms'.[21]

Two other things stand out about Wyclif's ecclesiology: it is individualistic and it is egalitarian. Everyone stands before God to be judged according to his or her own conscience, and the only standard against which conduct may be compared is Scripture. There is little, if any, sense of the action of the community or the fellowship of believers. Workman points out that Wyclif neither raised nor answered the question of who is to interpret Scripture.[22] As we shall see, taking this idea to its logical conclusion would lead to rampant individualism in the Church a few hundred years later.

Early Reformers

Martin Luther

In his *Treatise on Good Works* (1966) Luther states that the second work of the fourth commandment (Honour your father and mother) is

> to honor and obey the spiritual mother, the holy Christian Church, the spiritual authorities, so that we conform to what they command, forbid, appoint, order, bind and loose. We must honor, fear and love the spiritual authorities as we do our natural parents, and yield to it in all things not contrary to the first three commandments.[23]

These, on Luther's division, are 'you must have no other gods', 'you must not make wrong use of the name of the Lord', and 'remember to keep the Sabbath day holy'. Unfortunately, the Catholic Church was busy selling indulgences at the time. The pope and the cardinals were living in splendour and ruling over their subjects like princes. The only sin for which a believer was punished, Luther tells us, was non-payment of a debt to the Church, which could lead to exclusion. Adultery, unchastity, usury, gluttony, worldly show, and excessive adornment, by contrast, were left unchallenged and unpunished. The spiritual condition of the Church had become worldlier than the world. There was much spiritual power, but no spiritual government. Luther believed himself duty–bound to resist the authorities, as pious

19   Workman (1926), volume 1, pp. 132–3.
20   Winn (1929), p. 61.
21   Thatcher (1907), volume IV, p. 380.
22   Workman (1926), volume 2, pp. 19–20.
23   Luther (1966), p. 87.

children would resist parents who had become insane. We should honour Roman authority as our highest father, but we should not allow the cardinals to seek their own improvement at the expense of Christendom, for this would risk its destruction. Rome, he thought, had put up a bar against all reform to keep protection for the liberty of the hierarchy to act corruptly, and in the process had deprived others of their Christian liberty.

Luther explores this subject further in *The Freedom of a Christian* (1970b). He explains that 'A Christian is a perfectly free Lord of all, subject to none; a Christian is a perfectly dutiful servant of all, subject to all'.[24] He derives these apparently contradictory statements from 1 Corinthians 9:19 and Romans 13:8a. Christian liberty, according to Luther, is the result of justification brought about by faith. This faith exalts every believer to the extent that spiritually he is lord of all things, and therefore nothing whatever can harm him. This power, however, is not temporal: such power belongs to kings and princes. Rather it is the spiritual power that is made perfect in weakness. Since Christians are all priests, they all have this liberty.[25] Luther believed that the Church hierarchy had produced such a pompous display of corruption, power and tyranny that it was worse than any earthly government. Liberty had been replaced by bondage to human works and laws. 'We have become … servants of the vilest men on earth, who abuse our misfortune to serve only their base and shameless will'.[26]

There is no excuse to turn liberty into licentiousness. Paul tells us that everything is lawful, but not everything is beneficial.[27] As Christians, however, we are responsible for the effects of our actions upon those who are new or weak in the faith. We should do everything we can to avoid causing them to stumble.[28] Thus, Luther thinks, though we should boldly resist the teachers of tradition and of Canon Law, we should observe the laws and traditions so as not to offend the weak.[29] We should note that Luther's view of liberty is not individualistic. He recognises that there must be limits on liberty to preserve the integrity of the Church community. Within a Church, there must be a substantial area of shared faith and common mind if factions and disputes are to be avoided. Those weak in or new to the faith may be discouraged if they see anarchy and disorder in the Church. The liberty of the individual must be limited to some extent by the needs of the Church, if the Church

---

24 Luther (1970b), p. 277.

25 Luther also argues that all Christians, as priests, have the power of the keys, which can only be used to deal with sin. See ibid., pp. 203–4 and 244.

26 Ibid., p. 292. Luther also believes that a wise ruler will govern better by a natural sense of justice than by law (p. 226).

27 1 Corinthians 6:12, 10:23.

28 Matthew 18:6, Mark 9:42, Luke 17:2.

29 Luther states that 'it would be a good thing if canon law were completely blotted out, from the first letter to the last, especially the decretals … The study of canon law only hinders the study of the Holy Scriptures. Moreover, the greater part smacks of nothing but greed and pride' (pp. 94–5).

is to retain cohesion as a community of the faithful, without dissipating its energies or fragmenting.

Luther's view is in many ways similar to Paul's view. For Paul, freedom was release from the bondage of sin and adoption by the Spirit of God.[30] Paul's analogy is with Roman slavery laws. A slave could gain freedom in two ways. He or she could buy his or her own freedom, or someone else could buy them and set them free. In the latter case, they would be under obligation to their benefactor. Paul believes that since Christ has bought our freedom at Calvary, we must act as Christ directs: 'For whoever was called in the Lord as a slave is a freed person belonging to the Lord, just as whoever was free when called is a slave of Christ (*doulos estin Christou*)'.[31] In slavery to Christ there is perfect freedom, since everything is permitted to the believer,[32] if done rightly. This freedom is not for self-indulgence, but for loving service to other Christians.[33] Thus while Christians can live as they like, their lives should glorify God and build up the Church.

Both Luther's and Paul's concepts differ significantly from Aristotle's idea of liberty, which stated that each person had the freedom to take up any of the roles defined by society. Once one had taken up a particular role, however, one was bound to obey the rulers exactly.[34] A more Biblical view might be that in Christ, believers are freed from the restraints of society to become what God wants them to be. They should then use this liberty to build up the fellowship of the Church so that it can serve in the world. We should also note that Luther retained a respect for the authority of the offices of senior Churchmen. There is no suggestion of replacing the episcopacy with a set of councils to rule the Church. Incumbents may have behaved corruptly, not to mention disgracefully, but this did not nullify their offices. The existence of corrupt bishops does not invalidate the office of episcopacy. Luther spoke out against the behaviour and teaching of those who placed Canon Law and tradition above the Bible, often vigorously denouncing them. Nevertheless, he believed that Christians should obey the authorities, provided that in doing so their behaviour did not conflict with the Scriptures.[35]

Luther sets out his view of righteousness (*gerecht*)[36] in the *Preface to Romans* (Woolf, 1956). He includes his comments on justice in his treatment of faith, which he described as 'a living and unshakeable confidence, a belief in the grace of God so

---

30   Romans 8:12–23.

31   1 Corinthians 7:22.

32   1 Corinthians 6:12, 10:23.

33   Galatians 5:13–15.

34   Aristotle (1996), pp. 134–5.

35   See in particular *That a Christian Assembly has the Right and Power to Judge all Teaching* ... in Luther (1970a), pp. 305–14. We should note in passing that Luther did not accept the whole of the New Testament as canonical.

36   *Gerecht*, like *tsedaqah* and *dikaiosunē*, carries the twin connotations of justice and righteousness. Compare Messinger (1982).

assured that a man would die a thousand times for it'.[37] This is a gift of God through the Holy Spirit. Luther continues:

> Righteousness means precisely the kind of faith we have in mind, and should properly be called 'divine righteousness', the righteousness which holds good in God's sight, because it is God's gift and shapes a man's nature to do his duty to all … he pays God the honour that is due to Him, and renders what he owes. He serves his fellows willingly according to his ability, so discharging his obligations to all men. Righteousness of this kind cannot be brought about in the ordinary course of nature, by our own free will, or by our own powers.[38]

Righteousness, or justice, then, is giving everyone his or her due in the sight of God: giving everyone what God through Christ has told us is due to him or her. This link between justice and faith distinguishes Luther from Plato and Aristotle, who regarded justice as giving everyone what humans think is their due. In fact, Luther utterly rejects Aristotle's philosophy. In section 25 of *To the Christian Nobility of the German Nation* (1970b), he stresses his grief that 'this damned, conceited, rascally heathen has deluded and made fools of the best Christians with his misleading writings. God has sent him as a plague upon us on account of our sins'.[39] It seems that Luther is concerned to remove Aristotle's influence from theology and return to a more Augustinian, and therefore Neoplatonic, position. Luther also argues that the secular authorities are neither inferior to nor subject to the pope. They are free to pursue their calling, just like other Christians. All Christians, however, are subject to the secular authorities.[40] Luther argues his case entirely from Scripture, rather than from secular writers, and he does not seem to be concerned with the details of Church structures. His main concern is to resist greed and tyranny, and replace them with faith and liberty.

He was condemned on 15 June 1520 by the Bull *Exsurge Domine*.[41] However, while Luther's ideas about the power of the pope bear some similarity to those of Marsilius, a point strongly emphasised by his opponents, who tried to accuse him of Marsilianism, and to rebut him accordingly,[42] it seems that they are not derived from them. Luther appears consistently to argue primarily from the Bible, with only occasional references to the Fathers, particularly Augustine. He also seems to be consistent in his rejection of Aristotle in favour of Augustine. We must therefore

---

37 Woolf (1956), p. 289.

38 Ibid.

39 Luther (1970b), pp. 92–4. In *Table Talk* (1911), section 479, pp. 211–2, Luther accuses Thomas Aquinas of placing Aristotle above Scripture. I have already argued that this is not true. See above, chapter 4.

40 1 Peter 2:13–15.

41 Excerpts of this Bull are translated in Rupp and Drewery (1970), pp. 36–40. Formal excommunication followed in the Bull *Decet Romanum* on 3 January 1521 (pp. 62–7).

42 *Exsurge Domine*, for example, accused Luther of being Wycliffite. Wyclif had already been condemned for adopting some of the teachings of Marsilius, 'in changed terms'.

conclude that Luther's ecclesiology is not greatly dependent on either Marsilius or Aristotle.

John Calvin

Calvin's approach to authority is more structured than Luther's approach. In book 4 of the 1559 edition of the *Institutes* (1957), he argues that the only acceptable form of Church government is 'the order in which the Lord has been pleased that his Church should be governed'.[43] The ministers, in Calvin's view, operate as Christ's substitutes. They are the Church's safeguards, through whom Christ discharges His gifts to the congregation, thus exhibiting Himself through the energy of the Holy Spirit to prevent the Churches from being vain or fruitless. He believes that of the five offices of Church Government named by Paul, only pastors (*poimenas*, also translated 'shepherds' elsewhere) and teachers (*didaskaloi*) have an ordinary office in the Church. The others were necessary for the formation of the Church, but the offices died out with their bearers in the early Church. God only raises up prophets and evangelists now when necessary to deal with specific situations.[44]

The Church can never dispense with pastors and teachers, and Calvin believed that while a teacher could only interpret Scripture, the office of pastor included teaching, presiding over discipline, and administering the sacraments. Deacons, who could be men or women, administered alms and cared for the poor. In the early Church, he tells us, pastors and teachers were called presbyters, and they elected one of their number as bishop, to preside over debates when dissension arose. The bishop, however, had no dominion over his colleagues. As evidence for this, Calvin points out that Jerome wrote to Evangelus that the Epistles to Timothy and Titus conflate the functions of bishops and presbyters, the only difference being that only bishops could ordain other clergy.[45]

Calvin admitted that each province had had an archbishop, and that patriarchs were set over the Council of Nicea. He believed, however, that their function was to preserve discipline, and that they were appointed very rarely. This, of course, was the start of the hierarchy Calvin rejected, but he denied that the ancient bishops wished to order Church government in an unscriptural manner. It is, however, difficult to sustain the view that Christ laid down a single order of Church government in the Bible. Ignatius of Antioch, in the epistles generally accepted as genuine, wrote in the early Second Century to the bishop and deacons at Ephesus and Tralles, and the bishop, presbyters and deacons at Magnesia. He wrote to the bishop with the presbytery and deacons at Philadelphia and Smyrna, and made no mention of the order of government in his letter to Rome. This would suggest that there were a

---

43   Calvin (1957), volume 2, p. 315.

44   Ibid., pp. 315–8. Calvin believed that since God, through Moses, set out the order of government for Israel, Christ cannot have done anything less than set out the order of government for the Church.

45   Schaff and Wace (1999), volume 6, pp. 288–9.

number of variations on the theme of the threefold ministry, with different Churches assigning authority differently among those in positions of ministry. Nevertheless, Calvin seems correct in his contention that the episcopacy in the Roman Catholic Church at the time of the Reformation bore little resemblance to Church government in the New Testament.

Calvin's approach to Christian liberty is in many ways similar to Luther's treatment, but he develops the subject further. Calvin also believes that unbridled liberty often leads to licentiousness. He divides liberty into three parts. Firstly, believers must renounce the righteousness of the law, and look only to Christ. This does not mean abandoning the law altogether: it still reminds the faithful of their duty and encourages them to purity and holiness. Secondly, believers voluntarily decide to obey the will of God. Thirdly, believers are free to use or omit things not necessary to salvation, according to whether or not they find them useful. This liberty is a spiritual matter, which gives peace to troubled consciences. It frees the faithful from constant worry about whether or not they have sinned. It does not, however, give them licence to act without consideration for their weaker brethren.

Calvin's view of liberty is no more individualistic than Luther's view. Christians are still subject to one another in love. Calvin also shared with Luther a respect for the offices of the Church. Calvin, however, regarded the episcopacy as a corruption of Biblical Church government, and therefore sought to abolish it. The authority of the Church, for Calvin, is a purely spiritual power to be used for edification not for destruction. It is to be used only by those who are servants of Christ, and at the same time servants of the people in Christ: in other words, ministers. The authority is given to their ministry, not to the people who exercise it. It is only to be used in the name and according to the Word of the Lord. Thus those who teach must expound the Bible, and test all their teaching against it. They must not frame new doctrine, or admit any new doctrine framed by others. This applies both to individuals and to the Church as a whole. Inerrancy was the crux of Calvin's argument with Rome over Church authority. He believed that his opponents had added new doctrine, which went beyond Scripture, and claimed inerrancy for the Church, no matter what pronouncements she made, on the grounds that the Holy Spirit would lead her into all truth and preserve her from error. Calvin, by contrast, believed that the Church was only infallible when she discarded human wisdom entirely and relied solely on the Holy Spirit.[46]

Calvin explains his views on justice in *A Harmony of the Gospels* (1994). In his commentary on Matthew 1:19, which describes Joseph as a righteous man, he tells us that 'the righteousness here commended consists in a hatred and detestation of wickedness'.[47] He goes on to say that Matthew 7:12 gives a short and simple definition of what fair-dealing (*aequitatum*) means: 'In everything do to others as you would have them do to you; for this is the law and the prophets'[48] Calvin's

---

46 Calvin (1957), volume 2, pp. 393–8.
47 Calvin (1994), p. 62.
48 Ibid., pp. 231–2.

view of justice, then is both prescriptive and proscriptive. Positively, we should treat others as we would want them to treat us; negatively, we should abstain from evil.

Calvin shares some elements of Luther's view of Aristotle. In book 1 of the *Institutes*, he denounces those who 'led away by absurd subtleties, are inclined, by giving an indirect turn to the frigid doctrine of Aristotle, to employ it for the purpose both of disproving the immortality of the soul, and robbing God of his rights'.[49] Calvin, however, was prepared to use Aristotle to support his case where Aristotle was helpful. A few chapters later, Calvin, while dealing with the faculties of the soul, distances himself from what he sees as confusions and subtleties in Aristotle, but uses Aristotle as support for his view that the intellect governs the will. In book 2, when Calvin treats of the bondage of the will, he uses Aristotle's distinction between incontinence (forgetting morals in the heat of the moment) and intemperance (obstinacy – persisting in the evil choice once made) to illustrate Augustine's treatment of the ease with which the intellect can hold that murder or adultery in general is wrong, while simultaneously conspiring to commit the offence.

These examples do not appear to support any charge of inconsistency against Calvin, but rather it appears that he was using Aristotle intelligently here. Aristotle's name carries weight, so it seems eminently sensible for Calvin to use Aristotle's views where they both make sense and support his case, provided they do not conflict with the Bible. However, when discussing philosophy, Calvin refers more often to Plato and Cicero than he does to Aristotle.[50] He was greatly influenced by humanism, a school of thought to which Scholasticism was anathema, and therefore his theology was dominated by a sense of being laid hold of by God's Word. It therefore seems unlikely that the Aristotelian Marsilius had a significant influence on his thought. He seems to have seen Aristotle as a distraction from theology, rather than an aid to it.

Huldrych Zwingli

Luther and Calvin were highly influential in the Reformation, and both ensured that their theology was thoroughly grounded in their understanding of the Bible. The more radical of the Reformers, however, whose views we shall consider shortly, and who I believe distorted Luther and Calvin's theology, grew up in the circle of Huldrych Zwingli. I shall later argue that they developed Zwingli's work in a direction that gave less weight to Scripture than the early Reformers did. We will therefore need to examine Zwingli's thought more critically and in more detail.

Zwingli was opposed to any suggestion that human teaching or statutes had any salvific value. Article 16 of *The Defense of the Reformed Faith* (1984a), states that 'In the gospel we learn that human teaching and statutes are of no use to salvation'.[51] We

---

49   Calvin (1957), volume 1, p. 53.

50   This is at its clearest in his discussion of the faculties of the soul (Calvin, 1957, volume 1, pp. 166–8), in which he discusses the ideas of Plato and Cicero at length without mentioning Aristotle. Compare Vos (1985), pp. 120–121 and 170.

51   Zwingli (1984a), p. 62.

might reasonably conclude from this that Zwingli would reject Aristotle's teaching as useless, but in fact this is not the case. In *An Exposition of the Faith* (Bromiley, 1953), Zwingli explains that the Church needs government, 'whether of princes or of the nobility',[52] to punish flagrant sinners, and that without civil government a Church is maimed and impotent. Zwingli then goes on to summarise Aristotle's theory of civil government, which he recognises and commends, although he also recognises the right and duty of the Church to criticise secular rulers who misbehave, using Biblical examples to support this teaching. He then summarises his position: in the Church, both government and prophecy are necessary, but prophecy takes precedence. Just as humans are made up of body and soul, with the soul taking precedence, 'there can be no Church without government, although government supervises and controls those more mundane circumstances which are far removed from the things of the Spirit'.[53]

Zwingli offers a parallel argument in articles 36–39 of *The Defense of the Reformed Faith*, this time arguing from a Biblical perspective that all the faithful are bound to obey the rulers, except when they command things contrary to the faith. In the title of article 43, he states that the dominion of a single ruler under God is the best and most stable order, while one who rules by his own whims is the worst.[54] He then argues from the Old Testament that when the Jews adhered to God and obeyed His commandments, they prospered, but whenever they turned away, disaster followed. The emphasis here is on the ruler being obedient to God, rather than on the polity he or she leads, and Zwingli does not seem to be unduly concerned what polity is in place, as long as the ruler(s) are Godly.

The gospel, as Zwingli understands it, is God's will made known to humans and required of them: a mixture of commands, prohibitions and promises. It does not include the Mosaic Law, which, Zwingli believes, has been cancelled, or indeed, any human law: 'Those who trust in the Lord Jesus Christ with all confidence will no longer be damned by any law'.[55] The moral principles behind the law, however, which were instituted by God and not by humans, continue in force and will always do so. He is emphatic, however, that the Word of God is 'certain and can never fail. It is clear and will never leave us in darkness. It teaches its own truth. It arises and irradiates the soul of man with full salvation and grace. It gives the soul sure comfort in God'.[56] This understanding is open to all that seek to learn from the Scriptures, rather than seeking to justify their own opinions. Since God's word is so sure and clear, there is no need for other teachers, guides or interpreters.

---

52 Bromiley (1953), p. 266.

53 Ibid., p. 268. Ulrich Gäbler (1987, p. 37) states that Zwingli was a Scotist, and his thought was therefore in the Aristotelian tradition, yet the consequences of this have not been investigated thoroughly. W.P. Stephens (1992, p. 14) adds that in a letter of 1511 Zwingli is spoken of as an Aristotelian.

54 Zwingli (1984a), pp. 249–69 and 281–2.

55 Zwingli (1984a), p. 66.

56 Bromiley (1953), p. 93.

Law, Zwingli argues, comes from human reason, and is therefore carnal. From such things, nothing good can come. Therefore human laws cannot be good, and to present them as such is hypocrisy. Worse, to suggest that any human invention is of divine origin is 'blasphemy of God, an abomination, and despicable folly'.[57] True Christians have the Spirit of God, Who gives them perfect freedom. Those begotten of the Spirit can no longer be dependent on any written law.[58] Article 34 states that 'So-called spiritual authority cannot justify its pomp on the basis of the teaching of Christ'.[59] This article is a challenge both to spiritual pride, and to any doctrine of authority which gives one person power over another. Nowhere in the words of Jesus, Zwingli tells us, do we find Christ giving anyone power over others. By contrast, the most humble, submissive and childlike is the most prominent. Thus, the greatest in the Kingdom of Heaven, which Zwingli equates with the Church, is the servant of all. Those who seek power over others exclude themselves from the Kingdom, and therefore from the Church, in the process. Even Peter did not claim authority over his fellow elders, but appealed to them as equals to look after the flock of God.[60] This, Zwingli thought, forbade priests and clerics to rule. 'Priest' for Zwingli, meant an older, well-disciplined or earnest person. 'Bishop' meant simply a guardian. Neither priests nor bishops should force anyone to obey them, but persuade them to obey willingly and gladly. They should govern only in spiritual, not worldly matters. Christ refused to pass judgement when asked to adjudicate in a dispute over an inheritance,[61] and so priests should not judge others: rather they should suspend judgement until Christ's return on the last day.[62]

Zwingli accepted Paul's argument that Christians should sort out their own disputes, rather than taking them to secular magistrates.[63] He did not believe, however, that such disputes should go to the priest. Rather, he thought, the warring parties should go to the humblest and simplest of the congregation who would decide the issue. Priests should not judge, but admonish others to live together in peace according to God's word. Unfortunately, Zwingli is not entirely consistent on this point. If we take article 34 as the qualification for the priesthood, as I believe he intends, the humblest, if not necessarily the simplest, members of the congregation would be the priests. When it comes to the power of the keys, his view seems even more extreme. He did not accept that Christ gave the keys to Peter in any

---

57   Zwingli (1984a), p. 69.

58   Ibid., p. 66.

59   Ibid., p. 243.

60   1 Peter 5:1–3.

61   Luke 12:13ff.

62   Article 36, pp. 249–51. We should note that this is an egalitarian view. Hans von Campenhausen (1997, p. 13) argues that this position is not apostolic: 'In the primitive community freedom reigns, but not equality. At no time is there a lack of outstanding personalities'.

63   1 Corinthians 6:1–11.

straightforward sense, but rather that Peter's profession of faith opened the door for Jesus to found the Church on Himself.[64]

Zwingli thought the pope had confused Peter with Christ, the only foundation on which the Church could stand. He accused the pope of preaching that Peter alone was the foundation of the Church, and explained that the power of the keys was given, not to Peter, but to the whole Church. This power enables Christians to preach that 'we are impotent on our own account and incapable of doing anything'.[65] When sinners repented, the disciples loosed their sins through baptism, assuring them of God's forgiveness. Whenever the Gospel was rejected, they bound sins by shaking the dust off their feet, as a testimony that Sodom and Gomorrah would fare better on the Day of Judgement. Anyone who claims to forgive sins beyond this is usurping God's honour, which is idolatry.[66]

Finally, we come to Zwingli's views on human and divine righteousness. Human righteousness, he tells us, is generally defined as giving to each his own. God's righteousness, however, differs from human righteousness, because it is entirely free from selfishness and desire. Since everything is God's and nothing is ours, God can owe us nothing. Divine righteousness, then, is as far above human righteousness as God is above humanity. Nevertheless, the Bible has spelt out what is required of humans. For Zwingli, Christ has summed it up in Matthew 5:8: 'Blessed are those whose hearts are pure; they shall see God'. Zwingli expounded this in the form of ten challenges, parallel to the Decalogue, which he regarded as God's commandments. He believes that God calls us to forgive, not to kill or to be angry, to refrain from quarrels or lawsuits, to shun adultery and lust, not to swear, to give away our possessions, to do good to all – even enemies, neither to steal or to covet, to refrain from speaking evil or unnecessary words, and to love our neighbours as ourselves. This, he believes, is giving each his or her due. Only through Christ can we keep these commandments.[67] He believed that magistrates should restrain those who failed to do so. If all together endeavoured to keep God's word, they could expect to live in God's peace. Bromiley points out that while, on specifically Christian issues, Zwingli appeals exclusively to Scripture, on other matters he is open to both reason and revelation as sources of instruction. In consequence, he is not as consistent as Luther or Calvin, and his teaching includes elements that at times may be alien to the Evangelical Gospel he is trying to preach.[68]

We have seen, then, that while these three Reformers differed on matters such as the status and content of the Bible, and the nature of episcopacy, a consistent stream of thought on some matters runs through their writings. They were all agreed that the episcopacy of the time was corrupt, and needed reform. They sought to replace an authoritarian system of Church government with a system more centred on

---

64 Article 50, pp. 299–300.
65 Article 50, p. 311.
66 Article 51, p. 315.
67 Zwingli (1984b), pp. 5–11.
68 Bromiley (1953), p. 242.

servanthood. They all wanted to give more emphasis to the Bible than was customary in the Church at the time, although they differed on exactly what position the Bible should have. None of them was particularly keen on Aristotle, although Zwingli was less consistent on this point than Luther or Calvin. They all, with varying degrees of success, tried to reinvent the Church in a form closer to primitive Christianity, and they all sought to be true to their principles. These principles, however, were not always held by their successors. I shall argue that later Reformers corrupted the views we have discussed by adding ideas from variety of other sources to them. We shall now consider some later Reformers.

Later Reformers

In the centuries that followed, there were many competing voices arguing about the true nature of the Church. Among these voices, three names stand out as particularly influential representatives of their traditions: Walter Travers, John Knox and John Owen. David Cornick (1998) explains that many English Presbyterians drifted into rationalism and Unitarianism in the late eighteenth century,[69] and that those who remained Trinitarian were influenced substantially by Scottish Presbyterianism. If we are to understand the thought of the United Reformed Church in the twenty-first century, then, in addition to examining Congregationalism, we need to examine the roots of the Scottish Presbyterianism that fed into it, through the work of the most prominent Scottish Presbyterian, John Knox, as well as the work of his English counterparts. English Puritan thought had a much greater effect on radical Protestants, so we must also consider arguably its most influential, if not its most famous, spokesman on Church authority in the sixteenth century, Walter Travers.[70] John Owen was Congregational in his churchmanship, and was highly influential in the development of the Congregational tradition. He is sometimes seen as the finest Congregational theologian. When it comes to later Separatists, I have chosen those whose views seem most extreme, to show how far some Separatists were prepared to push their case. They also provide what seem to me the clearest indications of the undercurrents I have tried to identify in mainstream Congregational thought. Once I have set out their views, I will contrast them with the views of those of a more orthodox mindset, in an attempt to place them in their proper context. We begin, however, with Travers.

---

69 Cornick (1998), pp. 90–93, Compare Cragg (1970), pp. 135–8. Geoffrey Nuttall (1957, p. 112) believes that the requirement for Congregationalists to testify to their experience as well as their faith when joining the Church protected them from the rationalistic tendencies that proved so destructive in Presbyterianism.

70 Stephen Brachlow (1988, passim), shows that while Thomas Cartwright was more famous, Walter Travers took a harder line, and therefore had a greater influence on the more radical Puritans.

Walter Travers

Walter Travers, in *A full and plaine declaration of Ecclesiasticall Discipline* ...
(1574), sets out his Presbyterian views on Church government. Travers saw much
to criticise in his mother Church, and proposed a return to apostolic discipline. He
believed that if any form of government, Church or secular, was set up correctly in
the first place, changing it could only lead to ruin. He argued that Christ would have
abrogated His Kingly office if He had not established an order of government for the
Church. God ordered Israel's worship through Moses, Christ is greater than Moses,
and so He must have provided for the ordering of His Church, and done so better
than the Mosaic Law provided for Israel. Travers concurs with Calvin that Christ did
so by establishing a single order for the Church. Discipline, however, was gradually
changed, and with it, Travers thinks, doctrine was corrupted.[71] He saw a link here
– if Church discipline was decreed by Christ, and people had changed it, what was
to stop them from altering Christ's other commands? The Church of England had
reformed its doctrine, but adopted Roman discipline and tyranny wholesale, so that
'all the gouernment of our churche is not taken out of Goddes worde but out off the
cannon lawe and decrees off Popes'.[72] Travers believes the Consistory, made up of
pastors, doctors [teachers] and elders, should rule in the name and authority of the
Church. This council was modelled on the Sanhedrin, and it had authority to correct
and, if necessary, suspend members from Communion or expel them altogether.[73]

   This authority requires the consent and agreement of the congregation, so that
the Church is governed by all. Note the difference here. Luther thought the bishops
governed as ordained leaders of the Church. Calvin thought the ministers governed
as God's representatives. Zwingli thought the ministers governed by persuasion.
None thought that lay people should be involved in Church government. Travers
thought that popular election of Church leaders was the key to good Church
Government.[74] Travers argues, based on the account of the Council of Jerusalem in
Acts 15:1–29, that the early Church was governed by all its members. The key to
this passage is verse 22: 'Then, with the agreement of the whole church, the apostles
and elders resolved to choose representatives and send them to Antioch with Paul
and Barnabas'. Travers clearly believes that authority can only be exercised with
the consent of the people, and that the community exercises authority, in a mix of
aristocracy and democracy, under Christ's sovereignty. The Church is governed by
a heavenly order:

> for it is the best state off all whereas all these thre meete in one kinde of gouernment: as
> both Plato thought and Aristotle and the other chiefe and excellent Philosophers: that state
> I say / wherin all the cytezins obediently submit themselves to god which commandeth /
> as kinge and monarch / and the assembly which decreeth by his will and authoritie / where

71   Travers (1574), pp. 6–13.
72   Ibid., p. 16.
73   Ibid., pp. 160–161.
74   Compare O'Donovan (1991), p. 125.

also the assembly decreeth no weighty matter without the consent and approbation off the reste off the churche and people.[75]

In other words, Travers has drawn his ideas about Church government from both the Bible and the ideas of philosophers. The only philosopher I have found, however, who advocated a mixed system of government of this sort is Cicero, and his proposed division of power is totally different to that proposed by Travers.[76] Certainly, neither Plato nor Aristotle took this view. Aristotle held that an elected monarchy is the ideal, while democracy is the least damaging if the ruler is corrupt, because it gives the maximum freedom to the most people. Yet even he believed that the people should obey the leaders without question after electing them. He did not allow for debates – the leaders ruled, the people obeyed. Plato did not view either liberty or democracy as good things – he regarded the philosopher-king, a benevolent tyrant, obeyed by all, as the ideal. Nor did he require consultation in the sense Travers seems to think, any more than Aristotle did. Plato also believed that the people should obey the authorities without question.[77]

It may be instructive here to compare Aristotle's democratic ideas with the dynamic of the Council of Jerusalem. Democracy, for Aristotle, was based on liberty. One effect of this liberty, he thought, was that all should rule and be ruled in turn, and that what the majority approved must be considered right and just. Since everyone was equal in a democracy, the poor had more power than the rich did, because there were more of them, and the will of the majority was supreme. Another effect was that people could live as they liked, since conformity or obedience to another's will was indistinguishable from slavery.[78] The Council of Jerusalem operated rather differently. Following a dispute in Antioch, Paul and Barnabas went to Jerusalem to consult the apostles and elders. There was much debate, and Peter then made a speech, which was received in respectful silence. James, who seems to have been both the host and the chairman of the meeting, summed up, found scriptural backing for Peter's position, and decided what to do. The apostles and the elders, together with the whole of the congregation then selected delegates to deliver the decision to Antioch.

Notice that this was not a democratic meeting. The leaders of the Church discussed the issue, and a consensus seems to have emerged. The chairman decided what to do, and the whole Church was involved in the selection of the delegates to Antioch, not in the decision itself. This is rather different both from Aristotle's view of democracy, and from the way many Churches organise themselves today. Often, Churches hold a meeting at which everyone may speak, and then a vote is taken,

---

75   Ibid., p. 178. Thomas Aquinas comes to a similar conclusion. Compare ST IaIIae.105.1.

76   Cicero (1928), pp. 81–107. See particularly p. 105.

77   See above, chapter 3.

78   Aristotle (1996), p. 154.

the result being binding on all.[79] The Council of Jerusalem seems to have been a discussion by the leaders, under the guidance of the Holy Spirit, leading to a decision by consensus. There is no suggestion that a vote was taken, or that the rest of the Church was consulted. By contrast, Aristotle believed that the will of the majority should decide an issue, and that what they decided was, by definition, right and just. Travers's view of the role of the laity, however, seems to differ from the Council of Jerusalem in two ways.

First, he believed that lay people should be consulted on the substance of the matter in question, second, that they should be consulted before the decision was made. Neither appear to have happened in Jerusalem, where the congregation was consulted about the implementation of the decision, but seemingly not the decision itself. Travers seems to be moving the goalposts gently here. Before Travers, the will of God as discerned by the clergy or elders was the main factor in ecclesiastical decision-making. This was the practice in both Episcopal and Presbyterian Churches at the time. Travers sought to move the emphasis to the will of God as discerned by the people, but in the process, he seems to have introduced elements of Aristotle's democratic ideas into Church decision-making.

John Knox

Knox does not appear to have produced such a developed theory of the Church. The three main ecclesiological documents to which he contributed are *The Confessioun of Faith Professit and Beleivit be the Protestantis Within the Realme of Scotland ...*, *The Buke of Discipline* (Laing, 2004a, both written in Old Scots), and *The Confession of our Faith, which are assembled in the Englishe Congregation at Geneva* (Laing, 2004b, written in English, hereafter the *Geneva Confession*).[80] Knox was very strict about ceremonies and discipline, and he clearly expected offenders to be dealt with: in addition to the books of discipline, he wrote an *Order of Excommunication and Public Penance* (Laing, 2004c).

In *The Confessioun of Faith*, Knox explains that 'we maist constantlie belief, that God preservit, instructit, mulitpleit, honourit, decoirit, and frome death callit to lyfe his Kirk in all aiges, fra Adam, till the cuming of Chryste Jesus in the flesche'.[81] Knox clearly believes that the Jews who lived before Christ were members of the Church. Knox defines the Church, which he restates has always existed and will always continue to exist, as 'A company and multitude of men choisin of God, who rychtlie worschip and embrace him, by trew fayth in Christ Jesus'.[82] This, as

---

79   Such Churches do, however, emphasise the need to seek a consensus under the Holy Spirit before taking a vote. Experience suggests this does not always happen.

80   The closest Knox got to writing a political theory seems to have been his infamous *First Blast of the Trumpet against the Monstrous Regiment of Women* (Laing, 2004b, pp. 365–422).

81   Laing (2004a), pp. 98–9.

82   Ibid., p. 108.

we might expect, is a description of the Church Invisible, albeit one in which the position and contribution of the Jews is more highly visible than usual, and certainly more explicit than in Travers's understanding of Church. With this understanding of Church in mind, then, we move on to *The Buke of Discipline* and the *Geneva Confession.*

The fourth and seventh sections of the *Buke* concern ministers and their lawful election, and ecclesiastical discipline respectively. It is Knox's view that each congregation should elect its own minister. Should they fail to do so within 40 days of a vacancy, the Superintendent and his council may present them with 'a man quhom thai judge apt to feade the flock of Christ Jesus'.[83] If a local Church refused to accept the Superintendent's nominee, after finding nothing reprehensible in his doctrine or conduct during a public examination, and without presenting their own candidate, they would then incur the censure of the Council and the wider Church. If both the local Church and the Superintendent presented suitably qualified candidates at the same time, the candidate of the local Church would be appointed.[84]

On ecclesiastical discipline, Knox believes that no commonwealth can flourish or endure for long without 'gude lawis, and scharp execution of the same'.[85] The *Buke* divides crimes into those that should be punished by the state, and those that should be punished by the Church. Knox produced at least three such lists during his career, and no two lists are the same, so we should not read too much into their contents, but all three are agreed that activities described by the Bible as sinful should be punished by the Church, even if they are not civil crimes. The Church must draw the sword against such offenders, cursing and excommunicating them, but the road to such action should be grave and slow.

The *Geneva Confession* also expects sinners to be punished by the Church. It explains: 'what so ever it be that might spott the Christian congregation, yea, rather what so ever is not to edification, oght not to escape either admonition or ponishment'.[86] According to the *Buke*, for offences that had not caused public scandal, the first stage was a private admonition by the offended party. If the offender repented at this stage, that was the end of the matter. If not, the next stage was a private admonition by the minister. Again, if the offender repented, the matter was closed. If the offender did not repent after this, the matter went to the Church, who were informed of the offender's conduct, and from this stage on, public penance was required. If, after three weeks, the offender had shown no signs of penitence, he was excommunicated. If the offence was widely known, the first stage of discipline was a summons to appear before the minister, elders and deacons to be admonished. If the offender repented and performed public penance, he was restored to fellowship. If not, the matter went

---

83   Ibid., p. 189.

84   Ibid., pp. 189–91. Knox wanted to avoid the imposition of ministers if at all possible.

85   Ibid., p. 227.

86   Laing (2004b), p. 205.

to the Church as before.[87] Similarly, the *Geneva Confession* mandates private and public rebukes before excommunication, and exhorts Churches not to seem more ready to expel than to receive sinners after repentance. They should not forbid the excommunicate to hear sermons, which might help bring them to repentance. It concludes with an exhortation that no punishment, correction, censure or admonition should go beyond what God's word, applied with mercy, could lawfully bear.[88]

According to the *Buke*, after excommunication had been pronounced, no one except the offender's wife and family were permitted to have any kind of conversation with him, in eating or drinking, buying or selling, or for any other reason except as commanded or permitted by the minister for his conversion. The sentence was published throughout Scotland, so that no one could feign ignorance. If the offender had any children between excommunication and repentance, they could not receive baptism until they reached the age to make their own profession of faith, unless the mother or other friends offered and presented the child, abhorring and damning the iniquity and obstinacy of the impenitent.[89] Knox argues that this sanction, though severe, is justified, because 'the sacramentis appertene onlie to the faithfull and to thair seade: but suche as stuburnlie contempt all godlie admonitioun, and obstinatlie remane in thair iniquitie, can nocht be accompted amangist the faithfull'.[90]

Knox, then, advocated a strict and severe form of Calvinism. He thought that each congregation should choose its own minister, who should then govern the congregation, assisted by the elders and deacons. He was particularly severe when it came to discipline, in some cases visiting the sins of the fathers on their children. Knox's polity is more conservative than Travers's. He follows the traditional line that the ministers and elders should discern the will of God, and that their conclusions should form the main factor in ecclesiastical decision-making. Knox also set up Presbyteries, each with a Superintendent and a council, to supervise the local ministers. While the people had the final say in who led the local congregation, once leaders had been appointed, the people were morally obliged to follow where they led.

John Owen

John Owen, who unlike Travers and Knox, was of a Congregational persuasion, dealt with the polity of the Church in general in the second part of his *True Nature of a Gospel Church and its Government* (Goold, 1968). The Church, Owen tells us, can only exercise the authority of Jesus Christ, given to it according to His laws and directions, and for the edification of the faithful. This power rests fundamentally in

---

87   Laing (2004a), pp. 227–30.

88   Laing (2004b), pp. 205–6.

89   Compare Calvin (1957), volume 2, pp. 452–71. Calvin never suggests here that children should be punished for the sins of their fathers. It is not clear what Knox thought should happen if the impenitent sinner was the child's mother.

90   Laing (2004a), p. 231.

the Church itself, but it is exercised by those called to ministry. Each believer has the power, given to him when he first believed, to become a Son of God. This gives him the right to all the privileges and duties of membership in the family of God. This is the foundation of all Church power, but the individual cannot exercise it individually, it must be used by the congregation. Where two or three are gathered, they have the power to meet together in the name of Christ for their mutual edification, to exhort, instruct and admonish one another, and to pray together. Where many are gathered, they may perform all Church duties, and make joint solemn confession of their faith. This, however, does not complete the Church-state, because it cannot attain its ends without ministry. These rights and powers do not constitute authority. This is exercised by those called, chosen, appointed and set apart by the congregation. They can only be appointed to offices instituted by Christ, and therefore those appointed to such offices receive the authority granted to their ministry by Christ. It is Christ's command, Owen continues, that the whole Church submits to the authority of their ministers, and obeys them in matters concerning 'the performance of all duties which the Lord Christ requires, either of the whole church or of any in the church'.[91] Despite this requirement of obedience to the ministry, '[e]very individual person hath the liberty of his own judgment as unto his own consent or dissent in what he is himself concerned'.[92]

In *An Inquiry into the Original, Nature, Institution, Power, Order, and Communion of Evangelical Churches*, Part 1 (Goold, 1965), Owen explains that this authority is quite unlike worldly authority: those outside the Church have no right to its privileges and no obligation to perform its duties. Nor can they participate in this authority, because Christ alone has the power to send people out to do what He commands. The Church should not be subject to political pressure. Equally, those within the Church cannot import structures similar to civil government, like Canon Law, into the polity of the Church.[93] Finally, in *The Duty of Pastors and People Distinguished* (Goold, 1967), Owen warns his readers not to cut themselves off from the Church or disobey their ministers in the name of liberty.[94]

Owen was active in the 1640s, and clearly saw a need to restrain the excesses of some of his fellow dissenters, which we shall discuss shortly. He did not, as far as I am aware, comment on how the congregation should make decisions in their meetings. Presumably he thought that this was a matter for the local Churches to decide themselves. He does not seem to have advocated democracy in the same way as Travers. Owen clearly thought of the believers as individuals, but argued that they should act collectively. While there is individualism in his thought, it is tempered by

91   Goold (1968), p. 40.
92   Ibid.
93   Goold (1965), pp. 237–42. Interestingly, there is no mention of democracy as a structure of civil government here.
94   Goold (1967), p. 45.

his corporate view of the Church.[95] His view that the authority of ministers comes from the nature of their ministry, rather than being a consequence of their ordination, is, of course, Calvinist. In Owen's thought, then, we have several ingredients of the Congregational tradition that followed. The Church makes decisions as a body, involving the participation of the whole congregation, each Church may appoint its own minister, but having done so must accept his spiritual leadership; and no one is forced to act against his or her conscience.

Radical Protestants

Stephen Brachlow, in his *Communion of Saints* ... (1988), devotes a chapter to the government of the gathered Church between 1570 and 1625. He explains that early Stuart Puritans tried to balance the power of clergy and laity, although they often disagreed about where the balance should lie. Paul Baynes, for example, one of the non-separating Puritans, believed that Luther and Melanchthon were too radical in allowing any power to the congregation. Baynes, in fact, believed that the Church officers derived their authority directly from Christ, not through the Church.[96] On the other hand, William Ames and Robert Parker, who did leave the Church of England to gather new Churches, believed that the every member of the Church had the power of Christ.

Parker argued that in Matthew 16:19, Christ gave the keys to the whole Church. Peter, he thought, symbolised the person of the church not of bishops but of all the faithful. Both Ames and Parker, in fact, considered that the people were superior to the ministers, yet even so, they believed that ministers received their authority directly from Christ. Parker in particular was ambivalent concerning the power to govern the Church. He sometimes argued that power rested more with the rectors than with the people, sometimes the reverse.[97]

Brachlow believes that the key to resolving this apparent contradiction is a distinction between possession of power, which was the position of the congregation, and use of power, which was the prerogative of the ministers. The congregation, however, should not be entirely passive, but should approve action and appoint officers. Despite this ambiguity, however, we can see that certain features of what was to become Congregational government are beginning to appear here. The participation of lay people in approving or rejecting ministerial proposals, the

---

95   Geoffrey Nuttall (1957, p. 54) states that Owen thought that causeless separation from the established Church was a grave sin, although he also thought it wrong to remain in a gravely disordered Church.

96   Brachlow (1988), p. 169.

97   Ibid., pp. 171–2. Brachlow quotes Ames saying that 'as all sense and motion of a sensitive creature is derived from the head and into every particular member, so also all his spiritual virtue is derived by influence from Christ into his church'. (Ames, 1659, p. 144). Ames also said that 'the authority of administering divine things is immediately communicated from God to all lawful ministers'. (Ames, 1643, volume 1, p. 154).

appointment of Church officers, and perhaps even a rudimentary version of the conciliar model of the Church are detectable.

It is not clear that either Ames or Parker supported democratic Church structures, or that they thought the congregation could make proposals of their own; nevertheless, their views lead in this direction. In the Separatist Churches, however, democracy played a much larger part, although according to Brachlow they were far from the democratic extremist mould into which they were often cast. Robert Browne, who was sometimes seen as subordinating the ministry to the congregation, considered that the congregation should be stricken with the ministers' worthiness, and abase themselves according to their own unworthiness. They should yield to the ministers, gladly suffer correction, and put into practice any duty the ministers assigned them. Nevertheless, there was a strong democratic streak in Browne's thought.[98] This tension here between the aristocracy – we might say autocracy – of ministerial government and the democracy of government by the congregation led to squabbles in his Church which eventually resulted in Browne's ejection by his own congregation. It would, however, be dangerous to conclude from this that the congregation reigned supreme in Separatist Churches. They, like the non-separating Puritans, tried to balance ministerial authority with the authority of the congregation, but were no more successful in drawing a precise boundary between the two.

Puritans, both Separatists and non-Separatists, were united on one point here: participation by the congregation did not extend to the administration of the sacraments. This was solely the duty of the ministers. The Baptists were the first to cross the line and deny this. Ordination, similarly, should only be carried out by elders, unless a Church had no elders of its own, and no other elders lived nearby. Although the Separatists emphasised democratic government, they were not egalitarian, in that they insisted that everything be done in order, with due respect for the ministerial hierarchy. Brachlow points out that Puritans of all stripes were opposed to the Episcopate, which they saw as tyrannical. Baynes and Ames believed that ecclesiastical power resided in each local congregation. If synods were held, they could only advise.[99]

Only Parker was prepared to allow synods authority, and he argued that synods had only the authority the participating Churches delegated to them. These positions, like their positions on authority in the local Church, are ambiguous. Brachlow tells us that Ames for example, would allow for synods to censure and even excommunicate for open heresy or similar crimes, yet Ames is silent about the necessity of consent from the local minister. This is a surprising omission, given the strength of the link between minister and congregation in Puritan thought. Similarly, Baynes allowed that the temple at Jerusalem had certain reserved powers over the synagogues, and

---

98   Ibid., pp. 175–6. While Brachlow uses the word 'democratic' throughout this section, it is clear that Browne thought the people held 'the power of government immediately under Christ' (p. 176). This form of democracy is therefore not entirely government by the people, but also contains theocratic elements.

99   Ibid., pp. 177–81.

therefore that a synodical body might have powers over a local Church in some situations. Most Separatists took a more openly Congregational line – that synods, while useful as forums for debate and encouragement, should not challenge the autonomy of a local Church. Yet Browne reasoned that if many Churches joined together, the synod's authority must be greater than that of its constituent Churches, a seemingly Presbyterian approach that was not always well received by other Separatists.[100]

To summarise, Puritans were agreed that authority in the local Church should be shared between the minister and the congregation, in a mix of aristocratic and democratic government under Christ's Kingship. They did not, in general, think that synods had authority over local Churches. Their views on where the balance of power should lie were ambiguous, and covered a range of different options. They were generally Congregational in ethos. While in some ways their views on authority overlapped with the Presbyterian Walter Travers, the radicals seem to have drifted further towards democratic government.

While we seem to have established a historical link between Travers and Aristotle, we have not established such a link between Travers and his successors, or between later Puritans and Aristotle. Nevertheless, Travers had influence, and his views are strikingly similar to the more developed views of many Puritans 50 years later. It would be surprising if they had not incorporated Travers's views into their thought. This may have encouraged them to adopt democracy, a form of government that had at best a limited place in the civil government of the time, as the form for lay participation.[101] The next major development in this story, however, was caused as much by political events over which few Churchmen had control as by philosophical or theological development. We now turn our attention to events during the turbulent years of the English Revolution.

Ranters, Seekers and Levellers

In *The World Turned Upside Down* (1975), Christopher Hill[102] explores the development of radical ideas caused by the unprecedented freedom of speech during the English Revolution from 1640 to 1662. Hill traces some of the more extreme views back to Luther, and his doctrine of the priesthood of all believers. In the mediaeval Church, the priests ruled. They could easily convince the frustrated,

---

100 Ibid., pp. 211–7.

101 Only male property owners were able to vote at the time. The majority was excluded from the franchise. Compare Hill (1975), p. 15.

102 Hill, as far as I know, has written the only published history of ideas for this period. Unfortunately, he seems to have a Marxist agenda, which appears at times to colour his interpretation unduly. Nevertheless, I have yet to find anyone who disputes the facts Hill presents. Many histories of the Reformation do not discuss these radicals, as most historians regarded them as part of the lunatic fringe. Therefore, few histories can be used to provide alternative viewpoints. The only exception I have found is by Kenneth Hylson-Smith (1996), whose views we shall consider shortly.

seemingly helpless masses that they were sinful, and then discourage them from trying to resolve the problem, instead encouraging them to confess, pay the appropriate fee for an indulgence, and be absolved. This commercialisation was widely recognised as an abuse, prompting much of the popular backing for Luther's protest. Since Luther's doctrine internalised the sense of sin, priestly mediators were no longer needed. Inward penitence replaced outward penance. This set some free from the terrors of sin. God spoke directly to the consciences of the elect, without priests or sacraments, and so the old hierarchy became unnecessary. The reprobate were sunk in sin, but the elect, and the elect alone, were truly free, since they understood and co-operated with God's purposes.[103] This freedom, as we have seen in our discussion of Luther, is Christian liberty rather than Aristotelian democracy.

This situation led to the emergence of what Kenneth Hylson-Smith (1996) describes as the 'temporary but interesting spectacle of the radical sects of the Interregnum period',[104] from which only the Quakers survived. This, he tells us, was largely the result of Oliver Cromwell's promotion of liberty of conscience. Those who were honest, Godly and conscientious, who were genuine in their profession of Christianity, and who genuinely sought their own salvation should be allowed to form a Godly nation, without the constraints of an authoritarian and didactic Church. Parliament duly set about reforming the Church of England, dismantling Laud's doctrinal, disciplinary and liturgical system, and purging the lower clergy, many of whom had Royalist sympathies.[105]

Hill concentrates on the extreme fringe of the left wing of the Church – groups like the Ranters, Seekers and Levellers, who insisted in various different ways that ministers should be elected by the congregation and paid for by voluntary contributions. They agreed that all Protestant sects should be tolerated, and that discipline should be Congregational with no coercion behind it. They denied the importance of the sacraments, and of synodical structures. Many denied the need of clergy altogether, and would happily accept the leadership of a layman.[106] Hylson-Smith sets out the context in which these groups operated. In seventeenth century England, most people believed that God and the devil intervened daily in the details of their lives. Most believed in witches, fairies and charms. In due course, Protestantism helped eliminate these views, but in the 1640s, many were still deeply superstitious. This encouraged them to accept religious prophecy. If, as many believed, God spoke directly to the elect, it was their duty to publish His message.[107] This, then encouraged the rise of both prophets and Messianic figures.

Hill, however, believes that the liberal views of the radicals owed as much to politics as to theology. Censorship during the Commonwealth was lighter than it had ever been before or would be again for a considerable period, largely due to

---

103 Hill (1975), pp. 152–3.
104 Hylson-Smith (1996), p. xiv.
105 Ibid., pp. 193 and 223–5.
106 Hill (1975), p. 36.
107 Hylson-Smith (1996), pp. 203–4.

the tolerant views of Oliver Cromwell. Charles I had tried to rule on his own for 11 years, and when he summoned the Long Parliament in 1640, it rebelled against his authoritarian rule, and eventually executed him. Since Parliament had successfully rebelled against an authoritarian king, the people felt more secure about rebelling against an authoritarian Church. This led them to believe that they could say what they liked without fear of censorship, and it was a small step from this position for them to argue that their beliefs were not subject to examination by others. If one was justified by faith, and that faith was known only to oneself and God, what right had others to judge by appearances? This personal relationship with Christ gave people inner hope, and this in turn gave them the confidence to seek greater religious and political freedom.[108] If all were priests, all had equal claim to discern the will of God, everyone's opinion was equally valid, and all had the right to be heard. This view encouraged the laity to seek a more democratic style of Church government.

When it came to the Bible, Hill tells us, the radicals adopted two main approaches: they either treated its stories as myths, which could be interpreted however the reader chose, not necessarily considering the original meaning, or they denied its infallibility and subjected it to close textual criticism.[109] Some Ranters even supported the burning of Bibles. The halfway house was selective use of the Bible, picking out helpful sections and ignoring the rest. Some thought that the Bible could be subordinated, not merely to human conscience, but to human convenience. Since in their eyes the text was clearly corrupt, it could not be relied upon as a guide, leaving only reason as a trustworthy guide. Reason, according to this theory, possessed greater illumination than Scripture.[110]

These views are clearly extreme, but I would submit that we can usefully learn from them nevertheless. Heretics and extremists have often taken an undercurrent of mainstream theology and carried it to its logical conclusion, ignoring the tension inherent in the fact that God is both more and less than anything we can say about Him. God is greater than any theology, and both human language and human thought have their limitations. In some ways, however, mainstream Christianity has benefited from what it might consider the lunatic fringe through gaining clarity and understanding from the ensuing debates on where to set the boundaries of acceptable belief.[111] These views may help us to understand mainstream Christian thought of the time. Lest anyone think that they disappeared entirely at the Restoration, we

---

108 Ibid., p. 152. Even the Levellers, arguably the most politically active group, did not appear to seek a universal franchise, although some Levellers may have been in favour of this. In their manifestos, Levellers sought to ensure that all financially independent men, except certain supporters of Charles I, were able to vote. C. B. MacPherson argues that the Levellers' main aim was to repeal the provision introduced by Henry VI which restricted the franchise to men who owned land worth more than 40 shillings a year. See Aylmer (1975), pp. 9 and 162–8, Brailsford (1961), pp. 96–138 and MacPherson (1962), pp. 107–59.

109 Hill (1975), p. 261.

110 Ibid., pp. 262–4. Compare Hylson-Smith (1996), p. 208. Advocates of this approach included John Milton and Henry Parker.

111 Compare Augustine (1984), book XVIII, chapter 51.

should note that the Quakers emerged from, and have their roots in, this period of turmoil. Some of these ideas also survive in modified form in the Congregational tradition. In all these groups, the radical edge of the surviving Separatist views has become considerably more moderate now. Furthermore, as we shall see shortly, respectable members of society were prepared to publish similar views, and in some cases even more extreme views, several years later. Hill may well be correct in his conclusion that the views of radicals such as these were in part a product of the political atmosphere of the time. It would seem, however, that other influences were also at work. Hill does not mention Zwingli at all, which suggests he may not have been aware of Zwingli's views, but there are some striking similarities between Zwingli's thought and these radical ideas.

The most obvious is that the Separatists share Zwingli's view that the elect, those begotten of the spirit, are able to discern God's will without needing other teachers, guides or interpreters. The Separatists, however, went much further than Zwingli, and claimed that the faithful could form their own views in the light of reason, under the guidance of the Holy Spirit. Some of them did not even believe that the faithful were dependent on the Bible, which, as we have seen, Zwingli thought was essential. They believed, like Zwingli, that everyone had freedom of conscience under the Holy Spirit, that no one had any power over the consciences of others, although they understood this in a much more individualistic way.[112] Both denied the need for clerics. Both believed that the keys were given to the whole Church, not just to the pope or the hierarchy. Finally, neither placed much stress on the sacraments, although Zwingli never totally abandoned them in the way that some later radicals did. These similarities do not establish a historical link, but the number and closeness of the resemblances between Zwingli's thought and that of the radicals suggests that he had at least some degree of influence on their thought, although the radicals went some way beyond what he thought was acceptable. Certainly, they were closer theologically to Zwingli than to Luther, Calvin or the prominent followers of either. It seems highly unlikely that all the radicals' views could be the result of merely political influences.

Later Separatists

As we have said, those on the fringes of society were not the only ones to hold radical views. Even men as respected as Joseph Priestley, the chemist and Unitarian minister, were prepared to argue that responsibility in the Church is assigned to individuals by individuals, and that the limit of that authority was expulsion of those unable to accept this. Those expelled should not be considered Christians, but must be treated as human beings. They should not suffer civil punishment. Priestley was

---

112 Compare Zwingli (1984a), Article 34.

opposed to all restrictions on dissenters.[113] Richard Watson[114] espouses a similarly libertarian and individualistic view in his pamphlet *A Brief State of the Principles of Church Authority* (1773). He argues that liberty is the supreme virtue. No one should judge anyone else, and no group is subject to inspection by another. His definition of the Church is instructive:

> We may define a Christian Church, to be, a Voluntary assembly of men acknowledging the truth of the Bible and meeting together for the public worship of God. A Church is a voluntary Assembly; and, as such, subject to no external superintendence or jurisdiction: but as no business can be commodiously transacted in any Assembly without the establishment of certain rules, appointing the time and places of convention, and regulating the proceedings of the Members when met, every Church must be subject to an internal jurisdiction, must have an internal power of framing such ordinances as may be thought most conducive towards the attaining the end of their meeting.[115]

Watson goes on to say that this internal jurisdiction is limited to the power of expulsion. He refuses to divide the believers into clergy and laity, and asserts that anyone can preach, subject only to the requirement for decency, order and mutual edification. The ministers must perform tasks enjoined by the Bible in accordance with the Bible, but should perform other tasks as directed by the Church. Here we have democracy in matters of administration and individualism in matters of faith and conscience taken to great lengths. Watson says nothing about the Kingship of Christ here. It is almost as if he sees the Church as a society worshipping God for the mutual edification of its members, a rather unconventional view of the reason for worship. Expediency seems to be the driving force behind this form of Church order. Not surprisingly, many within the Congregational tradition were much more cautious about full-scale democracy and individualism than Watson was, and their views developed into mainstream Congregationalism, which we now consider.

Congregationalism

The Development of the Congregational Churches

Geoffrey Nuttall (1957) tells us that the principles of fellowship, separation, freedom and holiness were determinative for Congregationalists.[116] The Church, for them, was a local, voluntary association of believers, who knew and manifested the gifts and graces of the Spirit, gathered together to worship God. While they maintained fellowship with other similar Churches, they believed that all the essential marks of Church were contained within the local Church. The Anglican view at the time

---

113 Priestley (1769).

114 The Methodist Richard Watson we will meet in the next chapter, lived from 1781 to 1833. He is not the author of this tract.

115 Watson (1773), pp. 6–7.

116 Nuttall (1957), p. viii.

that the Church of England was coterminous with the nation of England, leaving everyone with the right to be baptised, was therefore anathema to them. Since the Church of England was, in their eyes, corrupt, they felt as obliged to separate from it as they felt obliged to separate from the world. They were also convinced that set prayers and liturgy restricted the Holy Spirit, denying them freedom of worship, and that the Scriptures required of them a greater holiness than was evident in many of their fellow men and women. They believed that compulsion in matters of conscience was intolerable. [117]

They were called Congregationalists because they held it as both a right and a duty that all members of the congregation should share in decision-making. Given this standpoint, it was impossible for them to define the Church in terms of its ministry or the sacraments as administered by ministers, since the Church existed, and in places continues to exist, without a minister.[118] Not surprisingly, this stance, with its implicit criticism of the Church of England, led to opposition and persecution by the Anglican authorities, beginning with the 1662 Act of Uniformity. During the late seventeenth century, dissenters were frequently fined or imprisoned for holding assemblies. Ministers who refused to accept everything contained in the Book of Common Prayer were ejected from their parishes and thrown out onto the streets. Lay people unwilling to attend worship at, and receive Communion in, the parish Church were debarred from holding municipal office by the Test and Corporation Acts.[119]

Tudur Jones (1962) tells us that the Congregational Churches were exposed to both radical and conservative influences arising from the early years of Congregationalism. The political agitation of their forebears, in a successful campaign to force the repeal of the Test and Corporation Acts,[120] left many nineteenth-century Congregationalists in dread of talk of revolution, and therefore conservative. At the same time, they were sympathetic towards social problems, increasingly aware of the political activities of seventeenth-century Puritans, and therefore radical. While Congregationalists may have been reluctant to get involved in politics, they were quite prepared to help the socially deprived. Jones tells us that this action arose from their concern for personal salvation, from their interpretation of divine providence, and from their continual insistence on the usefulness of Christianity.

The attitude of Congregationalists at this point was highly individualistic. This social action was not just intended to improve the economic and social position of the poor, although it undoubtedly did so: its main aim was to convert the heathen, to save individual souls. For nineteenth-century Congregationalists, Jones tells us, providence overruled everything. It was responsible for all things from the gambler's throw to Christ's crucifixion. It follows from this that society was also governed

---

117 Ibid., pp. 104–5. Compare Nuttall and Chadwick (1962), p. 166 and Nuttall (1967), pp. 57–9.

118 Compare Nuttall (1967), p. 62.

119 Compare Jones (1962), pp. 46–71 and Nuttall and Chadwick (1962), pp. 151–87.

120 Jones (1962), pp. 143–5.

by providence. The distribution of wealth and social class was not accidental. Providence, however, is God in action. Nothing, therefore, can be static. By co-operating with God to change society, and encouraging new converts to do the same, we can learn something of His purposes. This should be the goal of all Christians.[121] Thus, we see that their individualism was intimately connected with their doctrine of providence. Traditionally, of course, the doctrine of providence has been seen in a much more corporate sense – that God provides for His people and the world. It seems that Congregationalists at that stage focussed more on the individual than the corporate aspect of salvation.

Finally, we come to the conflict of ideas that beset the Congregational Churches in the 1920s. This conflict was a response to the theological liberalism that had developed in the free Churches in the early twentieth century. Biblical criticism had, by the turn of the century, become widely accepted. It had become clear that the Bible was written by a number of different authors over a span of several centuries. This made it more difficult to claim that the Bible was the infallible word of God. Accordingly, it became increasingly fashionable to emphasise experience at the expense of doctrine. The 'quest of the historical Jesus' began with the suspicion that the apostles, and Paul in particular, had distorted the original image of Jesus by wrapping Him up in garments woven by their own convictions about Him.[122]

If they could find the true historical figure, Christianity could be remoulded in a way that might attract sceptics into the Church. One result of this approach was that 'Christ' became seen not as a title of Jesus designating his unique role in the salvation of humanity, but as a quality attainable by anyone who achieved humanity in all its fullness. This extremely liberal view was not well received by Evangelicals. In response to this, two trends in Congregational thought came to the fore: first, there was a revival of interest in the Reformed tradition, with its emphases on ordered worship, doctrinal orthodoxy, respect for the ministry and the value of the sacraments. Secondly, there was a reaffirmation of the earlier Separatist tradition, which, as we have already noted, had great similarity to earlier radical thought. It emphasised the voluntary character of a Church and the freedom of the congregation. Each individual was encouraged to seek ultimate truth, and not to restrict the action of the Holy Spirit. Worship was sincere, spontaneous and charismatic. Since all believers were equal, it followed that the minister's role should not receive undue emphasis. This view, Jones tells us, was adopted by most Congregational writers and leaders at the time. The majority of these scholars were also historians who were well aware of the situation of the early Puritans and Congregationalists. They were not ignorant people unwittingly destroying the Church of their fathers, Jones tells us, but promoting what they believed to be the authentic Congregational tradition.[123]

Congregationalism has drawn from many sources, ranging from the Separatist tradition to Baptists, Methodists and Presbyterians. It took part in the Evangelical

---

121 Ibid., pp. 191–2.
122 Ibid., p. 347.
123 Ibid., pp. 367–8.

Revival in the eighteenth century, and drew ministers from many other communions in the nineteenth.[124] Consequently, its theology has been enriched by other traditions; indeed it might be considered a theological melting pot. We should not, therefore, be surprised to find the effects of non-theological influences on the Church in its theology. We have found ideas in the modern Church which are strikingly similar to earlier ideas that I have argued came from extra-Biblical sources, and in some cases seem to conflict with Biblical views. This adds support to the case that these ideas, once imported into the doctrine of the Church, have become undercurrents of mainstream Christian thought.

P.T. Forsyth

Peter Taylor Forsyth was a Congregationalist theologian of the early and middle twentieth century. While he was of Independent persuasion and a supporter of liberty, he was wary of democracy, he was strongly opposed to individualism, and his views of authority and liberty were closely linked. Chapter 1 of *The Principle of Authority* (1952) begins 'There is only one thing greater than Liberty, and that is Authority'.[125] Forsyth then explores several aspects of authority at length. He states that it is impossible to argue for unlimited latitude of belief. This 'canonises liberty at the cost of truth',[126] leaving no room for revelation. Without such revelation, the Church cannot stand, as no one has any right to claim freedom '*from* the apostolic word, but only *for* that word'.[127] The Gospel comes before freedom. Christianity requires obedience first, and only the obedient are truly free. The Church only has liberty to be faithful to its trust or in it. Forsyth sees a confusion in the Church between secular and Christian ideas of liberty, however, and suggests that some sections of the Church have acted like 'a democracy with no other standard than the hour's majority of votes merely counted'.[128] Were any Church to abandon the guidance of God, or the deposit of faith, in the name of democracy, it would cease to be a Church. Ultimately, however, Forsyth concludes that there is a fundamental difficulty with democracy in the Church. Numbers do not create genuine authority in the Church, while in democracy there is no other authority. Democracy, in this sense, is both individualistic and subjective. The Church, for Forsyth as for so many, is fundamentally theocratic, not democratic.[129]

Of course, Forsyth's criticism still has weight. While all the free Churches we consider in this study emphasise in their official documents the need to seek a consensus under the Holy Spirit, as we shall see in the next chapter, there is still an inclination in many people and some Churches to make decisions using secular

---

124 Ibid., p. 464.
125 Forsyth (1952), p. 17.
126 Ibid., p. 217.
127 Ibid., p. 253. Italics Forsyth's.
128 Ibid., pp. 248–9.
129 Ibid., pp. 236–7.

forms of democracy. The antidote to this tendency, of course, is to bring deliberations before the throne of Grace, and to ensure that such discussions are grounded in the Gospel. Godly decisions can only be made under the guidance of the Holy Spirit, while in a democratic meeting in which everyone has their say and a vote is taken, it is all too easy to lose sight of God. It seems that the Churches are right to resist this form of democracy.

Forsyth, perhaps surprisingly, is grateful for the contribution of eighteenth-century individualism, which he describes as 'an extreme but necessary protest'.[130] He recognises, however, that individualism can easily develop into egoism, and become antisocial and anti-Christian. He identifies individualists with truants and anarchists. He acknowledges that Christianity should develop, sanctify and perfect the whole person, but argues that it does so only in a Church of people in 'loving, absolute, and corporate obedience to God in Jesus Christ, the Saviour of the race'.[131] The cure for such individualism, in other words, is corporate growth under submission to a superior authority, namely Jesus Christ. While Congregationalists have, at times, been individualists in both Forsyth's sense and mine, there seems to be a trend towards a more corporate understanding of the local Church in more recent Congregational thought. Forsyth is not always easy to read, and therefore his work has often received less attention than it deserves, but the direction of his argument seems to follow the trends Tudur Jones identifies in the Reformed tradition within Congregational thought, and can therefore be said to reflect at least part of the Congregational mainstream.

Conclusion

We have seen that the early Reformers, like their successors, rebelled against the authoritarian rule of the bishops, believing that Canon Law had deprived the faithful of the liberty that is theirs in Christ Jesus. It is clear, however, that neither Luther nor Calvin believed that Christian liberty allowed for individualism. They expected the Church to act corporately. Zwingli may have opened the door to individualism by suggesting that no one's conscience was subject to judgement by anyone else. This view was later extended by his more radical successors, who placed human conscience above Scripture, and therefore allowed the faithful total freedom in their interpretation of the Bible. Similarly, both Luther and Calvin believed that the ministry played an essential part in the Church, and that only ministers could use the authority possessed by the whole Church. Zwingli had no great respect for clericalism, and believed that anyone prepared to serve the Church could do so, provided the Church agreed. Since the ministry played no great part in Zwingli's

---

130 Ibid., p. 268. Forsyth is mainly talking here of individualism in the sense that the individual is more important than the community, but his comments apply equally well to individual freedom of conscience. He credits eighteenth century individualism with helping to produce modern constitutionalism and fostering the early stages of political liberty.

131 Ibid., p. 269.

schema, he believed that authority in the Church was shared among its members. This again tended towards individualism, and, since for Zwingli everyone was equal, it may in part have accounted for the growing democracy in the Churches of the Reformation over succeeding centuries. Clearly, other factors were involved. Travers's championing of Aristotle in his view that Church government should be a mix of the monarchical, aristocratic and democratic had influence among Puritans, and Marsilius may also have had an effect. The political situation in the seventeenth century, when radicals were at their most active, certainly helped the development of Independent views. Both factors encouraged democratic and individualistic views of the Church. Later Congregationalists tried to restrain the more extreme elements of these doctrines, but their influence in the Church is still visible.

It remains an open question how much direct influence the views of Aristotle and Zwingli had on the Church in the years after the Reformation. We have only seen one direct link, that between Travers and Aristotle. Nevertheless, the Churches of the Reformation have diverted steadily more power from their ministers to their members over the centuries, although they have retained their emphasis on seeking the guidance of the Holy Spirit. While the modern form of Church government – by discussion among the members followed by a vote – differs greatly from the form Aristotle proposed, it can be seen as a logical development of Aristotle's ideas. Equally, the similarity between Zwingli's views and those of radicals active generations later is striking. It seems to me that in many places these later views are logical developments of Zwingli's thought – the sort of developments we should expect to find if Zwinglian ideas had become an undercurrent of mainstream thought in the meantime.

It is clear, however, that democracy as an idea did not originate in the Church, and it is difficult to find evidence of democracy in the Bible or in the early Church, even a theocratically-oriented democracy under God in the modern sense.[132] It is therefore reasonable to classify democracy as an outside influence that has been incorporated into Christianity. Similarly, individualism does not feature prominently in the Gospels. It may have been a problem at Corinth, but Paul and others were eager to discourage it. It does not seem to have played a major part in the Church before the Reformation. It also seems reasonable to classify individualism as an outside influence. Democracy, when used to seek consensus under the guidance of the Holy Spirit, is probably not a harmful influence. It may be beneficial in many situations. Individualism, however, if taken to excess, can be as destructive of the Church as the narrow sectarianism that declares that only Church X is the true Church, and everyone else is wrong, deluded or heretical. It is difficult to see individualism as a harmless innovation. This, then, is how the situation of the Churches of the Reformation developed. We have seen that they abandoned Canon Law in favour

---

132 There are, of course, references to voting in the New Testament (see, for example, Acts 26:10 and the accounts of the trial of Jesus before the Sanhedrin). The religious leaders, however, rather than the ordinary people, took these votes, and therefore they do not represent democracy in the sense I use it.

of individual liberty. We must next consider how they regulate themselves, whether they have developed other structures that perform the same function as Canon Law, and if so, how they operate.

Chapter 7

Do the Free Churches
Also Have Canon Law?

Introduction

As we saw in Chapter 4, James A. Coriden (2004) defines Roman Canon Law as 'the rules that govern the public order of the Roman Catholic Church ... ecclesiastical regulations.'[1] This definition can easily be adapted to suit the Church of England, and perhaps to fit other Churches too. While the Church of England expresses many of its rules as Canon Law, the Free Churches do not. Early views on this subject are summed up by a statement of the 'trewe markes of Christes churche', made by Richarde Fytz, minister of the 'privye churche' in London, to Queen Elizabeth I, probably in 1571:

> Fyrste and foremoste, the Glorious worde and Euangell preached, not in bondage and subiection, but freely, and purelye. Secondly to haue the Sacraments mynistered purely, onely and all together accordinge to the institution and good worde of the Lorde Iesus, without any tradicion or intention of man. And laste of all to haue, not the fylthye Cannon lawe, but dissiplyne onelye, and all together agreable to the same heauenlye and allmighty worde of oure good Lorde, Iesus Chryste.[2]

We must now study the rules of the Free Churches, and their views on Church Law. We must also examine how important Church order and consistency of doctrine are to each Church, and how this is reconciled with its doctrine of liberty, particularly freedom of conscience.

As we saw in Chapter 3, the Methodist Church is organised nationally. Its decision-making body is its annual Conference, which makes decisions binding on all districts, circuits and local Churches. Although its decision-making body is national, all decision-makers are delegates of local Churches, circuits or districts, and therefore it sees its organisation as bottom-up.

Baptist Churches are organised locally. Wider structures exist, but their functions are largely (for some Baptists, exclusively) advisory. For Baptists, the local Church

---

1   Coriden (2004), p. 4.

2   Quoted in Harrison (1959), p 21. The original is in the Public Records Office, under the PROCAT reference SP 15/20, number 107 (1). Harrison's spelling is slightly different, and he cites another secondary source. This view was fairly widespread at the time. Cf. chapter 18 of John Knox's *Confessioun of Faith ...* of 1560 (Laing, 2004a, p 110).

contains all the necessary elements of the universal Church, and the Church Meeting, which is properly all the members gathered together and led by the minister and elders, makes decisions concerning the Church. This organisation is also bottom-up.

The United Reformed Church (URC) has both national structures, which tend to be Presbyterian, and local structures, which tend to be Congregational. General Assembly can make policy or decisions affecting the whole Church, and similarly Provincial Synods and District Councils can make policy or decisions concerning their area of influence. No such decision, however, can be implemented without the consent of the local Church. Each congregation is led by a minister and elders, who also represent the Church in its wider councils, but the Church Meeting is the final decision-making body locally. This structure is hybrid, with both top-down and bottom-up elements.

With these structures in mind, we begin with a more detailed consideration of the regulations of the Methodist Church.

The Methodist Church

John Wesley

Wesley was wholly committed to the Church of England. He saw himself as an Anglican priest, and encouraged the members of Methodist societies to remain Anglicans. Since doing so would place them under the Canon Law of the Church of England, Wesley had no need to set up an alternative. There is no evidence that he ever preached against English Canon Law. Albert C. Outler (Kirkpatrick, 1964) comments that Wesley deliberately designed Methodist services so that they were liturgically insufficient, leaving the people dependent on the Church of England for what was missing, and that he never tired of insisting 'We are *not* dissenters; we are *not* Sectarians; we will *not* separate!'[3]

Methodist discipline consisted of admonition, followed by the refusal to renew the membership tickets of disorderly Methodists at the quarterly visitation.[4] While there was no need to set up a system of discipline for lay Methodists, the same was not true of itinerant preachers. The first Conference, held in London in 1744, set up a disciplinary structure for their supervision. These rules were modified in 1753, and entitled *The Twelve Rules of a Helper*.[5] Rule 10 states 'Be punctual. Do everything exactly at the time. And do not mend our Rules, but keep them; and that for conscience' sake.'[6]

---

3   Kirkpatrick (1964), p. 13. Italics original.
4   See Sermon 107, *On God's Vineyard*, section IV.2–3 in Wesley (1986), p. 512. Such expulsions were usually carried out quietly. Those causing scandals, however, were liable to have their expulsion announced in the meeting.
5   CPD, pp. 77–8.
6   Ibid., p. 77.

Much like the Church of England at the time, ministers had to follow certain rules that did not apply to lay people, although these rules were not expressed in the terminology of law, and they do not seem to have been understood as Canons in the Anglican or Roman sense. This situation changed when the authorities expelled Methodists from the Church of England after Wesley's death, forcing Methodists to produce their own procedures for Church government. These procedures largely took the form of resolutions of Conference, and they were generally reported and circulated as Conference minutes. The most influential document to emerge from this process was a series of resolutions adopted by the 1820 Wesleyan Methodist Conference.

The Liverpool Minutes

This Conference, held in Liverpool, adopted a series of Resolutions on Pastoral Work. This document has become known as the *Liverpool Minutes*.[7] It makes two important references to law. The first, in *Resolution III: The Pulpit*, restates Wesley's doctrine that grace does not do away with the need for righteousness, and urges preachers to resist antinomian abuses. The second, on *Official Meetings*, develops the place of law in the Church further:

> Let us remember that the only way to live in peace is to walk by rule; and in the administration of all our affairs, in the Society and in the Circuit, let us cultivate the spirit and exhibit the manner of men who are acting for God in the service of His Church.[8]

This seems to be a development of the tenth rule of a helper. We should note that this resolution is, at least implicitly, much wider in scope. If the only way to live in peace is to walk by rule, it would seem to follow that everyone, not just ministers, should follow the rules. It was for later Conferences to develop these rules, and to comment on how they should be interpreted.

While the *Liverpool Minutes* were influential, events thereafter were chiefly influenced by individuals. Two people played key roles: the Biblical scholar Adam Clarke, whose work is not relevant here, and Richard Watson, who has been described as 'the chief theological spokesman for nineteenth century British Methodism in the transition from Wesley.'[9]

Richard Watson[10]

In his *Theological Institutes* (1840), Richard Watson sets out what he sees as the three legitimate uses of Church authority. These are firstly, the preservation and the

---

7   Ibid., pp. 79–87. The current resolutions date from 1971, are much shorter, and do not discuss law.

8   Ibid., p. 86.

9   Langford (1998), p. 18.

10 This is not the Congregational Richard Watson whose 1773 tract we reviewed in the last chapter.

publication of sound doctrine; secondly, the regulation of worship, the management of the affairs and direction of the general conduct of the whole society; and thirdly, the infliction of censures.[11] We have already discussed the first and third,[12] and we now come to the second, the regulation of the members of the society. This, Watson tells us, 'consists in making canons or rules for those particular matters which are not provided for in detail by the directions of Scripture.'[13]

Watson states that this power has been used to excess in many Churches, leading them into legalism, but he also concedes that 'there is a sound sense in which this power in the church must be admitted, and a deference to it bound upon the members.'[14] Scripture plainly requires believers to engage in public worship, for example, but it does not state when, how often, and in what style it should be conducted. It is for the local Church to decide these matters and produce regulations. The Church may do so, however, only provided the rules she prescribes are aimed at the edification of the Church, practical purity, order and decorum in worship, and usefulness to the world. They must be controlled by spirituality, simplicity and the practical character of Christianity, and derived from piety, wisdom and singleness of heart.[15]

It seems to follow from this that Watson would support the Church's right to regulate, and would accept that such regulations must bind worshippers. He clearly did not support any form of Church government based on a rigid legal framework of rules. Thus, while he left the door open to some form of Canon Law, it seems he excluded any detailed and prescriptive legal framework that could become a straitjacket. He did not, however, rule out a system of flexible regulations, which could be subject to annual revisions, and this was the path the Methodist Church eventually took. From the legacy of Wesley and Watson, then, we see that that the Methodist Church was open to the use of law as a way to regulate the conduct of members. We must now examine how the Methodist Church has applied this legacy.

Methodist Conference

The Methodist rulebook is *The Constitutional Practice and Discipline of the Methodist Church* (CPD, 1988/2005). Volume 1 contains the fixed texts, and volume 2 the Standing Orders of Conference and other important Methodist documents. Sections 8(1) and 8(2) of The Methodist Church Union Act, 1929 empowered the uniting Churches to declare and define the constitution of the united Church, by enacting a Deed of Union. Conference had full discretion over the structures and doctrine of the Methodist Church with only one restriction: it had (and has) no power 'to alter or vary in any manner whatsoever the clauses contained in the

---

11 Watson (1840), volume 2, pp. 596–605.
12 Above, chapter 3.
13 Ibid., p. 599.
14 Ibid.
15 Ibid., p. 600.

Deed of Union which define the doctrinal standards of the Methodist Church.'[16] Clause 5 of the 1934 Deed of Union states that 'The Conference shall be the final authority within the Methodist Church with regard to all questions concerning the interpretation of its doctrines.'[17] Clause 24 of the Deed states that 'Resolutions ... including the confirmation of provisional legislation ... shall be presented first to the Conference in its Ministerial Session.'[18] It follows from this that Methodists regard at least some resolutions of Conference as legally binding, just as Roman Canon Law is legally binding on members of the Roman Catholic Church.[19]

For further explanation, we need to go to the Standing Orders of Conference. At 1 September 2005, there were 536 such Standing Orders. They cover a wide range of subjects, some in great detail. They fill 456 pages, against 386 pages for the 1983 Roman Catholic Code of Canon Law, which contains 1,752 Canons. The Deed of Union directs us to SO 122 for details of provisional legislation. This Standing Order is entitled *Provisional Resolutions*, and includes a note about amendments to provisional legislation.[20] It therefore seems that Conference resolutions are taken as legislation by the Methodist Church. This is confirmed by SO 128, entitled *Extent of Legislation*, which states that General Resolutions of the Conference have effect throughout the Home Districts unless Conference directs otherwise.[21] SO 338 deals with the Law and Polity Committee, which is appointed annually by the Methodist Council. Its responsibilities include advising the Conference 'as to the interpretation of its laws and Standing Orders and, in the case of necessity, suggest any alteration or modification or put forward other proposals for legislation.'[22] It therefore seems that the Methodist Church does have a body of Church Law, but that it is not, as we might expect, the Standing Orders of Conference, rather it is the resolutions and declarations of Conference. It is interesting to note that Standing Orders seem to perform the same function as the sections in the 1983 Roman Code dealing with the various synods of the Church,[23] but in much greater detail.

While the Methodist Church would probably not accept that its Standing Orders are a form of Canon Law, there is a good case for interpreting them as such, since they fulfil a similar function. There is a certain ambiguity here, in that amendments to Standing Orders can only be made by a resolution of Conference. This would suggest that such amendments have the effect of legislation, even though the instruments

---

16 The Methodist Church Union Act, 1929, section 8(2). CPD, p. 97. The doctrinal standards are on pp. 213–4. The uniting Churches adopted a Deed of Union in a Uniting Conference in 1932.

17 Ibid., p. 214.

18 Ibid., p. 226.

19 Those who join a society are bound by its rules, and the courts have treated such agreements as contracts. The status of English Canon Law is different: it is part of English Civil Law. See above, chapter 5.

20 Ibid., pp. 373–4.

21 Ibid., pp. 378–9.

22 SO 338 section 3. Ibid., p. 441.

23 Canons 334, 336–48, and 460–468. Canon Law Society (1997), pp. 75–8 and 106–8.

they amend seemingly do not, but this ambiguity could easily be resolved by a declaration of Conference. Church councils have a duty to ensure that all voices are heard before making decisions. This seems designed to protect freedom of conscience by ensuring 'a proper representation of all the diversities present in the local Church, including those who are newcomers to it'[24] in the government of each local Church. Since members of the Circuit Meeting are elected by the local Church Council, members of the District Synod are elected by the Circuit Meeting, and most members of Conference are elected by Synod, it is presumably expected that Conference will represent the diversity of views in the Methodist Church.

Nevertheless, if a member cannot accept a decision of Conference, he or she has just two options: raise the issue again after a suitable interval, in the hope of reversing or changing the decision, or leave the Church. Thus, the Methodist Church seeks to consider all shades of opinion before reaching decisions, and thereby to make decisions which take account of the diversity of views within the Church, but once decisions have been made, its members are expected to follow them.

The United Reformed Church

The URC, as we saw in Chapter 3, combines both Presbyterian and Congregational elements in its ecclesiology. We also saw that alongside executive and consultative functions, the URC has a legislative function. We now need to examine this function, which seems to be restricted to General Assembly, in more detail. Section 2.(5) A of *The Structure of the URC* sets out the functions of General Assembly. The relevant sections are as follows:

> vi. to make regulations respecting theological colleges belonging to the United Reformed Church, to appoint the principal, professors and other members of the teaching staff, Board of Studies, and bursar, and to superintend their work;
>
> x. to interpret all forms and expressions of the polity practice and doctrinal formulations of the United Reformed Church including the Basis and the Structure and to determine when rights of personal conviction are asserted to the injury of the unity and peace of the United Reformed Church;
>
> xi. to alter, add to, modify or supersede the Basis, Structure and any other form or expression of the polity and doctrinal formulations of the United Reformed Church …
>
> xii. to make, alter or rescind rules for the conduct of its own proceedings and of those of other councils and commissions of the United Reformed Church and such other rules, bye–laws and standing orders as General Assembly may from time to time think desirable for the performance of its functions and the carrying into effect of any of the provisions contained in the Basis and

---

24 SO 602. CPD, p. 555.

the Structure and for the conduct of the business and affairs of the General Assembly and of the other councils and commissions of the United Reformed Church;

xvi. to make, alter or rescind rules of procedure for the submission and conduct of references and appeals to and by the councils of the United Reformed Church.[25]

We should note that three of the five functions listed above refer to the *Basis* and *Structure*. However, with the exception of the single reference to bye-laws in function xii, none of these functions of General Assembly express the URC's legislative function in legal language. To the best of my knowledge, there are no such bye-laws in force, and nor have any ever been proposed. Despite this, we still might reasonably conclude that the *Basis* and the *Structure* are good candidates for Canon Law substitutes in the URC. Before we explore this further, we need to examine the formative documents of the URC, to discover the traditional Presbyterian and Congregational views of Canon Law. We can then consider whether the URC has moved away from its roots or introduced new perspectives. We shall first examine the *Westminster Confession* and then the *Savoy Declaration*.

Chapter 19 of the *Confession* deals with the law of God. It states that while the ceremonial and judicial law of the Old Testament has been abrogated, the moral law is forever binding on everyone. Christians are not bound by it as a covenant of works, but as a 'perfect rule of righteousness'[26] which is of great use to them. Chapter 20 deals with Christian liberty and freedom of conscience. This consists of 'freedom from the guilt of sin, the condemning wrath of God, [and] the curse of the moral law [treating it as a means of salvation by works].'[27] It adds that to permit rules on matters not required by Scripture is to destroy both freedom of conscience and reason. Nevertheless, because authority and liberty are not intended to destroy each other, those 'who, upon pretence of Christian liberty, shall oppose any lawful power, or the lawful exercise of it, whether it be civil or ecclesiastical, resist the ordinance of God.'[28] There is thus a balance to be struck between submitting to the doctrines of men and opposing lawful authority.

The *Savoy Declaration* takes much the same position as the *Confession*, although its wording is slightly different in a few places.[29] Two such changes are relevant. When discussing freedom of conscience, the *Declaration* states that 'God alone is the Lord of the conscience, and hath left it free from the doctrines and commandments

---

25 United Reformed Church (2000), p. B13.

26 Sections 2–6. Thompson (1990), p. 30.

27 Section 1. Ibid., p. 31.

28 Section 4. Ibid., p. 32.

29 Chapter 19 in both is *Of the Law of God*. The *Confession* has *Of Christian Liberty, and Liberty of Conscience* as chapter 20, while the *Declaration* inserts an extra chapter *Of the Gospel, and the Extent of the Grace thereof*, before returning to Christian liberty in chapter 21. I am again indebted to Bray (1994) for his comparison of the *Westminster Confession* and the *Savoy Declaration*.

of men which are in any thing contrary to his Word, or not contained in it.'[30] The *Declaration* omits the section on opposing any lawful power or its exercise, but since this section appears to be a restatement of Romans 13:1–8, Hebrews 13:17 and 1 Peter 2:13–17, Congregational Churches seem bound to uphold it. As we can see, these differences are not significant for our purposes. The *Confession* and the *Declaration* take the view that in matters to which Scripture is indifferent, no rule is permissible. This contrasts with the view generally taken by the Episcopal Churches that they are free to legislate on such matters. The *Confession* and the *Declaration*, then, evidently see no need to legislate on matters that are contained in Scripture, and they oppose the imposition of any rule not found in Scripture. Thus, they stand squarely against Canon Law.[31]

The URC is currently reviewing its position on authority. As part of this process, General Assembly adopted a report in 1999, which dealt with the resolution of contentious issues. It states that:

> It is inevitable that there are occasions when some in the church plead for freedom while others are seeking a prescriptive ruling. The stress which this sometimes produces is to be preferred, in the opinion of this group, to the development of a detailed 'canon law'; we believe that such sustaining of stress affirms the doctrinal principles which are foundational for the United Reformed Church.[32]

The reference to a detailed Canon Law here is intriguing. It seems that the authors had in mind the 1983 Roman Code of Canon Law, which is indeed detailed and prescriptive. If one compares the *Basis* and the *Structure* with the *Canons of the Church of England*, however, one is struck by the similarities. Clauses 1–10 of the *Basis* set out the place of the URC in the Church as a whole; Canon A1 of the Church of England, while much shorter, performs the same function. Clause 11 of the *Basis* explains the purpose of the URC, the only section for which there is no equivalent Anglican Canon. Clauses 12–18 set out the faith of the URC; Canons A2 to A5, while much shorter, do the same.[33] Sections 19–25 of the *Basis* deal with ministry in the URC; Canons C1 to C28 do the same at greater length. The *Structure* and Canons H1 to H3 also deal with similar issues in equivalent ways. Despite the URC's reluctance to identify its rules as Canon Law, it does seem that the *Basis* and *Structure* fall within the definition with which we began this chapter.

The *Basis* states that the URC 'shall uphold the rights of personal conviction. It shall be for the Church, in safeguarding the substance of the faith and maintaining the unity of the fellowship, to determine when these rights are asserted to the injury of its unity and peace.'[34] There is therefore a tension here between freedom of conscience

---

30 Chapter 21, section 2. Ibid., p. 101.

31 John Owen also took this position. See above, Chapter 6.

32 United Reformed Church (1999b), p. 60.

33 These Canons point to the Book of Common Prayer, the Thirty-Nine Articles and the Ordinal, which set out the Anglican position at much greater length.

34 United Reformed Church (2000), p. A2.

and maintaining unity. While the URC tries to give its members as much freedom as possible, it reserves the right to limit that freedom rather than lose its unity. To date, it has not made any such limits, although it has considered doing so and may do so in the future. Like the Methodist Church, the URC, while recognising the tension between unity and freedom, has tended to place more emphasis on the former.

The Baptist Union

Baptists, in general, have not had much to say about Canon Law. Issues of Church discipline have always been the responsibility of the local Church. Beyond frequent references to the Law of Christ [the principles of the Gospel] in Baptist documents, very little has been written on the subject of Canon Law, either by the Baptist Union or by individual Baptist writers. Baptists have always emphasised that the local Church is the manifestation of the universal Church, and have stressed the importance of freedom of personal conscience. They have generally been reluctant to accept anything that might be seen as a rule imposed from on high. The Baptist *Declaration on the Church* of 1948 spells this out:

> Our conviction of Christ's Lordship over His Church leads us to insist that Churches formed by His will must be free from all other rule in matters relating to their spiritual life.[35]

Given this, it is highly unlikely that Baptists would willingly embrace any form of Canon Law originating outside the local Church. When it comes to law within the local Church, I can find only three statements that seem relevant in British official Baptist documents. The first comes from *The Faith and Practice of Thirty Congregations*, published in 1651 (Lumpkin, 1969). Article 28 states that '*Iesus Christ* was not only the Lawmaker, but the Law giver to every man that liveth in the world, in that he giveth every man therein some measure of light.'[36] If Jesus has made the law, and given it to everyone, it would seem to follow that no other form of law is necessary in the Church.

Secondly, B. R. White (1976) comments that 'It seems highly unlikely that the New Testament writers intended to *legislate* for Church organisation in their generation let alone for any others after them.'[37] Thirdly, the Baptist Union of Scotland (1985) has much the same view: 'It has been doubted whether any part

---

35 Hayden (1980), p. 11. In its original context, this refers to state influence over Churches, but given the advisory nature of associations and the emphasis on the local Church in Baptist theology, it clearly has wider implications. The same declaration states (p. 6) that local Churches 'are gathered by the will of Christ and live by the indwelling of His Spirit.' We might reasonably conclude from this that these local Churches should also be free from rules imposed by associations.

36 Lumpkin (1969), p. 179. Emphasis original.

37 White (1976), p. 22. Emphasis original.

of the New Testament was intended to be taken as ecclesiastical legislation for the future.'[38]

Other Baptists, however, have not always been so reticent. Charles Williams (1882) wrote that there are two principles behind Baptist theology. Firstly, no one has authority to legislate in religious matters, or in any way to exercise lordship over human consciences or the Church of God. Secondly, God is the 'one Lawgiver,' to whom every man owes allegiance, and whose will shall be done on earth 'as it is in heaven.'[39] This view, which is consistent with and expands upon the Baptist Union declarations above, seems to leave no room for Canon Law. If Christ is the only lawgiver, the only law binding on Christians is the law of love as expressed in the Gospels. As Williams puts it, for Baptists, 'their statute book is the New Testament.'[40]

This, however, does not stop individual Baptists from using their freedom in Christ to choose to follow any system of Canon Law they want, or to decide to obey a particular minister of the Church. In practice, were anyone to do so, their actions would be likely to attract disapproval from their fellow Baptists. In Baptist theology, no such system is necessary, and nor is it right to try to impose one without the consent of the local Church. Given the resistance of many Baptist Churches to anything that might limit the Spirit, however, this seems a most unlikely contingency. It is clear, then, that Baptists do not accept the need for Canon Law, either within the local Church, or in any wider context. While it is difficult and dangerous to generalise too far, the emphasis on freedom of personal conscience within Baptist circles would seem to preclude the establishment of Canon Law or any equivalent structure in a Baptist Church.

In Baptist Churches, then, freedom of conscience takes precedence over regulation. Church order is a matter for the local Church, and no Church or individual can be induced to accept a decision for the sake of wider Church unity. This does not mean that Baptists can believe what they want. Any individual renouncing believer's baptism, for example, or promoting doctrine contrary to the Gospel can expect swift expulsion, and any Church doing so can expect to be disowned by other Baptist Churches. Nevertheless, provided Baptists and Baptist Churches remain reasonably orthodox in their theology, they recognise no authority that can restrict their freedom of conscience.

Conclusion

It seems, then, that the Methodist and United Reformed Churches have set up structures of varying flexibility that act like Canon Law. They have also reserved the right to place limits on freedom of conscience for the sake of Church unity. In the Methodist Church, freedom of conscience is expressed in wide consultation of all

---

38 Baptist Union of Scotland (1985), p. 6.
39 Williams (1882), p. 1.
40 Ibid., p. 69.

sections of the Church in the procedures leading to Conference resolutions, which are binding on all Methodists. In the URC, freedom is expressed in a similar manner, but in addition, local Churches are not obliged to accept or implement resolutions of Assembly. Of the major Churches we discuss here, only the Baptist Churches have neither established regulatory structures nor established limits on freedom of conscience. We have seen that the secular views of justice as law, justice as reason and justice as liberty have been added to the Biblical view we identified earlier. These views have affected the ideas of authority in these Churches, and their structures have evolved or been designed to reflect their views on authority. The structures of the Churches are all intended to get people into a right relationship with God. They all succeed to some extent. Law, reason and liberty are all aspects of righteousness, but I have argued that where one or more of these has been emphasised to the detriment of righteousness, the Churches have drifted away from the ideal.

Chapter 8

Where Now?

If existing views of authority fall short of the Biblical standard as set out in the New Testament, we must ask what a more Biblical view might look like. Our examination in chapter 1 of the main passages dealing with authority enabled us to develop a critique of the current views of the major Churches. We will need to build on what we learned there if we are to develop an alternative model. This will require us to refer to a wider range of texts. Fortunately, most of the other texts to which we shall refer are far less controversial than the texts we examined earlier.

Firstly and most importantly, all authority comes from God the Father,[1] Who is the source of all things, and in Whom all things find their being. Human authority, therefore, derives from and shares in the Father's authority. As we saw in chapter 1, the New Testament sees such authority as limited, and exercisable only within a legally ordered context. It cannot be exercised in an arbitrary manner, but only justly and righteously, in accordance with God the Father's will. Any other use of authority would, in my view, more properly be called an abuse or usurpation of power, since I have argued that authority connotes delegated power together with accountability to the source of that power.

The New Testament tells us that the Father has committed full authority to Jesus Christ,[2] as Son, Who acts on behalf of the Father and according to His will. It tells us that Christ has in turn delegated limited authority to leaders in the Church, sending them out to preach the Gospel and to make disciples and baptise in His name.[3] Some will become rulers in the age to come, and will have authority to judge the faithful.[4] Those who persevere in doing God's will to the end will be given authority over the nations,[5] and therefore all Christians, not just the leaders of the Church, will have a share in Christ's authority in the Kingdom. However, Christians, whether Church Leaders or not, whether ordained or lay, cannot use their authority for any purpose they chose: the purpose of authority in the Church is not to exalt individuals, but to build up the faithful as a whole.[6] The New Testament makes it clear that the Father has also delegated limited authority to secular governors to punish wrongdoers and

---

1   John 19:11 and Romans 13:1.
2   Matthew 9:6–8 and 28:18, John 5:26–27 and 17:1–5, Ephesians 1:20–22 and Colossians 2:8–10.
3   Matthew 28:19–20.
4   Matthew 19:28, Luke 22:28–30 and Revelation 20:4.
5   Revelation 2:26–27.
6   2 Corinthians 10:7–9 and 13:10.

protect those who act justly. Provided they do not ordain things contrary to the will of God, such as idolatry, Christians are urged to submit to secular rulers for the sake of the Lord.[7]

Turning specifically to authority in the Church, some are appointed to positions of leadership, which bring with them a degree of authority. The Church has traditionally, and I believe correctly, understood leadership as a vocation of loving service, to which some are called (*klētoi*) by God.[8] Service, however, does not imply inferiority, and it need not be menial: In Ephesians 3:7, St. Paul describes himself as a servant (*diakonos*) of the Gospel. The call to leadership is mediated through the Church. The personal perception that one is being called by God to exercise a particular ministry is necessary, but not sufficient. The wider Church must also participate in a process of discernment, seeking the will of God under the leading of the Holy Spirit, to verify this calling. Hence the calling is both individual and corporate. The candidate is called to a particular ministry by God, and trained for and called to a particular ministry in a particular place by the Church. Both parts of this calling bring authority with them: in the first part authority is conferred by God, in the second it is delegated by the Church.

The candidate, then, receives authority as a minister through his or her calling from God. This authority can only attach to the person being called, since it precedes any appointment to a position that may carry authority, and it may precede a clear understanding of the type of ministry to which the candidate is called. In my view, such authority lasts for life. While this authority is logically and temporally prior to authority over a congregation, I do not believe that it can be exercised until the minister is appointed to a particular ministry in a particular place. Such an appointment conveys authority over a congregation, which comes firstly through ordination, in which the candidate receives authority to act as a minister of the wider Church, and secondly through a calling from the Church to a particular pastorate, through which the minister receives authority over a congregation. Authority therefore comes from both the local congregation and the wider Church. These kinds of authority come with the position of ministry, and the position of leadership in a particular congregation. In the latter case, the authority is attached to the particular ministry, not to the minister who exercises it. Thus, while a minister has authority over a particular congregation while he or she is authorised to lead it, that authority lapses when he or she leaves, and passes to his or her successor. Since both the wider Church and the local congregation are involved in the calling of a minister, and they act together in the appointment, they delegate authority to the minister jointly. Since authority as I understand it is power combined with authorisation and accountability, it follows that those to whom authority in the Church is delegated are accountable to God, to the wider Church and to the local Church for the use they make of it.

---

7   John 19:11, Romans 13:1–4 and 1 Peter 2:13–17. Those to whom such authority is delegated are also, in my view, accountable to the Father through Christ.

8   Compare Romans 1:1–7.

Priesthood, however, is not confined to the ordained, or to other Church leaders. 1 Peter 2:5–9, echoing Exodus 19:6, describes the people of God as a holy and royal priesthood. This suggests that the Church as a whole exercises priesthood, albeit of a different sort from that exercised by Church leaders.[9] Martin Luther combined verse 9 with the elders' song to the Lamb in Revelation 5:9–10, and argued that since Christ has made His people a royal house of priests, in addition to forming them into a royal priesthood, each individual believer becomes a priest through baptism.[10] It seems to me that we must maintain a tension between the individual and the corporate elements here, without becoming individualistic. Each Christian, and the Church as a whole, is responsible for co-operating with and participating in Christ's priestly work of bringing salvation to the world. Thus, for example, both the Christian and the Church have a duty to make Christ known through the way they live, thus living out their calling as Christians to be salt and light to the earth.[11] While Christians may act individually, however, their activities should be seen in a corporate light, as a part of the activity of the Church as a whole. Christians are similarly accountable to God, individually and corporately, for their actions.

Traditionally, bishops, priests and deacons have exercised authority on behalf of the Church as a whole. I do not wish to suggest that this is the only viable form of Church order: clearly it is not. As we saw in Chapter 7, this order did not exist in anything like its current form in the Primitive Church, and there were a number of variations on the theme of the threefold ministry, with different churches assigning authority differently among those in positions of ministry. However, I do think that episcopacy is the preferable system. It is an ancient structure that has stood the test of time. It began to emerge towards the end of the New Testament period,[12] and was universal from the second century to the Reformation. Throughout that period, the bishops were guardians of the faith, entrusted to protect it against attacks from without and within, to be bulwarks against heresy, a function they have performed with a large measure of success.

Similarly, the use of presbyters and deacons to assist the bishop in his ministry is of ancient provenance. Traditionally, presbyters have assisted bishops with pastoral work and have deputised for them in celebrating the Eucharist. Deacons, however, have had many different rôles over the years. The diaconate in episcopal Churches has for centuries been a transitional stage as a pastoral worker and assistant at the Eucharist for those training as priests, rather than a permanent ministry of service to others.[13] The Roman Catholic Church and the Church of England have begun to

---

9　Best (1971, p. 108), Goppelt (1993, pp. 141–2) and Achtemeier (1996, pp. 156 and 165) are agreed that 'priesthood' in verses 5 and 9 should be understood in a corporate sense, not an individualistic one.

10　Luther (1970b), pp. 12–16 and 244–5. Both Aune (1997, pp. 47–9 and 362) and Charles (1920, pp. 16–17 and 148) interpret *basileias kai hiereis* in this passage and *basileias, hiereis* in Revelation 1:6 as statements that each believer is a priest.

11　Compare Matthew 5:13–16 and Rahner (1975), pp. 1282–3.

12　Compare Hanson and Hanson (1987), pp. 130–131.

13　Compare Acts 6:1–6.

rediscover the distinctive ministry of the deacon, and have restored the permanent diaconate, while still requiring prospective priests to become deacons first. This emphasises the need for leadership in the Church to be underpinned by a ministry of loving service, and is a development I welcome. While the way bishops function, and their relationships with presbyters and elders, have clearly changed over the centuries, it seems to me that the threefold ministry has generally, under the guidance of the Holy Spirit, maintained the integrity of the faith successfully.

The existence of the ordained ministry, however, does not deprive lay people of authority, even though they are not in positions of formal leadership. I have already emphasised the importance of calling in the authority of Church leaders. The writer to Ephesus states that all Christians are called by God to 'maintain the unity of the Spirit in the bond of peace.'[14] If calling brings with it authority, as I believe it does, then all Christians have at least some authority within the Church. While leaders have authority to lead, other Christians have authority at least to maintain unity and foster peace within the congregation, as far as it lies within their power.[15] The writer to Ephesus adds that Christ gives those who lead the Church authority 'to equip the saints for the work of ministry, for building up the body of Christ.'[16] This ministry is described in 1 Peter 2:9: Christians should 'proclaim the glorious deeds of him who has called you out of darkness into his marvellous light.' The ministry of Christians, therefore, is to build each other up in the faith, and to undertake mission to bring the faith to others. While leaders will obviously have a prominent rôle in such activity, it is the duty of the whole Church, not just its leaders. In matters affecting mission or the peace of the congregation, responsibility and authority are shared between the minister and the congregation. In practice, it seems likely that any contentious issue will fall into one of these categories.

This authority should not be exercised the way that secular rulers exercise power. Christ was at pains to point out to the Twelve that seeking personal prestige or position, imposing one's will on others, or generally behaving in an authoritarian or oppressive manner is not His way.[17] Instead, the way to greatness in the Kingdom, and therefore in the Church, whose structures, I believe, should prefigure the Kingdom at least to some extent, is through sacrificial service. The model for this service should be the ministry (*diakonia*) of Christ,[18] Who came as bearer of the message of release from bondage to sin, as an ambassador for the Father, and as one

---

14 Ephesians 4:3 NRSV.

15 In some situations where others refuse to behave reasonably, believers may be unable to exercise this authority effectively.

16 Ephesians 4:12 NRSV. I agree with Ernest Best (1998, pp. 395–9) and Markus Barth (1974, pp. 439–40 and 477–84), *contra* John N. Collins (1990, pp. 30–32 and 233–4) that there should be no comma between 'saints' and 'for', as this would imply that the work of ministry, like the work of equipping the saints, was reserved to those in positions of leadership. The New Testament shows that lay people had more ministerial functions than this would suggest (see, for example, Romans 15:14, 1 Corinthians 14:26–33 and Philippians 1:15–18).

17 Matthew 20:20–28, Mark 10:35–45 and Luke 22:24–26. Compare 1 Peter 5:1–3.

18 Compare Matthew 20:28 and Mark 10:45.

who attended on those in need of salvation. John N. Collins (1990) sees message, agency and attendance upon a person or household as the key uses of *diakonia* in the Christian tradition, and believes that the word refers to a mode of activity, not a status. He states that waiting at tables is just one possible application of such activity, and that such service need not be menial: both a Roman procurator and a general could be seen as *diakonoi* of the emperor. He also points out that the *diakonos* was an agent of the bishop, not a servant of the needy person or the congregation.[19] As John L. McKenzie, S. J. (1966) puts it, authority can only be exercised effectively in a spirit of love, which can produce a much greater response than attempts to rule and dominate.[20]

Those with authority are always subject to the twin temptations of using it too little, possibly leading to anarchy, and over using it, and risking tyranny. On the one hand, it would be possible to overemphasise the freedom that is ours in Christ to the extent that authority ceased to operate altogether. This could easily lead to controversial issues being fudged in an attempt to avoid conflict, and to a general lack of clarity in doctrine and practice. On the other hand, one might overstate authority to the extent it becomes rigid, authoritarian and legalistic, inhibiting Christian love and obstructing the Holy Spirit. Both situations are characterised by a lack of accountability: in the first case upward accountability to wider Church structures, in the second, downward accountability to those being governed. Clarity is essential if the Church is to pursue its mission effectively: Christians need to know what the Good News is before they can share it effectively. Flexibility is essential if pastoral needs are to be met well: one size fits all solutions rarely work. Accountability is essential if leaders are to have legitimate authority rather than coercive power. Those called to leadership in the Church should seek to lead in a way that avoids both extremes, and should refrain from leading in ways that tend to exalt the leader or to diminish others. Instead, they should try to serve and build up the fellowship. They should lead through authentic preaching, through a holy lifestyle, reflecting Christ through the way they live, through administering the sacraments, and through pastoral care, encouraging and supporting the faithful through the joys and sorrows of life.

Authority has traditionally been exercised mainly in the local Church. Those called by God, however, whether or not they are in positions of leadership, are part of the whole Church in addition to being part of a local Church. Similarly, those called to leadership are ministers of the whole Church, not just ministers of their local congregations or dioceses, a fact attested to by the movement of leaders from one congregation or diocese to another, and by the input of the wider Church in the discernment of calling. This implies that authority has a wider dimension than just the strictly local, and that it is shared on a wider basis. As I have already explained, ministers derive some of their authority from the local congregation and some of it from the wider church, both of which delegate this authority to them through a call

---

19 Collins (1990), sections II and III. See also pp. 335–7.
20 McKenzie (1966), p. 61.

to a particular ministry. Thus, when issues affecting the wider Church arise, Church leaders can, in my view, legitimately convene a synod to discuss the matter, and, having reached a common mind, can make binding decisions on behalf of the wider Church.

Historically, shared authority has been used, through such means as synods and councils, to defend the faith against distortions of the truth, and to offer mutual support and encouragement between widely dispersed groups of Christians. However, it is also important to preserve a degree of local autonomy regarding decisions on matters that are not theologically necessary, and to recognise that some such decisions that may be right for the whole Church may not necessarily be right for a particular congregation. It therefore seems right that the minister should consult the congregation, or their representatives, about how, when, and, where appropriate, if such decisions should be implemented, or what alternatives might be more suitable. While it is essential to maintain unity within the Church, this does not necessarily entail uniformity. Decisions should not be imposed on reluctant Churches without good reason. Instead, they should be implemented with pastoral tact, to help the Church to grow into fuller unity. Hanson and Hanson (1987) express this thought well by saying that the Church is the people of God, but it is called to be the body of Christ.[21]

While the Bible states the principles on which authority should be based, it does not spell out all the details. These are therefore left to the Churches to decide for themselves. As a visible organisation, the Church needs a structure and a means of governing itself. In practice, its only feasible option was to develop appropriate structures by learning from secular practice, adopting and adapting what seemed the most useful elements of it that seemed to fit best with the Biblical description of authority.[22] While adopting some secular structures might be seen to be sensible and perhaps necessary, I have argued earlier in this study that the Church has been inclined at times to adopt secular models of government rather less critically than it might have done, embracing the theory as well as the practice, even when the theory sat uneasily with elements of Christianity. While Christianity cannot and should not be entirely divorced from the world, the lifestyles of Christians should be distinctively different from those of their secular contemporaries, and this applies as much to the way Church structures are operated as to any other part of the Christian life.

It is essential that the structures of the Church reflect the power of grace and love, rather than the power of domination based on position that underlies many secular models of authority. As Meneo Afonso (1996) puts it, a theory of authority that is not founded on God's self-communication in the Spirit and grace is likely to look like a secular theory of authority, thereby distorting the uniquely Christian concept of authority.[23] Therefore, it seems to me, the Church should look carefully at secular

---

21 Hanson and Hanson (1987), p. 43.
22 Compare Timms and Wilson (2000), pp. 120–121.
23 Afonso (1996), p. 62.

structures of authority before adopting them, and ensure that they are modified to fit Christian doctrine before being put into practice.

For Church leaders, then, authority and leadership should be underpinned by loving service, which is the standard in the Kingdom, as it was in the earthly ministry of Jesus. Leaders should use their authority to build up the faithful and strengthen the weak, heal consciences, reclaim the lost, encourage sinners to repent, and do all in their power to restore everyone who comes to them to the right relationship with God. Leaders should also recognise that their authority is both limited and shared.[24] Only Christ has full authority in the Church, and while He has delegated some authority to Church leaders, He has not given them full authority. Leaders derive some of their authority from the congregation, with whom they share authority over some matters, and to whom they remain accountable for the way they use that authority. Those not in positions of leadership should also look forward to the time when they will share Christ's authority in the Kingdom, and should act in a manner that builds up the fellowship, proclaims the Gospel to those around them, and prefigures the justice, peace and joy that will be found in the Kingdom.[25]

This, then, is my position on authority. The principles that follow seem to me to illustrate the points on which this divergence from this model and between the models used by each Church is most serious. It seems to me that many of these divergences have at least been exacerbated, if not actually caused, by either/or thinking. This, to my mind, concentrates too much on what divides Christians, and may sometimes obscure what unites us. I will set out these principles, as far as possible, in terms of both/and thought, which I hope will counteract this tendency. I will then apply the principles to the five Churches, explaining how each Church differs from this view, and setting out the challenges the principles pose to each Church.

The Principles

1. Structures of Church Government should maintain a balance between top-down and bottom–up authority and accountability.

The current structure of the Roman Catholic Church seems almost exclusively top-down. Clergy take oaths of canonical obedience to their hierarchical superiors, and particularly the pope. Lay people, while they do not take such oaths, are expected to obey the priests. There is no similar requirement, except in certain specific situations, for the clergy even to consult non-priests, let alone to give lay people an account of their conduct. Structures of upward accountability are highly visible, but there is no clear mechanism for downward accountability. While Canon Law encourages priests to consult the laity about matters on which they are experts, they have little or

---

24 Compare de George (1985), pp. 224–7.
25 Compare Romans 14:17.

no share in authority.[26] In this structure, with its strict separation between ordained and lay, it can be easy to forget that the clergy too are members of the *laos*, the people of God. Since Vatican II, the Church has sought to develop a theology of the laity, but while this may have created a different atmosphere, encouraging lay people to participate more fully in the life of the Church, it seems to me that the fruits of this work have not yet become easily visible in official structures.[27] The Roman Catholic Church does not yet appear to have paid enough attention to the part played in authority by lay people, and this seems to have led it to an unbalanced view of authority.

While the Code allows for parochial structures that include lay members, these are not required by the Canons, and they do not exist everywhere. The diocesan synod does exist in each diocese, and it is perhaps the easiest vehicle through which lay involvement could be increased. It is made up of priests and lay members, with the latter group being selected by the (mainly lay) pastoral council. The bishop decides how many lay members the synod will have, and how they are to be elected. In addition, he can co-opt other members if he wishes. Currently, the pastoral council meets at least once a year,[28] while the synod only meets when the bishop, 'after consulting the council of priests, judges that the circumstances suggest it.'[29] He need not consult it, and he can ignore its advice if he sees fit. Greater lay involvement could be ensured by requiring a significant percentage of lay members on the synod, and by making both the pastoral council and the diocesan synod permanent standing committees. The bishop should then be given a duty to consult the synod on all important matters affecting the diocese.[30] This arrangement would retain the bishop's right of veto and maintain his position as diocesan legislator. It would also ensure that the synod is consulted regularly and its advice is not lightly discarded, thereby enabling lay people to have appropriate input into decisions affecting the mission and peace of the Church.

The Church of England seems to have achieved a legitimate balance between top-down and bottom-up government and accountability, with its episcopal leadership and synodical government allowing for both clerical and lay involvement in decision-making. This balance, however, seems to favour the bishops a little too much at the

---

26 Gerard Mannion, by contrast, argues that the laity is the *de facto* and should be the *de jure* source of authority in the Church. See Hoose (2002), pp. 32–4.

27 See *The Priest, Pastor and Leader of the Parish Community* (Congregation for the Clergy, 2002), which, while trying to encourage lay participation in Church administration, restates the position that the priest is the sole decision-maker within the parish and rejects any lay-involvement in decision-making that might interfere with this situation.

28 Canons 511–4.

29 Canon 461 §1. Diocesan synods are governed by Canons 460–468.

30 Compare Canon 127, Timms and Wilson (2000), pp. 99–100, and Francis A. Sullivan (Hoose, 2002, p. 90). Hoose (2002, pp. 235–6), suggests that parish councils would encourage lay involvement more effectively, because people are more likely to take part in parochial initiatives than in diocesan councils. I take his point, but I do not think lay involvement will be effective unless it also occurs at diocesan level.

moment. As doctrinal guardians, bishops should be able to block unsound doctrinal measures. However, there are usually competent theologians in the House of Laity who are more than able to form their own views on these matters, and who may in some cases be more expert on the Anglican Tradition than some bishops. The bishops currently do not need to consult them before sending amended instruments back to Synod for final approval. Where the bishops feel changes are required, there could be advantages in an extra stage of consultation with expert members of the House of Laity, perhaps through the Doctrine or Liturgical Commission, before the bishops submit an amended doctrinal or liturgical measure to Synod for final approval. This would preserve the Bishops' right and responsibility to define doctrine, and would also ensure that the laity could better play its part in Synodical Government, without appearing to be marginalised on the most important issues.

Methodist theology views authority in the Church as bottom-up, with members delegating their authority to a series of committees, which in turn make decisions binding on its local Churches. In this structure, authority flows up from the roots to representative committees, which then act with executive authority on behalf of the whole Church. However, in my opinion, the balance between top and bottom would be enhanced by some checks and balances on the powers of the President of Conference during his or her year of office. As we have seen, these powers allow the President, should he or she think it expedient or necessary, to appoint, remove or transfer any minister in any manner he or she sees fit.[31] There seems to be no right of appeal against unjust use of these powers, and therefore they would appear to be rather excessive. While they may be very useful if used properly in an emergency, the potential for abuse is enormous. If the claim that the Methodist doctrine of authority precludes autocracy is to be sustained, some method for reviewing such presidential decisions would seem to be highly desirable. Otherwise, the Methodist Church seems to have achieved a legitimate balance of the top-down and the bottom-up.

The United Reformed Church also has both top- and bottom-up elements in its ecclesiology, the former from its Presbyterian heritage, the latter from its Congregational roots. It is not clear, however, that these are properly balanced. The URC understands itself primarily as a conciliar Church, and its structure reflects this. In the local Church, the Church Meeting is the governing body, and no decision can be implemented in the Church without its consent. It elects elders to ensure the spiritual life of the Church and the fabric of the Church building are kept in good order, and to represent the local Church in the wider councils of the URC. In the URC, however, the elders are responsible to the Church meeting, rather than being the Church's governing body, as they would be under the traditional Presbyterian arrangement. Therefore, no decision made by any of the wider councils of the URC can be implemented without the consent of the Church Meeting of the relevant local Church. The fact that people who are ultimately delegates of their Local Churches make decisions on behalf of the local Churches does not guarantee the implementation

---

31 Above, Chapter 2.

of any such decision,[32] although an unreasonable refusal to implement such a decision would inevitably lead to a pastoral intervention. This effectively makes the decisions of the wider councils of the URC unenforceable, which can only impede strategic decision-making. It is to be hoped that the review of structures currently under way in the URC will resolve this issue, but it is difficult to avoid the conclusion that the URC will eventually have to adopt some kind of Presbyterian model for its local Churches if this issue is ever to be resolved.[33]

Baptists have traditionally regarded the Bible, as the written word of God, as the supreme authority, and provided local Churches have organised themselves in a reasonably Biblical manner, they have resisted any other external authority. They have, however, always believed that just as Christians have a duty to form associations, in the form of local Churches, local Churches also have a duty to form associations for mutual support and fellowship. Thus the top-down element in Baptist theology is the belief that all authority comes from Christ, and the Bible is the supreme (or for some Churches sole) authority for faith and conduct. There is no requirement for associations to have authority to do more than give advice. In Baptist thought, each Church has liberty under the Holy Spirit to interpret and administer God's laws as revealed in Scripture. Since the New Testament does not describe a single, uniform Church structure, Baptist Church structures have tended to be fairly flexible. They have, however, been predominantly bottom–up, in that the members choose the elders and minister to lead them. These leaders have only personal authority. While Baptists are always likely to resist what they might see as excessive structure, it seems to me that they have an insufficient awareness that a calling by God to a position of leadership in itself carries with it a certain authority, in addition to any personal authority a particular leader may have. This authority, conferred by God, entails a sharing in the authority of the Father, and is therefore top-down. This is additional to the bottom-up authority conferred by the congregation, and the personal authority arising from the personality and training of the minister.

2.   There should be a proper balance between the local and the universal Church.

The Roman Catholic Church formally recognises this proposition, but it sometimes seems that the its structures tip the balance in favour of the universal Church to the detriment of the local. Many important decisions are reserved to Rome, of which the appointment of bishops is one of the most visible and controversial issues, but by no means the only one. Vatican II recognised the principle of subsidiarity: that decisions should be taken as locally as appropriate, but this principle is less visible in the current structures of the Church than it is in the documents of the council.

---

32   While from time to time local Churches refuse to accept decisions made by the wider Church anyway in other Communions, the URC is the only Church, as far as I am aware, in which the structures allow for this possibility.

33   I see no problem, however, in retaining the Church Meeting as the governing body of the local Church within this structure.

There is a strong case for devolving a great deal of decision making to the provincial or diocesan level,[34] with the Vatican retaining the right to approve local decisions before implementation.

It seems to me that in the Church of England, authority is distributed well between national, diocesan and parish level. The most important decisions are made by General Synod, on behalf of the Church, although in certain important areas Parliament has a veto over Church legislation. Leadership is exercised by the bishops, who delegate authority within the parish to the parish priest. Generally, bishops can exercise their authority without requiring the approval of the archbishop, and each diocese has a synod to advise the bishop. Incumbents, after consultation with the Parochial Church Council, can also make appropriate decisions concerning the local Church. This allows those affected by decisions to contribute to decision-making at the appropriate level.

Similarly, the relationship between local Church, circuit, district and national Church among Methodists seems well balanced, with local Churches sending representatives carrying the delegated authority of the Church to a succession of councils with increasingly wide geographical remits. These councils, acting on behalf of the local Churches, can then take decisions binding on the appropriate Churches. I have already stated my reservations about the relationship between local and wider Church in the URC, but the balance between its district, synod and national bodies also seems good.

It seems to me that the Baptist Churches understate the universal aspect of authority.[35] I have already argued that those called to leadership are ministers of the whole Church, not just the local Church. In my view, ministers share in the apostolic ministry, which was directed towards the whole Church and the whole world, not just a part of it, and that therefore their ministry, while focussed in a particular local Church, is directed towards the whole Church and the whole world, not just a part of it. It follows from this that in some sense the authority associated with ministry extends beyond the local Church.

Baptists, however, do not seem to accept this. They tend to identify the local Church with the universal Church, although they also believe that Churches have a duty to form associations. However, Baptists frequently describe their Churches using the model of the Body of Christ. This model, at least as used in Romans 12 and 1 Corinthians 12, seems to presuppose a stable and organically united, but diverse structure, the keynotes of which are mutual union, mutual concern and mutual dependence. Augustine, for example, develops this image with particular stress on

---

34 For a similar view, see Hugh Lawrence's article on *Ordination and Governance* (Hoose, 2002, pp. 73–82). Edmund Hill (1988, pp. 6–8) argues that the Church should be governed regionally, not globally.

35 Article XXVI of the Second London Confession refers to the 'Catholick or universal Church', but this seems to refer only to the Church Invisible. The declaration makes no reference to the universal Church when discussing particular congregations. See Lumpkin (1969), pp. 285–9.

the communion that binds together all who are enlivened by the grace of Christ. Yet in practice, Baptist Churches are free to leave one association and join another if they feel it right to do so. This gives the impression that Baptist Churches only feel bound to those with whose doctrine they agree, a much looser bond than that understood by Augustine, and one that I believe is too loose.

While Baptists have tended to resist giving authority to any structure wider than the local Church, the Baptist Union argues that such structures are desirable as a means of building up fellowship, and seeking the Mind of God. I believe, however, that they are necessary. In Baptist theology, authority resides in the local Church, and since the local Churches do not, in general, delegate their authority to associations, the officers of such associations have no authority to act on behalf of the Churches. They are, nevertheless, appointed to particular committees, and expected to work for the Church, and they are influential as a result of their position. It would therefore seem that such officers have power without authority. If the officers of an association are to do their appointed jobs, they must act illegitimately, since Baptist theology does not allow them the authority they need to operate.[36] The simplest solution to this problem would be to authorise the officers to act and place them under the oversight of the local Churches. This will involve the development of some form of shared authority. Without this, officers of the associations will continue to be unable to act legitimately, since there are at present no structures of accountability beyond the local Church.

3. Structures of authority should maintain a proper balance between clarity and flexibility.

Authority in the Roman Catholic Church, as expressed through Canon Law, certainly meets the first condition of clarity, but it seems to lack flexibility, particularly, for example, in the area of matrimonial law. The bishops do have discretion in a wide variety of disciplinary cases, but the Code of Canon Law also contains detailed provisions for some situations that one might suspect arise fairly rarely.[37] The upshot of this is that bishops are often asked for dispensations from Canonical impediments to marriage, and the largest proportion of cases in the Ecclesiastical courts concern marriage nullity.[38] It is not clear that this is the best use of bishops' time. The fact that so much activity is devoted to providing exemptions from Roman Canon Law suggests that the Canons are unnecessarily detailed and over-prescriptive. There is, nevertheless, a lot to be said for a system that lays down the principles on which decisions should be made, rather than trying to spell out all the details. Such a system

---

36 Harrison (1959), pp. 60–62.

37 See, for example, Canon 1089, which declares invalid a marriage in which the bride has been kidnapped for the purpose, 'unless the woman, after she has been separated from her abductor and established in a safe and free place, chooses marriage of her own accord.'

38 See Doe (1996), p. 142.

would leave many of the decisions currently decided by the courts to the discretion of the bishops and parish clergy without the need for legal proceedings.

The law of the Church of England, by contrast, is a lot more flexible. Anglican Consistory Courts deal most often with disputes about property matters, particularly changes to the fabric of Church buildings for which permission has been refused by the Diocese.[39] These generally result from disagreements about how buildings should be used or disputes about the interpretation of faculty law, rather than attempts to bypass detailed Canonical provisions. The Church's model of authority, however, could be a lot clearer. As we have seen, the Church recognises many sources of authority, including Scripture, the creeds, the Thirty-Nine Articles, the Prayer Book and the Ordinal, not to mention the Canons of the Church of England, the Church Representation Rules, the standing orders of General Synod or any of the statements of the House of Bishops.[40] It is often far from clear to which of these documents reference should be made when deciding who has authority to do what. While this arrangement fits the Anglican ethos well, and while I agree with the 1948 Lambeth Conference that this system provides suitable checks and balances against abuse, I would submit that there is a strong case for the production of an official document (by General Synod or the Doctrine Commission) providing an overview of the whole system, arranged in a way that facilitates both clarity and understanding. While this would not, in itself, become the official doctrine of the Church of England, it would make it a lot easier to determine what that doctrine is.

The structure of authority in the Methodist Church is clear: authority comes from Christ, it is mediated through the members of the Church, and it is delegated to representative committees, which make decisions binding on the Churches. The structures are also flexible: *The Constitutional Practice and Discipline of the Methodist Church* sets out the membership, method of election, terms of reference and responsibilities of each committee. It does not, however, set out in detail how the committees must operate, or limit the subjects they can discuss. This, then, seems a good balance between clarity and flexibility. The structures of the URC are flexible, in that the *Manual* sets out policy and constitution in a similar way to CPD, and that the URC has explicitly disavowed the development of a detailed Canon Law.[41] They are not, however, as clear as they could be, due to the ambiguity we have already discussed between local and wider Church when it comes to decision-making. Baptist structures tend, by definition, to be flexible, since each local Church is entitled to structure itself according to its own interpretation of Scripture. They are also clear, in that the members of the Church both elect their own officials to lead, and make decisions collectively in Church Meetings. However, Baptist structures are sometimes so flexible that rampant individualism becomes a real possibility against which the Churches need constantly to be on their guard. Provided this tendency is avoided, the Baptist balance between flexibility and clarity also seems reasonable.

---

39 See ibid., pp. 142–3.
40 Above, chapter 2.
41 United Reformed Church (1999b), p. 60.

4. Church government should draw on the best secular practice, but avoid adopting secular management theory.

Rome, as we have seen, has been greatly influenced by Roman Law, and, I have argued, it has based its system of government on the imperial model, by developing the monarchical hierarchy with an elected pope at the top. In doing so, it seems to have adopted a great deal of Roman legal theory, at times apparently without due consideration of the consequences of doing so. Nevertheless, every pope since Gregory I has referred to himself as the servant of the servants of God (*servus servorum Dei*), even if the conduct of some popes has not matched these words. In the light of Vatican II, the commission revising Canon Law was instructed to adopt the servant model of leadership for the new Code. This suggests, at least, intent on behalf of the popes to adopt this model more fully. However, Vatican I aside, I have argued that the Roman Catholic Church has been influenced less by secular theory than one might expect, even when it has expressed its theology using Aristotelian language or structured its Canon Law like Roman Law. It seems, therefore, the Church has to some extent adapted the secular ideas it has adopted to reflect Christian values and remove values contrary to Christianity. Nevertheless, the tendency towards authoritarianism remains in Canon Law, and the current Code seems to need further revision to incorporate fully the reforms of Vatican II.

At the Reformation, the Church of England sought to retain as much of the Canon Law of the Roman Catholic Church as it could in the changed conditions of Reformation England, and to reform itself where it felt this was necessary. The episcopal, as opposed to archiepiscopal, structure survived this reform substantially untouched: the bishops still formed a college which received its authority through the Apostolic Succession. The sovereign, however, briefly replaced the pope as the head of the Church of England, and the Archbishop of Canterbury's role as primate of all England was substantially modified: the presidency of jurisdiction he had held before the Reformation was replaced by a presidency of honour. Instead of being the senior bishop to whom the others were subject, he developed into the first among equals.

The Church seems to have been greatly influenced by English Civil Law. Consequently, English Anglicanism places great emphasis on reason and equity, and the pragmatism that goes with it. I do not believe however, that the Church has adopted the utilitarianism evident in much contemporary Civil Law, and I therefore consider that it, too, has to some extent adapted the secular theory with which it works to reflect Christian values and remove values contrary to Christianity. However, the Church has modelled its General Synod on the Westminster Parliament, and General Synod's structure requires that decisions be taken by voting by houses, in a similar manner to the Houses of Commons and Lords. Unlike most secular democracies, sessions of General Synod are conducted in the context of worship, and members are encouraged to consider prayerfully each decision they make. These measures seem to be designed to lead to a consensus under the Holy Spirit.[42] Thus, while the Church of England has borrowed a secular structure for its governance, it has adapted the structure to some extent to reflect the Biblical testimony about structures in the Primitive Church. Nevertheless, the strong pragmatic streak in English Anglican thought sometimes creates the impression that the Church places too much emphasis on how reasonable its structures are, instead of concentrating on how effective they are at pointing the faithful towards God.

While the Methodist Church does not share the Parliamentary structure of the Church of England, it does make decisions through committees to which delegates are sent by the local Churches, circuits and districts. This again might seem like a democratic system, and one rather more like Aristotelian democracy than that of the Church of England. The Methodist system, however, is also a modified democracy, in which sessions are conducted in the context of worship and members are encouraged to consider prayerfully each decision they make. Following this path might again reasonably be expected to lead eventually to a consensus under the Holy Spirit, in which case the vote at the end of the process would merely confirm what had already been decided, rather than be a means of making a democratic choice.

The URC also organises itself around a series of councils. Again, this might look like a democratic system, but it is also a modified democracy, in which the intention is that decisions are taken in the context of worship, under the guidance of the Holy Spirit. In addition, the URC draws a sharp distinction between Church government and civil government, arguing that the former is not subordinate to the latter in spiritual matters, and that the civil authorities should respect the rights of conscience and belief of all.[43] While this view has a few similarities to the relationship between Church and state proposed by Marsilius, it is different in that Church and state are government are parallel, except in spiritual matters, where Church government takes precedence.

In Baptist Churches, decisions are made by the local Church, normally in its Church Meeting. This meeting 'has the privilege and responsibility of discovering the mind of Christ for his body in that place'.[44] Since the Holy Spirit can speak through the least as effectively as through the greatest, Baptist Church Meetings operate democratically, although Baptists tend to regard this type of organisation as a pure democracy, based on free discussion, through which the mind of God may be discerned, and unsullied by the compromises made by secular democracy.[45] Provided each local Church remains attuned to the Holy Spirit, this arrangement should guard against the secularisation of the Baptist theory of authority. However,

---

42 By consensus, I mean an agreement arising from a free and open (although not necessary public) discussion of the issues by all members of the appropriate forum. I am not advocating compromises brokered behind closed doors by a small number of the influential members of a committee.

43 *The Basis of Union*, Schedule D, section 8. Ibid., p. A18.

44 Fiddes (1994), p. 6. Compare White (1976), pp. 27–8.

45 Compare Harrison (1959), pp. 159–63. Baptists have always resisted delegate voting, because this may exclude someone through whom the Holy Spirit may choose to speak.

the lack of wider structures that might act as a check against error leaves this system open to the twin dangers that local Churches may wander from the faith, and that the modified form of democracy that Baptists seek to exercise may relapse into the secular form of democracy they see as corrupt.

Conclusion

We see, therefore, that while this view of authority overlaps substantially with those of the major Churches, it also challenges them to revise elements of their structures of government to bring them more into line with the expectations of the New Testament. We have explored where the Churches stand on authority now, how they have arrived at these positions, and how they might be improved. It only remains to draw some final conclusions.

Conclusions

1 Aristotle

As we have seen, Aristotle is widely, and correctly, acknowledged as a major influence on Scholastic theology. A great deal of theological effort was expended in the Middle Ages, most famously by Thomas Aquinas, in applying Aristotelian Categories to theology, in an attempt to develop it into a logical system. It is widely believed that Thomas based his theology on Aristotle and in the process developed an Aristotelian theology. Many think Thomas used reason as the foundation for his theology, and added grace as a superstructure on these foundations. It is, however, difficult to see how a fair study of Thomas' work could reach this conclusion. Arvin Vos (1985) thinks these ideas come from Cajetan's commentary on the *Summa Theologica*, rather than the ST itself.[1]

As we have seen, the accusation of Aristotelianism in Thomas seems to originate in one of Martin Luther's arguments against transubstantiation. This accusation, however, seems rather prejudiced, and I do not believe it is true. One cannot ignore Aristotle, of course, but a more careful study of the *Summa* than that evidenced by Luther's remark suggests that Thomas bases his theology on Scripture, which he uses Aristotle, and a number of other witnesses, to illustrate. Mark Jordan (1992) argues that to accuse Thomas of Aristotelianism is to misunderstand his view of philosophy, which he subordinates to Scripture: while Thomas often quotes Aristotle, he also corrects and judges him, placing him above other philosophers, but below all believers.[2] As we have seen, he refused to place Aristotle above revelation, and while he used Aristotle to support his case, he frequently argued against Aristotle as well. In fact, while Thomas used Aristotle widely to support his case, and arranged his arguments in the SCG and ST in an Aristotelian fashion, he does not appear to have adopted Aristotle's thought in his argument to the extent that some of his opponents would have us believe. It seems to me, therefore, that the dependence on Aristotle's thought of Thomas' theology, and therefore of much of the subsequent Roman Catholic theology founded upon it, is somewhat less than is widely assumed.

The Free Churches, and the Reformers to whom they are indebted, by contrast, rejected Aristotle's thought in theory, but continued to use it in their arguments when it suited them. Of the early Reformers, Luther rejected what he saw as Thomas' synthesis of Aristotle with Augustinian theology, and attempted to remove Aristotle's influence, thereby returning to a more Augustinian position. He, like Augustine, was therefore influenced more by Plato than Aristotle. Calvin was influenced by humanism, and was therefore much more interested in what the Word of God had to

---

1 Vos (1985), p. 154.
2 Jordan (1992), pp. 1 and 40.

say than in Aristotle's opinions. He saw Aristotle as a distraction, and sometimes as an anti-Christian distraction at that.[3] Zwingli's thought, however, was less consistent than Luther's or Calvin's, and he showed much greater Aristotelian influence, even though he believed that human teaching had no salvific value. Ultimately, while he relied on Scripture for specifically Christian matters, he was open to both reason and revelation in matters indifferent, a category which, for Zwingli, seems to have included some elements of Church structure. Provided the Church was not clerical, priestly, monastic or authoritarian, Zwingli did not seem too concerned about how it was organised. Some of the successors of these Reformers took a line that seems much more Aristotelian, the more radical of them arguing that the Bible was unnecessary.

Over the years, the Churches of the Reformation, while reasserting the importance of Scripture, have come to structure themselves in a steadily more democratic manner. This, of course, was the form of government recommended by Aristotle as the least harmful in practice, although the Churches would argue that the way they operate these structures is rather different to the way Aristotle proposed. While the evidence of Aristotelian influence is suggestive, rather than conclusive, we have seen evidence of democracy in the Church at least two centuries before it was a reality in the secular sphere. It is therefore difficult to argue that the Church gradually became democratic as secular government became democratic. It seems to me that the most likely explanation is that democracy in the Church comes ultimately from Aristotle, probably indirectly through such writers as Marsilius, Ockham, Wyclif and Zwingli, who gradually modified the idea on its way, adapting it to fit more easily into a Christian environment, where the will of God, rather than the will of the people, should be supreme. If this is a fair reading, it appears that the Free Churches are much more indebted to Aristotle than is often supposed, just as the Roman Catholic Church is rather less indebted to him than is sometimes alleged.

2 Law

Canon Law began as a number of collections of the accumulated wisdom of the early Churches, before developing into a structured collection of rules that the faithful are required to obey (Roman Catholic Church), or a series of applied principles by which the clergy and certain lay officials are governed (Church of England). Roman Canon Law has been subject to a variety of influences, including Roman and Germanic legal theory, and mediaeval political theory. As these influences took hold, Roman Canon Law became increasingly authoritarian and rigid, in part because Roman Law was authoritarian, and in part because the Church felt the need to make increasingly strident assertions of its authority in times of opposition from heretical factions and

---

3   Vos (1985, pp. 38–40, 116 and 157) points out that while Calvin often argues against the Schoolmen, he never mentions Thomas by name, and, in fact, shows no sign of having read his work. He therefore believes that Calvin is arguing against the Scholastics of his day, particularly the 'sophists' then teaching in Paris. Compare Calvin (1957), volume 1, p. 228.

civil authorities. At times this opposition developed into military conflict. Once the Canons had been arranged by Gratian and extended by Gregory IX, they largely reached a static form, subject to occasional amendments by decretal, and also by the Canons of the Council of Trent. After Trent, the Canons were used in increasingly literalistic ways to support the increasing centralisation of the Church, which reached its peak at Vatican I. By this stage, law was the dominant factor, and the Church seems to have lost sight of canon, in the sense of a guide or benchmark. Only since Vatican II has the Church begun to moderate this position in favour of a view closer to the original meaning of Canon. Even so, there still seems to be a greater emphasis on law than on Canon in the Roman Catholic Church.

While the Canon Law of the Church of England as it entered the Reformation was Gratian's *Decretum*, as extended by Gregory IX, since the Reformation, its development has taken a different path. In addition to the changes made during the reign of Henry VIII to remove what were seen as the undesirable elements of Roman Canon Law, English Canon Law was influenced by the reasonableness and pragmatism usually associated with English Civil Law. As we have seen, Richard Hooker, whose views reflected those of the Church of England in the seventeenth century, emphasised the close link between reason and Divine Law, a view shared by many practitioners of English Civil Law at the time.[4] The authorities therefore had little trouble integrating English Ecclesiastical Law (and therefore English Canon Law) within English Civil Law. Thus the two systems developed in parallel, and a measure of cross-fertilisation between the two became inevitable. However, the Church of England retained the view that natural justice and equity are founded in Divine Law, even when English Jurisprudence abandoned this idea and moved towards a more utilitarian concept of justice. It thereby retained the theological content in its view of justice, and escaped the worst effects of this secularisation in English legal theory. Despite this, it seems that pragmatism and reason have been overemphasised. The Church sometimes gives the impression that it is more concerned to avoid disharmony than it is to heal consciences, to cure sins, to reclaim offenders from iniquity, and to make them just by repentance,[5] its expressions of concern that authority should be used to build up the faithful notwithstanding. In general, however, the Church of England has sought to use its Canons to reconcile the various wings of the Church, rather than to control them. Nevertheless, the Church has also been authoritarian at times. In the early seventeenth century English Canon Law was seemingly more concerned to punish and isolate offenders at times than to restore them to the Church, even though the Canons emerged from an attempt to reconcile Puritans and Episcopalians.[6] Later, following the disruption of the

---

4   See Dowrick (1961), p. 53.

5   Hooker (1981), p. 15.

6   The 1604 Canons were, in many places, extremely severe on those who refused to conform.

English Revolution, authority was often exercised in a manner neither reasonable nor pragmatic, and, in fact, singularly lacking in Christian love.[7]

The Free Churches have traditionally rejected Canon Law as a corruption of the Gospel and a product of episcopal tyranny. They have, however, needed to establish structures of Church government themselves. While the structures adopted by the Methodist and United Reformed Churches have not generally been interpreted as forms of Free Church Canon Law, I believe that they perform many of the same functions, and are therefore good candidates for Canon Law substitutes. It is clear, however, that these Churches, resisting any tendencies to authoritarian rule, have not interpreted their regulations in any legalistic sense, and the regulations seem to be flexible enough to meet these Churches' needs. Only the Baptist Churches seem to have abandoned Canon Law altogether.

In the Episcopal Churches, Canon Law seems to have been one of the principal means by which secular ideas have influenced Church structures, not always to the benefit of the latter. At times, the structure of Roman Canon Law has been so rigid that almost all flexibility in the system has disappeared, and during these periods authoritarian structures of Church government have also developed. By contrast, the Church of England has, in its more inclusive phases, seemingly fudged disputed issues rather than trying to resolve them, and this, when combined with the effects of the dispersed model of authority, has often led to a certain lack of clarity, both in its Canon Law and in its structures. Both systems of Canon Law have had their failures as well as their successes. Despite the failures, however, there continues to be something to be said for this system of Church organisation, when everyone can see where he or she stands within the Church, and it is clear what is expected of him or her.

3   Liberty

The Reformers, by contrast, rebelled against what they saw as the excessive regulation of Canon Law and the authoritarian rule of the bishops, and some of the later Reformers rejected authority altogether. Instead, they sought to emphasise Christian liberty, drawing on the letters of Paul, and insisted that Christians had freedom of conscience. While Luther and Calvin placed limits on this freedom, Zwingli thought that it was not subject to supervision or restriction by others. The Reformers sought to replace the structures they saw as corrupt and authoritarian with more limited structures designed to shock sinners into repentance without subjecting them to civil penalties. While, in general, the Churches they founded set up looser structures than the Episcopal Churches, in the process giving their members more freedom, some went too far the other way and became libertarian, particularly during the Commonwealth period. Other Churches, emphasising that no one could judge another's conscience, concluded that anyone could form their own views in the

---

7   The great ejection of 1662, for example, caused severe hardship for many clergymen with no other source of income.

light of reason guided by the Holy Spirit, without regard to what others believed. Consequently, in some Churches, liberty developed into both democracy and individualism, despite the opposition of the major Reformers to these developments. While other, more moderate Churches opposed the extreme libertarianism of the left wing, the idea of democracy gradually worked its way into all the Free Churches, although some were more successful in restraining individualism than others.

We have seen Forsyth's concern that such individualism can lead to anarchy, and I have argued that it can also lead to sectarianism, since it allows any believer to conclude that he or she alone has the truth, and that anyone who disagrees is at least mistaken. It may have been part of the problem at Corinth, where the Church was split into factions claiming to follow Paul, Apollos, Cephas and Christ.[8] As such, individualism in the Church is a destructive influence, and one with a natural tendency to divide the Body of Christ. However, it is clear that the Free Churches we have studied have put structures in place to discourage this. In the Methodist Church, Conference has final authority to interpret Methodist doctrine. Similarly, in the URC, General Assembly has the authority to limit the rights of personal conviction when necessary to maintain unity and peace. While the Baptist Union recognises no authority beyond the local Church, it does recognise a duty of individual Christians to associate in local Churches, and a similar duty of local Churches to associate on a wider basis. In each of these structures, a corporate body is able to test conflicting views under the Holy Spirit, to seek common ground, and to maintain fellowship, even if in Baptist theology it ultimately lacks the authority to resolve the situation. This seems to be the safest way to restrain the excesses of individualism.

Democracy, as we have seen, is difficult to discern in the New Testament or the Early Church. Its origins seem to be secular, and the most prominent exponent of democracy in Western thought was Aristotle. In its original, secular sense, it meant rule by the people, ideally for the common good, but more often for the good of the rulers. This is clearly not the ideal way to run a Church, in which the will of God, not the will of the people, should be supreme. God's will, however, must be discerned by the people, and since the Holy Spirit can speak through the least influential believer just as easily as through the most influential, it makes sense to consult widely before making important decisions, whether such decisions are ultimately made by the leaders or the Church members. In most Free Churches, such discussions are held in an atmosphere of worship, and the intention is to reach agreement under the Holy Spirit. Democracy, in this sense, is not harmful in the Church, and may in fact be beneficial, provided it is used as a means to seek a Godly consensus.

4   Justice

Since authority is intended to heal consciences, to reclaim the lost, and to bring sinners to repentance, it needs to be supported by a Biblical view of justice and

---

8   1 Corinthians 1:12.

righteousness. I have argued that the variety of different approaches to authority has been contributed to by a variety of different understandings of justice. Justice in the Bible is a means of ensuring fairness and right conduct, ensuring no one becomes rich at the expense of others, and emphasising that property is held in trust for the Lord. In the New Testament there is a greater emphasis on generosity and servanthood than in the Old. Early Roman Law, by contrast, sees justice as a way of exacting vengeance on those who wrong others, and placing the guilty under the power of those they have wronged. This idea sees justice as retributive, in which vengeance belongs to the victim, a position that conflicts with Biblical ideas of justice, which are distributive, and in which vengeance belongs to the Lord, not to human legislators. Greek philosophy sees justice as a part of virtue and a way to achieve happiness. This also conflicts with Biblical ideas, in that it sees either humans or fate as sovereign, not God. While English Law at the Reformation used natural justice, which in turn was founded on Divine Law, as the basis of its jurisprudence, this developed into a utilitarian system in which the best result was the one that achieved the maximum happiness for the largest number of people. Again utilitarianism conflicts with the Biblical view, in that what makes humans happy is seen as more important than what God has revealed as just. All are agreed that giving each his or her due lies at the core of justice. However, the ideas of justice in Greek, Roman and more recent English Law have self at the centre, while Jewish ideas are centred on God. Thus, these secular ideas link justice with equity, not righteousness, and therefore move away from the Biblical ideal. As we have seen, Biblical ideas of justice include equity, while the other ideas see equity as a correcting factor, where a strict application of the law fails to produce justice.

Every Church seeks to root itself and its doctrine in the Bible. However, all of these ideas of justice have been adopted to some extent by at least one of the Churches we consider. The Roman Catholic Church has been greatly influenced by Roman legal theory, as witnessed by no less a figure than Pope Paul VI, in addition to the influence of Plato in late antiquity, and ideas from sources as diverse as Germanic legal theory, Aristotle and Cicero in the Middle Ages. The Church of England has also been influenced by English Legal theory, although the Church has largely managed to avoid adopting a utilitarian approach to justice. By harmonising its Canon Law with English Civil Law, the Church has largely removed the influence of Roman Law, although elements of Germanic influence remain.[9] Similarly, I have argued that the Free Churches are indebted, at least in part, to Aristotle, and therefore to the Greek idea of justice as virtue, although the extent of this influence is difficult to quantify. If this is a fair reading, all the Churches we consider have adopted non-Biblical elements into their concepts of justice, and this has distorted their views to some extent. To the extent that these ideas of justice have influenced Church structures, then, they have also distorted the structures of authority founded on them, and impaired the ability of the Church to exercise authority in appropriate ways.

---

9   Such as patronage, oaths of obedience and parishes as benefices.

5 Authority

All the approaches to ecclesiastical authority adopted by the Churches are based to some extent on the patterns of authority used in the Primitive Church and described in the New Testament. While these patterns were appropriate to their day, the development and growth of the Church required new structures to be found, and the Church therefore adapted and adopted secular structures as it grew. All these structures, however, have had effects that I have argued were harmful to the Church. The Roman Catholic Church, by adopting a monarchical system based on the Roman Empire,[10] in part as a defence against conflict, ended up with an authoritarian and inflexible system that seemed to exclude the majority of Christians from decision-making, although since Vatican II it has begun to increase the flexibility of its structures, and to seek to decentralise its structures and to increase the voice of the laity. However, outside the episcopal hierarchy there seems to be a consensus that this process has not gone far enough. While the Roman Catholic Church sees the ecclesiastical hierarchy as one of the essential marks of the Church, and it will not accept any lay involvement in decision-making that might interfere with this situation,[11] it seems that it also needs to find ways to empower lay people to exercise their common priesthood as the People of God more fully within the Church, as well as in the world.

The Church of England, having tried to retain as much Canon Law as it could, while distancing itself from what it saw as corrupt practices in the Roman Catholic Church, attempted to embody what it saw as the English virtues of reason and moderation by building in checks and balances at every stage of decision-making. In the process, it ended up with a view and structure of authority so diffuse that it is often difficult to discover where the Church of England stands on a particular issue, even when that issue is completely uncontroversial. While this approach gives the Church breadth, and enables it to accommodate Christians of many different types of Churchmanship, it can at times lead to issues being fudged rather than addressed, and it can leave members of the Church confused about where they stand theologically. While it is desirable for the Church to be as inclusive as it can be, it seems that greater clarity in its doctrine and structures would reduce such confusion, and make it easier for Anglicans to be effective witnesses for Christ.

The Free Churches, reacting against the authoritarian structures of the Episcopal Churches, adopted structures that are in principle democratic, in a bid to give more freedom to their members. They also shifted the focus of authority away from Church leaders and towards members, through such expedients as making the Church Meeting, rather than the minister, the governing body of the Church. This tendency towards personal freedom, if allowed to proceed without restrictions, could easily lead to rampant individualism or anarchy. However, in an attempt to ensure that their structures do not operate like secular democracies, in such a way that the members

---

10 See Southern (1970), pp. 24–6.

11 Congregation for the Clergy (2002), pp. 27–49.

feel able to do whatever they like, each Church has set up safeguards designed to ensure discernment of the will of God in decision-making. Nevertheless, it is essential to ensure that the corporate dimension of Christianity is always retained, and that the faithful are always aware that they are part of the Body of Christ, and not just individual Christians.

It therefore seems that there is potential for growth and reform in all these systems, and there is certainly scope for further work on authority taking account of the material we have examined. It is my hope that each of the Churches will find both encouragement and challenge in what I have said. In a fallen world, there can be no perfect Church order, and the only suitable response to the continuing imperfections of our structures is constantly to return to God in a spirit of repentance and to seek renewal through the Holy Spirit. As we do so, the Church, as the body of Christ, will be refashioned and redeemed so that it more accurately represents His image and more effectively reflects His glory.

Bibliography

Achtemeier, Paul J. (1996), *1 Peter: A Commentary*, edited by Eldon Jay Epp. Minneapolis: Fortress Press.

Afonso, Meneo A. (1996), *What is the Nature of Authority in the Church?* Lanham, Maryland: University Press of America.

Ames, William (1643), *Conscience with the Power and Cases thereof, Divided into Five Bookes, Written by the Godly and Learned William Ames, Doctor and Professor of Divinity in the Famous University of Franeker in Friesland. Translated out of Latine into English for more Publique benefit. Published by order [of Parliament]. 20 May 1641* (two volumes). London.

——— (1659), *The Substance of Christian Religion*. London: T. Mabb.

Anglican Communion (1948), *The Lambeth Conference 1948: The Encyclical Letter from the Bishops, together with Resolutions and Reports*. London: SPCK.

——— (1978), *The Report of the Lambeth Conference 1978*. London: CIO.

Aquinas, Saint Thomas (1975a), *Summa Contra Gentiles, Book 1: God*, translated by Anton C. Pegis, FRSC. London: University of Notre Dame Press.

——— (1975b), *Summa Contra Gentiles, Book 2: Creation*, translated by James F. Anderson. London: University of Notre Dame Press.

——— (1975c), *Summa Contra Gentiles, Book 3: Providence, Part II*, translated by Vernon J. Bourke. London: University of Notre Dame Press.

——— (1981), *Summa Theologica*, translated by the Fathers of the English Dominican Province. New York, Benzinger Brothers. Reprinted in five volumes by Christian Classics.

——— (1987), *Selected Political Writings*, edited with an introduction by A.P. d'Entrèves. Translated by J.G. Dawson. Oxford: Basil Blackwell.

ARCIC (1999), *The Gift of Authority: Authority in the Church III*. London: Catholic Truth Society.

Archbishops' Commission (1947), *The Canon Law of the Church of England: Being the Report of the Archbishops' Commission on Canon Law, together with Proposals for a Revised Body of Canons, and a Memorandum* 'Lawful Authority' *by the Honourable Mr Justice Vaisey*. London: SPCK.

Aristotle (1976), *Ethics*, translated by J.A.K. Thomson, revised by Hugh Tredennick. London: Penguin.

——— (1991), *The Art of Rhetoric*, translated with an introduction and notes by Hugh Lawson–Tancred. London: Penguin.

——— (1996), *The Politics and The Constitution of Athens*, edited by Stephen Everson. Cambridge: Cambridge University Press.

Augustine (1984), *City of God*, translated by Henry Bettenson with an introduction by John O'Meara. London: Penguin.

Aune, David E. (1997), *Revelation 1–5* (Word Biblical Commentary, volume 52). Dallas, Texas: Word Books.

Avis, Paul (2001), *Church, State and Establishment*. London: SPCK.

Aylmer, G.E., ed. (1975), *The Levellers in the English Revolution*. London: Thames and Hudson.

Ball, W.E. (1891), St. Paul and the Roman Law, *Contemporary Review*, volume 60: 278–93. London: Isbister and Company.

Baptist Union of Great Britain (1999), *The Baptist Union Directory for 1999–2000*. Didcot: Baptist Union of Great Britain.

Baptist Union of Scotland (1985), *Viewpoint: Authority, Ministry and Business in the Church*. Baptist Union of Scotland.

Barrett, C.K. (1960), *The Gospel According to St John: An Introduction with Commentary and Notes on the Greek Text*. London: SPCK.

Barth, Markus. (1974), *Ephesians 4–6: A New Translation with Introduction and Commentary* (The Anchor Bible). New York: Doubleday.

Bauer, W. (1979), *A Greek–English Lexicon of the New Testament and Other Early Christian Literature: A translation and adaptation of the fourth revised and augmented edition of Walter Bauer's Griechisch–Deutsches Wörterbuch zu den Schriften des Neuen Testaments und der übringen urchristlichen Literatur*, translated by William F. Arndt and F. Wilbur Gingrich. Second Edition, revised and augmented by F. Wilbur Gingrich and Frederick W. Danker from Walter Bauer's Fifth Edition, 1958. Chicago: Chicago University Press.

Baynes, Norman (1972), *Constantine the Great and the Christian Church: The Raleigh Lecture on History, 1929*, Second Edition. London: British Academy/ Oxford University Press.

Beal, John P., James A. Coriden and Thomas J. Green (2000), *New Commentary on the Code of Canon Law, Study Edition*. New York: Paulist Press.

Beasley-Murray, George R. (1987), *John* (Word Biblical Commentary, volume 36). Waco, Texas: Word Books.

Benedict XV, Pope (1949), *Codex Iuris Canonici, PII X Pontificis Maximi, Iussu Digestus Benedicti Papae XV Auctoritate Promulgatus*. Westminster, Maryland: The Newman Press.

Bentham, Jeremy (1789), *An Introduction to the Principles of Morals and Legislation*. London: T. Payne & Son.

Bernard, J.H. (1928), *A Critical and Exegetical Commentary on the Gospel According to Saint John*, volume II. Edinburgh: T & T Clark.

Bernard of Clairvaux, Saint (1976), *Five Books On Consideration: Advice to a Pope*. Kalamazoo, Michigan: Cistercian Publications.

Best, Ernest (1971), *I Peter* (New Century Bible). London: Oliphants.

——— (1998), *A Critical and Exegetical Commentary on Ephesians*. Edinburgh: T & T Clark.

Bettenson, Henry, ed. (1943), *Documents of the Christian Church, Selected and Edited by Henry Bettenson*. London: Oxford University Press.

Bevan, Edwyn R. (1913), *Stoics and Sceptics: Four Lectures Delivered in Oxford During Hilary Term 1913 for the Common University Fund*. Oxford: Clarendon Press.

Bible (1982), *The Holy Bible: 1611 Edition (King James Version)*. Nashville, Tennessee: Thomas Nelson.

—— (1984), *New International Version*. London: Hodder and Stoughton.

—— (1989), *The Revised English Bible*. Oxford and Cambridge: Oxford University Press and Cambridge University Press.

—— (1993), *Novum Testamentum Graece*, Nestle-Aland XXVII. Stuttgart: Deutsche Bibelgesellschaft.

—— (1994), *Biblia Sacra, Iuxta Vulgatem Versionem*, Fourth Edition. Stuttgart: Deutsche Bibelgesellschaft.

—— (1998), *New Revised Standard Version with Apocrypha*, Anglicized Edition. Oxford: Oxford University Press.

Boecker, Hans Jochen (1980), *Law and the Administration of Justice in the Old Testament and Ancient Near East*, translated by Jeremy Moiser. London: SPCK.

Borgeaud, Charles (1894), *The Rise of Modern Democracy in Old and New England*, translated by Mrs Birkbeck Hill [from two articles published in the *Annales de l'Ecole libre des sciences politiques*]. With a preface by C.H. Firth. London: Swan Sonnenschein & Co.

Botterweck, G. Johannes and Helmer Ringgren, eds (1990), *Theological Dictionary of the Old Testament*, volume VI: *yôbēl – yātar I*, translated by David E. Green. Grand Rapids, Michigan: Eerdmans.

Botterweck, G. Johannes, Helmer Ringgren and Heinz-Josef Fabry, eds (2003), *Theological Dictionary of the Old Testament*, volume XII: *pāsah – qûm*, translated by Douglas W. Stott. Grand Rapids, Michigan: Eerdmans.

Bouscaren, T. Lincoln, SJ, Adam Ellis, SJ, and Francis N. Korth, SJ (1963), *Canon Law: A Text and Commentary*, Fourth Edition. Milwaukee: The Bruce Publishing Company.

Bowden, John (1840), *The Life and Pontificate of Gregory the Seventh*, in two volumes. London: J.G.F. & J. Rivington.

Brachlow, Stephen (1988), *The Communion of Saints: Radical Puritan and Separatist Ecclesiology 1570–1625*. Oxford: Oxford University Press.

Brailsford, H.N. (1961), *The Levellers and the English Revolution*. London: Cresset Press.

Bray, Gerald, ed. (1994), *Documents of the English Reformation*. Cambridge: James Clarke & Co Ltd.

—— (1998), *The Anglican Canons 1529–1947*. Woodbridge, Suffolk: The Church of England Record Society and the Boydell Press.

Briden, Timothy and Brian Hanson (1992), *Moore's Introduction to English Canon Law*, Third Edition. Oxford: Mowbray.

Brierley, Peter (1999), *UK Religious Handbook: Religious Trends, 2000/2001, No. 2*. London: Christian Research and HarperCollins.

—— (2000), *The Tide is Running Out: What the English Church Attendance Survey Reveals*. London: Christian Research.

Bromiley, G.W. (1953), *Zwingli and Bullinger* (The Library of Christian Classics, volume 24). London: SCM Press.

Burton, Ernest de Witt (1921), *A Critical and Exegetical Commentary on the Epistle to the Galatians*. Edinburgh: T & T Clark.

Butterfield, Jeremy, ed. (2003), *Collins English Dictionary*, Sixth Edition. Glasgow: HarperCollins.

Calvin, John (1957), *Institutes of the Christian Religion* (two volumes), translated by Henry Beveridge. London: James Clarke and Co.

—— (1994), *A Harmony of the Gospels: Matthew, Mark and Luke*, Third Edition, volume 1, translated by A.W. Morrison. Carlisle: Paternoster Press.

Cameron, Averil and Stuart G. Hall, translators (1999), *Eusebius: Life of Constantine*. Oxford: Clarendon Press.

Campbell, R. Alastair (1995), Leaders and Fathers: Church Government in Earliest Christianity, *Irish Biblical Studies*, volume 17 (January 1995): 2–21.

Canon Law Society of Great Britain and Ireland in association with the Canon Law Society of Australia and New Zealand, and the Canadian Canon Law Society (1997), *The Code of Canon Law: New Revised English Translation*. London: HarperCollins.

Cartwright, Thomas (1575), *The second replie of Thomas Cartwright to Maister Doctor Whitgiftes second answer/touching the Church Discipline*.

Chadwick, Henry (1967), *The Early Church* (Penguin History of the Church, volume 1). London: Penguin.

Charles, R.H. (1920), *A Critical and Exegetical Commentary on the Revelation of Saint John*, volume 1. Edinburgh: T & T Clark.

Chilton, Bruce and Jacob Neusner (1995), *Judaism in the New Testament: Practices and Beliefs*. London: Routledge.

—— (1999), *Types of Authority in Formative Christianity and Judaism*. London: Routledge.

Chodorow, Stanley (1972), *Christian Political Theory and Church Politics in the Mid–Twelfth Century: The Ecclesiology of Gratian's Decretum*. Berkeley, California: University of California Press.

Church of England (1980), *The Alternative Service Book 1980*. London, Beccles and Cambridge: SPCK, William Clowes and Cambridge University Press.

—— (1992), *The Book of Common Prayer*. (including amendments by Measure from 1964 to 1968), Standard Edition. Cambridge: Cambridge University Press.

—— (2000), *The Standing Orders of the General Synod of the Church of England*, October 2000 Edition. London: Church House Publishing.

—— (2005), *The Canons of the Church of England*, Sixth Edition, incorporating First Supplement. London: Church House Publishing.

Cicero, Marcus Tullius (1913), *De Officiis*, translated by Walter Miller (Loeb Classical Library). London: Harvard University Press.

―――― (1928), *De Re Publica* and *De Legibus*, translated by C.W. Keyes (Loeb Classical Library). London: Harvard University Press.

―――― (1931), *De Finibus Bonorum et Malorum*, Second Edition, translated by H. Rackham (Loeb Classical Library). London: Harvard University Press.

Cochrane, Arthur C., ed. (2003), *Reformed Confessions of the 16th Century*. London: Westminster John Knox Press.

Cohen, Abraham (1995), *Everyman's Talmud: The Major Teachings of the Rabbinic Sages*, with a new foreword by Jacob Neusner. New York: Schocken.

Collins, John N. (1990), *Diakonia: Re–interpreting the Ancient Sources*. Oxford: Oxford University Press.

Collins, Paul (1997), *Papal Power: A Proposal for Change in Catholicism's Third Millennium*. London: Fount.

Congregation for the Clergy (2002), *The Priest, Pastor and Leader of the Parish Community*. London: Catholic Truth Society.

Coriden, James A. (2004), *An Introduction to Canon Law*, Revised Edition. New York: Paulist Press.

Cornick, David (1998), *Under God's Good Hand: A history of the traditions which have come together in the United Reformed Church in the United Kingdom*. London: United Reformed Church.

Cragg, Gerald R. (1970), *The Church and the Age of Reason 1648–1789* (Penguin History of the Church, volume 4). London: Penguin.

Cyprian, Saint (1964), *Letters*, translated by Sister Rose Bernard Donna, CSJ (The Fathers of the Church: A New Translation, volume 51). Washington DC: Catholic University of America Press.

Davies, Rupert (1968), *Religious Authority in an Age of Doubt*. London: Epworth Press.

Davies, W.D. and Dale C. Allison (1988), *A Critical and Exegetical Commentary on the Gospel According to Saint Matthew*, volume 1: *Matthew 1–7*. Edinburgh: T & T Clark.

―――― (1991), *A Critical and Exegetical Commentary on the Gospel According to Saint Matthew*, volume 2: *Matthew 8–18*. Edinburgh: T & T Clark.

―――― (1997), *A Critical and Exegetical Commentary on the Gospel According to Saint Matthew*, volume 3: *Matthew 19–28*. Edinburgh: T & T Clark.

de George, Richard T. (1985), *The Nature and Limits of Authority*. Lawrence, Kansas: University of Kansas Press.

Denzinger, Henricus, ed. (1932), *Enchiridion Symbolorum Definitionum et Declarationum de Rebus Fidei et Morum*, Editio 18–20. Friburgi Brisgoviae: Herder.

Doctrine Commission of the Church of England (1981), *Believing in the Church: The Corporate Nature of Faith*. London: SPCK.

Doe, Norman (1996), *The Legal Framework of the Church of England: A Critical Study in a Comparative Context*. Oxford: Clarendon Press.

Doe, Norman, Mark Hill and Robert Ombres, eds (1998), *English Canon Law: Essays in Honour of Bishop Eric Kemp*. Cardiff: University of Wales Press.

Dowrick, F.E. (1961), *Justice according to the English Common Lawyers*. London: Butterworths.

Dunn, James G. (1988), *Romans 1–8* (Word Biblical Commentary, volume 38A). Dallas, Texas: Word Books.

Dyson, R.W., trans. (2004), *Giles of Rome's 'On Ecclesiastical Power'*. New York: Columbia University Press.

Elliott, John H. (2000), *1 Peter: A New Translation with Introduction and Commentary* (The Anchor Bible). New York: Doubleday.

Engberg–Pedersen, Troels, ed. (1994), *Paul in his Hellenistic Context*. Edinburgh: T & T Clark.

English Reports (1903), volume 26: *Chancery 6*. London: Stevens.

Evans, C.F. (1990), *Saint Luke*. London: SCM Press.

Evans, Craig A. (2001), *Mark 8:27–16:20* (Word Biblical Commentary, volume 34B). Nashville, Tennessee: Thomas Nelson.

Evans, Craig A. and Stanley E. Porter (2000), *Dictionary of New Testament Background: A Compendium of Contemporary Biblical Scholarship*. Leicester: InterVarsity Press.

Evans, G.R. (1990), *Authority in the Church: a challenge for Anglicans*. Norwich: The Canterbury Press.

——— (1994), *The Church and the Churches: Towards an Ecumenical Ecclesiology*. Cambridge: Cambridge University Press.

Fiddes, Paul S., ed. (1994), *The Nature of the Assembly and the Council of the Baptist Union of Great Britain*. Didcot: Baptist Union of Great Britain.

Fitzmyer, Joseph A., SJ (1985), *The Gospel According to Luke, X–XXIV* (The Anchor Bible). New York: Doubleday.

Forsyth, P.T. (1952), *The Principle of Authority*, Second Edition. London: Independent Press.

Foster, Nigel (1993), *The German Legal System and Laws*. London: Blackstone.

Friedberg, Aemilius and Aemilii Ludouici Richteri (2000), *Corpus Iuris Canonici, Editio Lipsiensis Secunda, Curas ad Librorum Manu Scriptorum et Editionis Romanae, Fidem Recognouit et Adnotatione Critica* (two volumes). Lipsiae: Bernardi Tauchnitz. Reprinted by The Lawbook Exchange, Limited.

Gäbler, Ulrich (1987), *Huldrych Zwingli: His Life and Work*. Edinburgh: T & T Clark.

Gallagher, Clarence (2002), *Church Law and Church Order in Rome and Byzantium: A Comparative Study* (Birmingham Byzantine and Ottoman Monographs, volume 8). Aldershot: Ashgate.

Gerosa, Libero (2002), *Canon Law*. London: Continuum.

Gewirth, Alan (1951), *Marsilius of Padua: The Defender of Peace, volume 1: Marsilius of Padua and Medieval Political Philosophy*. New York: Columbia University Press.

Gibson, Edmund, DD (1713), *Codex Juris Ecclesiastici Anglicani: or, the Statutes, Constitutions, Canons, Rubricks and Articles of the Church of England,*

Methodically Digested under their Proper Heads. With a Commentary, Historical and Judicial. London: J. Baskett.

——— (1854), *Synodus Anglicana: or, the Constitution and Proceedings of an English Convocation, Shown From the Acts and Registers Thereof to be Agreeable to the Principles of an Episcopal Church*, edited by Edward Cardwell, DD Oxford: Oxford University Press.

Giles, Edward, ed. (1952), *Documents Illustrating Papal Authority: A.D. 96 – 454*. London: SPCK.

Goold, William H., ed. (1965), *The Works of John Owen*, volume 15. Edinburgh: Banner of Truth.

——— (1967), *The Works of John Owen*, volume 13. Edinburgh: Banner of Truth.

——— (1968), *The Works of John Owen*, volume 16. Edinburgh: Banner of Truth.

Goppelt, Leonhard (1993), *A Commentary on I Peter*, translated by John E. Alsup. Grand Rapids, Michigan: Eerdmans.

Granfield, Patrick (1980), *The Papacy in Transition*. Dublin: Gill and MacMillan.

Gratian (1993), *The Treatise on Laws*, translated by Augustine Thompson, OP, with *The Ordinary Gloss*, translated by James Gordley. Washington DC: Catholic University of America Press.

Halsbury, Lord (1975), *Halsbury's Laws of England*, Fourth Edition, volume 14: *Easements and Ecclesiastical Law*, edited by Lord Hailsham of Marylebone. London: Butterworths.

——— (1986), *Halsbury's Statutes of England and Wales*, Fourth Edition, volume 14: *Ecclesiastical Law*, edited by James Bowman. London: Butterworths.

——— (2000), *Halsbury's Statutes of England and Wales*, Fourth Edition, volume 41: *Solicitors, Stamp Duty and Statutes*, edited by Andrew Davies. London: Butterworths.

Hanson, A.T. and R.P.C. Hanson (1987), *The Identity of the Church: A Guide to Recognizing the Contemporary Church*. London: SCM Press.

Harrison, Paul M. (1959), *Authority and Power in the Free Church Tradition: A Social Case Study of the American Baptist Convention*. Carbondale, Illinois: Southern Illinois University Press.

Hayden, Roger, ed. (1980), *Baptist Union Documents 1948–1977*. London: The Baptist Historical Society.

Henderson, Ernest F., trans. and ed. (1965), *Select Historical Documents of the Middle Ages* (Bohn's Antiquarian Library). New York: Biblio and Tannen.

Hicks, Edward (1896), *Traces of Greek Philosophy and Roman Law in the New Testament*. London: SPCK.

Hill, Christopher (1975), *The World Turned Upside Down: Radical Ideas During the English Revolution*. London: Penguin.

Hill, Edmund, OP (1988), *Ministry and Authority in the Catholic Church*. London: Geoffrey Chapman.

Hill, Mark (2001), *Ecclesiastical Law*, Second Edition. Oxford: Oxford University Press.

Hooker, Richard (1977a), *Of the Lawes of Ecclesiasticall Politie*: The Folger Library Edition of the Works of Richard Hooker, volume 1: *Preface and Books I–IV*, edited by Georges Edelen. London: The Belknap Press of Harvard University Press.

────── (1977b), *Of the Lawes of Ecclesiasticall Politie*: The Folger Library Edition of the Works of Richard Hooker, volume 2: *Book V*, edited by W. Speed Hill. London: The Belknap Press of Harvard University Press.

────── (1981), *Of the Lawes of Ecclesiasticall Politie*: The Folger Library Edition of the Works of Richard Hooker, volume 3: *Books VI–VIII*, edited by P.G. Stanwood. London: The Belknap Press of Harvard University Press.

Hoose, Bernard, ed. (2002), *Authority in the Roman Catholic Church: Theory and Practice*. Aldershot: Ashgate.

Hylson-Smith, Kenneth (1996), *The Churches in England from Elizabeth I to Elizabeth II*, volume 1: *1558–1688*. London: SCM.

John Paul II, Pope (1983), *Codex Iuris Canonici, Auctoritate Ioannis Pauli PP. II Promulgatus*. Vatican City: Libreria Editrice Vaticana.

────── (1998a), *Apostolic Letter* Motu Proprio *of Pope John Paul II: Ad Tuendam Fidem, By Which Certain Norms Are Inserted into* the Code of Canon Law *and into* the Code of Canons of the Eastern Churches, Vatican Translation. Boston, Massachusetts: Pauline Books and Media.

────── (1998b), *The Theological and Juridical Nature of Episcopal Conferences: Apostolic Letter issued* Motu Proprio *by His Holiness John Paul II*. Sherbrooke, Québec: Médiaspaul.

Jones, Tudur (1962), *Congregationalism in England 1662–1962*. London: Independent Press.

Jordan, Mark D. (1992), *The Alleged Aristotelianism of Thomas Aquinas*. Toronto: Pontifical Institute of Mediaeval Studies.

Kagan, K. Kahana (1955), *Three Great Systems of Jurisprudence*. London: Stevens and Sons.

Kirkpatrick, Dow, ed. (1964), *The Doctrine of the Church: A Symposium prepared under the direction of the World Methodist Council*. London: Epworth Press.

Kittel, Gerhard, ed. (1964), *Theological Dictionary of the New Testament*, volume II: Δ–H, translated by G.H. Bromiley. Grand Rapids, Michigan: Eerdmans.

────── (1965), *Theological Dictionary of the New Testament*, volume III: Θ–K, translated by G.H. Bromiley. Grand Rapids, Michigan: Eerdmans.

Kittel, Gerhard and Gerhard Friedrich, eds (1968), *Theological Dictionary of the New Testament*, volume VI: Πε–P, translated by G.H. Bromiley. Grand Rapids, Michigan: Eerdmans.

Lacey, T.A. (1928), *Authority in the Church: A Study of Principles*. London: Mowbray.

Laing, David, ed. (2004a), *The Works of John Knox*, volume 2. Eugene, Oregon: Wipf and Stock.

────── (2004b), *The Works of John Knox*, volume 4. Eugene, Oregon: Wipf and Stock.

—— (2004c), *The Works of John Knox*, volume 6. Eugene, Oregon: Wipf and Stock.

Lake, Kirksopp, trans. (1912), *The Apostolic Fathers*, volume 1 (Loeb Classical Library). London: Harvard University Press.

Langford, Thomas A. (1998), *Exploring Methodism: Methodist Theology*. Peterborough: Epworth Press.

Law Reports (1868), House of Lords, volume 3. London: Clowes.

Long, A.A. and D.N. Sedley (1987), *The Hellenistic philosophers*, volume 1: *Translations of the principal sources with philosophical commentary*. Cambridge: Cambridge University Press.

Luibheid, Colm, trans. (1987), *Pseudo-Dionysius: The Complete Works* (The Classics of Western Spirituality). London: SPCK.

Lumpkin, William (1969), *Baptist Confessions of Faith*, Second Edition. Valley Forge, Pennsylvania: Judson Press.

Luther, Martin (1911), *The Table Talk of Martin Luther*, translated and edited by William Hazlitt. London: G. Bell and Sons.

—— (1966), *Luther's Works*, volume 44: *The Christian in Society I*, edited by James Atkinson. Philadelphia: Fortress Press.

—— (1970a), *Luther's Works*, volume 39: *Church and Ministry I*, edited by Eric W. Gritsch. Philadelphia: Fortress Press.

—— (1970b), *Three Treatises*, Second Revised Edition, edited by Helmut T. Lehmann. Philadelphia: Fortress Press.

Luz, Ulrich (1989), *Matthew 1–7: A Commentary*, translated by Wilhelm C. Linss. Edinburgh: T & T Clark.

—— (2001), *Matthew 8–20: A Commentary*, translated by James E. Crouch. Minneapolis: Fortress Press.

MacEoin, Gary, ed. (1998), *The Papacy and the People of God*. Maryknoll, New York: Orbis.

MacPherson, C.B. (1962), *The Political Theory of Possessive Individualism: Hobbes to Locke*. Oxford: Clarendon Press.

Mann, C.S. (1986), *Mark: A New Translation with Introduction and Commentary* (The Anchor Bible). New York: Doubleday.

Mannion, Gerard, Richard Gaillardetz, Jan Kerkhofs, and Kenneth Wilson, eds (2003), *Readings in Church Authority: Gifts and Challenges for Contemporary Catholicism*. Aldershot: Ashgate.

Marsilius of Padua (2001), *Defensor Pacis*, translated by Alan Gewirth, with a new afterword and bibliography by Cary J. Nederman. New York: Columbia University Press.

McGrade, Arthur Stephen (1974), *The Political Thought of William of Ockham: Personal and Institutional Principles*. Cambridge: Cambridge University Press.

McKenzie, John L., SJ (1966), *Authority in the Church*. London: Geoffrey Chapman.

Messinger, Heinz, ed. (1982), *Langenscheidt's Condensed Muret-Sanders German Dictionary*. Berlin: Langenscheidt.

Methodist Conference (1988), *The Constitutional Practice and Discipline of the Methodist Church*, Prepared by the Law and Polity Committee of the Methodist Church, volume 1: *Fixed Texts*, Seventh Edition. Peterborough: Methodist Publishing House.

——— (1999a), *The Minutes of Conference and The Directory of the Methodist Church*. Peterborough: Methodist Publishing House.

——— (1999b), *Called to Love and Praise: A Methodist Conference Statement on the Church*, Prepared by the Faith and Order Committee of the Methodist Church. Peterborough: Methodist Publishing House.

——— (2005), *The Constitutional Practice and Discipline of the Methodist Church*, Prepared by the Law and Polity Committee of the Methodist Church, volume 2: *Deeds, Standing Orders and Other Constitutional Documents*, Seventh Edition, 2005 Revision. Peterborough: Methodist Publishing House.

Moltmann, Jürgen and Hans Küng, eds (1981), Who Has the Say in the Church?: *Concilium*, volume 148. Edinburgh: T & T Clark.

Moo, Douglas J. (1996), *The Epistle to Romans*. Grand Rapids, Michigan: Eerdmans.

Morrisey, F.G., OMI (1978), The Spirit of Canon Law in the Teaching of Pope Paul VI. *L'Osservatore Romano*, 9 November 1978: 6–8.

Morrison, Wayne (1997), *Jurisprudence: from the Greeks to post-modernism*. London: Cavendish.

Mounce, William D. (1993), *The Analytical Lexicon to the Greek New Testament*. Grand Rapids, Michigan: Zondervan.

Neuner, Josef and Jacques Dupuis, eds (1996), *The Christian Faith in the Doctrinal Documents of the Catholic Church*, Sixth Edition. New York: Alba House.

Neusner, Jacob and Bruce Chilton (1997), *The Intellectual Foundations of Christian and Jewish Discourse: The Philosophy of Religious Argument*. London: Routledge.

Nuttall, Geoffrey F. (1957), *Visible Saints: The Congregational Way 1640–1660*. Oxford: Blackwell.

——— (1967), *The Puritan Spirit: Essays and Addresses*. London: Epworth Press.

Nuttall, Geoffrey F. and Owen Chadwick, eds (1962), *From Uniformity to Unity 1662–1962*. London: SPCK.

Ockham, William of (1992), *A Short Discourse on the Tyrannical Government Over Things Divine and Human, but Especially Over the Empire and Those Subject to the Empire, Usurped by Some Who Are Called Highest Pontiffs*, edited by Arthur Stephen McGrade, translated by John Kilcullen. Cambridge: Cambridge University Press.

——— (1995), *A Letter to the Friars Minor and Other Writings*, edited by Arthur Stephen McGrade and John Kilcullen, translated by John Kilcullen. Cambridge: Cambridge University Press.

——— (1998), *On The Power of Emperors and Popes*, translated and edited by Annabel S. Brett. Bristol: Thoemmes Press.

O'Connor, D.J. (1967), *Aquinas and Natural Law*. London: MacMillan.

O'Donovan, Joan Lockwood (1991), *Theology of Law and Authority in the English Reformation* (Emory University Studies in Law and Religion, Number 1). Atlanta, Georgia: Scholars Press.

Örsy, Ladislas (1992), *Theology and Canon Law: New Horizons for Legislation and Interpretation*. Collegeville, Minnesota: Michael Glazier.

Patrick, Dale (1985), *Old Testament Law*. Atlanta: John Knox Press.

Peters, Edward N., curator (2001), *The 1917 or Pio-Benedictine Canon Law in English Translation with Extensive Scholarly Apparatus*. San Francisco: Ignatius Press.

Pharr, Clyde, trans. (1952), *The Theodosian Code and Novels, and the Sirmondian Constitutions*. Princeton, New Jersey: Princeton University Press.

Pius XII, Pope (1943), *On the Mystical Body of Christ and our Union in it with Christ*. Boston, Massachusetts: Pauline Books and Media. Undated reprint.

—— (1950), *Some False Opinions Which Threaten to Undermine Catholic Doctrine*. Boston, Massachusetts: Pauline Books and Media. Undated reprint.

Plato (1970), *The Laws*, translated with an introduction by Trevor J. Saunders. London: Penguin.

—— (1987), *The Republic*, Second Edition, translated with an introduction by Sir Desmond Lee. London: Penguin.

Portalié, Eugène (1960), *A Guide to the Thought of Saint Augustine*. London: Burns and Oates.

Priestley, Joseph (1769), *Considerations on Church Authority,: Occasioned by Dr Balguy's Sermon on that Subject, preached at Lambeth Chapel, and Published by the Order of the Archbishop*. London: J. Johnson and J. Payne.

Rahner, Karl, ed. (1975), *Encyclopedia of Theology: A Concise Sacramentum Mundi*. Tunbridge Wells: Burns and Oates.

Richardson, Alan and John Bowden (1983), *A New Dictionary of Christian Theology*. London: SCM.

Roberts, Alexander, DD and James Donaldson, DD, eds (1999), *The Ante-Nicene Fathers* (ten volumes). Edinburgh: T & T Clark. Reprinted by Hendrickson.

Roman Catholic/Methodist Committee (1981), *Eucharist, Ministry, Authority: Statements Agreed by Roman Catholics and Methodists*. Abbots Langley: Catholic Information Services.

Rousseau, Jean-Jacques (1968), *The Social Contract*, translated by Maurice Cranston. London: Penguin.

Rupp, E.G. and Benjamin Drewery, eds (1970), *Martin Luther: Documents of Modern History*. London: Edward Arnold.

Salvian of Marseille (1962), *The Writings of Salvian, the Presbyter*, translated by Jeremiah F. O'Sullivan (The Fathers of the Church: A New Translation, volume 3). Washington DC: Catholic University of America Press.

Sanday, W. and A.C. Headlam (1908), *A Critical and Exegetical Commentary on the Epistle to the Romans*, Fifth Edition. Edinburgh: T & T Clark.

Schaff, Philip and Henry Wace, eds (1999), *The Nicene and Post-Nicene Fathers*, Series 2, (14 volumes). Edinburgh: T & T Clark. Reprinted by Hendrickson.

Schleiermacher, F.D.E. (1928), *The Christian Faith: English Translation of the Second German Edition*, edited by H.R. Mackintosh and J.S. Stewart. Edinburgh: T & T Clark.

———— (1958), *On Religion: Speeches to its Cultured Despisers*, translated by John Oman. London: Routledge and Kegan Paul. Reprinted by Harper and Row.

Scott, S.P., trans. and ed. (2001), *The Civil Law, including The Twelve Tables, The Institutes of Gaius, The Rules of Ulpian, The Opinions of Paulus, The Enactments of Justinian, and The Constitutions of Leo, in Seventeen Volumes*. Cincinnati: The Central Trust Company. Reprinted in seven volumes [preserving the original volume numbers] by The Lawbook Exchange, Limited.

Seneca, Lucius Annaeus (1917), *Epistulae Morales*, volume 1: *Letters 1 to 65*, translated by R.M. Gummere (Loeb Classical Library). London: Harvard University Press.

———— (1920), *Epistulae Morales*, volume 2: *Letters 66 to 92*, translated by R.M. Gummere (Loeb Classical Library). London: Harvard University Press.

———— (1925), *Epistulae Morales*, volume 3: *Letters 93 to 124*, translated by R.M. Gummere (Loeb Classical Library). London: Harvard University Press.

Southern, R.W. (1970), *Western Society and the Church in the Middle Ages* (Penguin History of the Church, volume 2). London: Penguin.

Sparkes, Douglas C. (1996), *The Constitutions of the Baptist Union of Great Britain*. Baptist Historical Society.

Stephens, W.P. (1992), *Zwingli: An Introduction to his Thought*. Oxford: Clarendon Press.

Tanner, Norman P., SJ, ed. (1990), *Decrees of the Ecumenical Councils*. London: Sheed and Ward.

Thatcher, Oliver J., ed. (1907), *The Library of Original Sources: Editors Edition* (ten volumes). New York: University Research Extension.

Thatcher, Oliver J. and Edgar Holmes McNeal, eds (1905), *A Sourcebook for Mediæval History*. New York: Charles Scribner's Sons.

Thompson, David M., ed. (1990), *Stating the Gospel: Formulations and Declarations of Faith from the Heritage of the United Reformed Church*. Edinburgh: T & T Clark.

Timms, Noel and Kenneth Wilson, eds (2000), *Governance and Authority in the Roman Catholic Church: Beginning a Conversation*. London: SPCK.

Todd, John M., ed. (1962), *Problems of Authority: An Anglo-French Symposium*. London: Darton, Longman and Todd.

Tollinton, R.B., trans. (1929), *Selections from the Commentaries and Homilies of Origen*. London: SPCK.

Travers, Walter (1574), *A full and plaine declaration of Ecclesiasticall Discipline owt off the word off God / and off the declininge off the churche off England from the same*, translated by Thomas Cartwright. Heidelberg: Michael Schimat.

United Reformed Church (1999a), *The United Reformed Church Yearbook 1999*. London: United Reformed Church.

——— (1999b), *Human Sexuality Report 1999*. London: United Reformed Church.

——— (2000), *The Manual*, Sixth Edition. London: United Reformed Church.

Virgil (1958), *The Aeneid*, translated by W.F. Jackson-Knight. London: Penguin.

von Campenhausen, Hans (1997), *Ecclesiastical Authority and Spiritual Power in the Church of the First Three Centuries*, translated by J.A. Baker. London: A & C Black. Reprinted by Hendrickson.

Vos, Arvin (1985), *Aquinas, Calvin and Contemporary Protestant Thought: A Critique of Protestant Views on the Thought of Thomas Aquinas*. Washington DC: Christian University Press.

Warmington, E.H. trans. and ed. (1938), *Remains of Old Latin*, volume 3: *Lucilius* and *The Twelve Tables* (Loeb Classical Library). London: Harvard University Press.

Watson, Richard (1773), *A Brief State of the Principles of Church Authority*. London: Bowyer and Nichols.

Watson, Richard (1840), *Theological Institutes: or, A View of the Evidences, Doctrines, Morals and Institutions of Christianity* (two volumes). New York: George Lane.

Weber, Max (1947), *Theory of Social and Economic Organization*. New York: Oxford University Press.

Webster, William (1999), *The Matthew 16 Controversy: Peter and the Rock*, Revised Edition. Battle Ground, Washington: Christian Resources.

Weekly Law Reports (1968), Second Quarter. London: Incorporated Council of Law Reporting for England and Wales.

Wesley, John (1976), *Explanatory Notes Upon the New Testament*. London: Epworth Press.

——— (1984), *The Works of John Wesley*, volume 1: *Sermons I, 1–33*, edited by Albert C. Outler. Nashville: Abingdon Press.

——— (1986), *The Works of John Wesley*, volume 3: *Sermons III, 71–114*, edited by Albert C. Outler. Nashville: Abingdon Press.

White, B.R. (1976), *Authority: A Baptist View*. London: Baptist Publications.

Williams, Charles (1882), *Principles and Practices of the Baptists*. London: Baptist Tract and Book Society.

Winn, Herbert E., ed. (1929), *Wyclif: Select English Writings*. London: Oxford University Press.

Winroth, Anders (2000), *The Making of Gratian's Decretum*. Cambridge: Cambridge University Press.

Woolf, Bertram Lee (1956), *Reformation Writings of Martin Luther*, translated with introduction and notes from the definitive Weimar Edition, volume II: *The Spirit of the Protestant Reformation*. London: Lutterworth Press.

Workman, Herbert B (1926), *John Wyclif: A Study of the English Medieval Church* (two volumes). Oxford: Clarendon Press.

Zwingli, Huldrych (1984a), *Writings*, volume 1: *The Defense of the Reformed Faith*, translated by E.J. Furcha (Pittsburgh Theological Monographs, New Series, volume 12). Allison Park, Pennsylvania: Pickwick Publications.

———— (1984b), *Writings*, volume 2: *In Search of True Religion: Reformation, Pastoral and Eucharistic Writings*, translated by H. Wayne Pipkin (Pittsburgh Theological Monographs, New Series, volume 13). Allison Park, Pennsylvania: Pickwick Publications.

Index